Pegan Diet Cookbook: 1000-Day of Natural and Environmentally Friendly Recipes for Your Whole Family | 4-Week Meal Plan to Speed up the Slim Process through Healthy Foods & Embrace the Pegan Lifestyle

ISBN 9798844588990

10 9 8 7 6 5 4 3 2 1

Pegan Diet Cookbook

1000-Day of Natural and Environmentally Friendly Recipes for Your Whole Family | 4-Week Meal Plan to Speed up the Slim Process through Healthy Foods & Embrace the Pegan Lifestyle

Sharon Rush

Table of Contents

Chapter 4: Pegan Diet - Dinner Recipes 73

Introduction

Buffalo chicken pizza may have first appeared weird, but it is now quite common. People went crazy when the cronut, a hybrid of a croissant & a doughnut, was made available to the general public a few years ago. Sometimes combining two things may produce exciting consequences, particularly if the result is something culinary.

The Pegan Diet, which combines the Paleo Diet with the Vegan Diet, is the most recent diet to gain popularity. The majority of you probably already know about well-known diets like the vegan and ketogenic diets, but the Pegan diet has slowly begun to gain popularity among health enthusiasts. The paleo and vegan diets, 2 of the most well-liked eating patterns, served as inspiration for the Pegan diet. The Pegan diet, according to its founder Dr. Mark Hyman, promotes ideal health by lowering inflammation and regulating blood sugar. Although the Pegan diet is based on both vegan and paleo ideas, it adheres to its own set of rules and is developed to be long-term sustainable. Fruits & vegetables make up approximately 75% of the Pegan diet. The remaining 25% is generally made up of eggs, meats, and healthy fats like nuts and seeds. Limited amounts of certain legumes and whole grains can be permitted without gluten. The Pegan diet strongly emphasizes nutrient-dense vegetables, fruits, and healthy fats, which may aid in illness prevention, health promotion, and inflammation reduction. The Pegan diet is a popular dietary regimen (not pagan, mind you; that's another matter). Dr. Mark Hyman initially used the phrase in 2014 on his blog, but it has only recently gained popularity. According to data from Pinterest, searches for the Pegan diet have increased by 337 percent over the last year. You're correct if you think it's difficult to eat like a caveman and avoid all animal products at the same time. The Pegan diet still has restrictions on whole grains, dairy products, and legumes, although allowing some fish, meat, and eggs.

Chapter 1: The Pegan Diet - A Complete Introduction

Based on the idea that whole, nutrient-dense foods help decrease inflammation, manage blood sugar, and promote optimum health, the Pegan diet integrates fundamental elements from the paleo and vegan diets. You're not alone if your first assumption is that adopting a paleo and vegan diet simultaneously seems practically impossible. The Pegan diet, despite its name, is distinct and follows its own set of rules. In fact, it's less limiting than a vegan or paleo diet taken on its own. Vegetables and fruit are prioritized, although modest to moderate quantities of meat, some fish, seeds, nuts, and certain legumes are also permitted. Although they are discouraged, highly processed grains, oils, & sugars are still permissible in very limited quantities. The Pegan diet isn't intended to be a standard, temporary diet. It strives to be more long-lasting so that you may adhere to it forever.

1.1 Pegan - The Combination of Two Diets

There are a few similarities between the paleo diet & a vegan one. One emphasizes meat, whereas the other does not. But if you combine some of the best aspects of both diets into one, what would happen?

The worlds of health & nutrition are buzzing with talk about fad diets. While most people are probably aware of the well-known ones, such as the vegan and ketogenic diets, the Pegan diet has slowly begun to gain popularity among health lovers. Some years back, Dr. Mary Hyman, the creator of the vegan diet, was participating in a doctor's panel discussion with two colleagues who had opposing nutritional philosophies: a strong supporter of the paleo diet and a committed vegan. Hyman cracked a joke about becoming Pegan, or a good middle ground between the two, to ease the tension.

Dairy, wheat, vegetable oils, gluten, and legumes must all be avoided or consumed in moderation while following this diet. This specific diet encourages the use of locally sourced, organic, & sustainably produced foods; all types of sugar should be consumed in moderation. The diet mainly comprises elements that must be included in a healthy eating plan. In order to promote beneficial changes in health, this diet relies on enhancing the number of fresh fruits, healthy fats & vegetables having omega-3 fatty acids and appropriate proteins. Additionally, foods labeled as "Low Glycemic Load" are emphasized. The Pegan diet was developed by functional medicine expert Mark Hyman, MD, who claims that it:

- Reduces inflammation and blood sugar levels, which may lower your chance of developing certain chronic diseases, including Type 2 diabetes & heart disease.
- It is eco-friendly since it emphasizes meals that are plant-based and sustainable.
- Accentuates nutrient-dense meals while minimizing or avoiding harmful options.

As paleo diet, this diet emphasizes foods that early people would have collected or hunted." But here's the twist: You'll be eating mostly vegetables on a regular basis. You consume a lot less animal-based food than you would if you followed the paleo diet.

When consuming Pegan:

- You consume plants, such as fruits, vegetables, nuts, and seeds, for 75% of your daily calories.
- Your diet should consist of 25% meat, poultry, eggs, and fish (preferably organic, grass-fed, or sustainably raised options).

Foods to eat:

Whole foods, or those that have gone through little to no process before reaching your plate, are a major component of the Pegan diet.

Eat a lot of greens

Vegetables and fruit should make up the majority of your diet, or 75%, according to the Pegan diet. It is important to prioritize low-glycemic fruits & vegetables like berries and non-starchy veggies to reduce your blood sugar reaction. For people who already have stable blood sugar levels before beginning the diet, a small number of starchy vegetables & sweet fruits may be permitted.

Protein should be obtained ethically

Even though the Pegan diet focuses mostly on plant foods, getting enough protein from animal sources is still advised. Remember that less than 25% of the diet is still made up of animal-based proteins since 75% of it consists of fruits and vegetables. As a result, you will consume far less meat than you on a conventional paleo diet but more on any vegan diet. The Pegan diet avoids consuming eggs or meat from traditional farms. Instead, it emphasizes beef, poultry, pork, & whole eggs from sources that are grass-fed & pasture-raised. Additionally, it promotes the consumption of seafood, particularly those with low mercury levels, such as sardines & wild salmon.

Limit your intake to hardly processed fats.

You should consume healthy fats from certain sources when following this diet, such as:

- Nuts, excluding peanuts
- seeds, except for refined seed oils
- Avocado & olives: You may also use cold-pressed avocado and olive oil.
- Coconut: It's okay to use unrefined coconut oil.
- Omega-3s, especially those derived from low-mercury algae
- Omega-3s, especially those derived from low-mercury algae
- Whole eggs and grass-fed, pasture-raised meats are additional sources of fat in the Pegan diet.

You could eat some beans and whole grains.

The Pegan diet discourages most grains & legumes because of their tendency to affect blood sugar levels. However, certain gluten-free legumes and whole grains are allowed in small amounts. Legumes should not be consumed in excess of 1 cup (75 grams) each day, whereas grains should not be consumed in excess of 1/2 cup (125 grams) per meal. You may consume the following grains and legumes:

- Grains include oats, black rice, amaranth, quinoa, millet, and teff.
- Legumes: black beans, Pinto beans, chickpea, and lentils

If you have diabetes or another illness that makes it difficult to regulate your blood sugar, you should further limit these items.

Foods to avoid:

The Pegan diet allows for the occasional consumption of practically any food, making it easier than a vegan or paleo diet. Nevertheless, a number of foods and dietary categories are strictly contraindicated. Depending on what it is for, some of these meals may be considered quite harmful, while others can be very healthy. On the Pegan diet, these items are often avoided:

Dairy: It is not recommended to consume cow's milk, yogurt, or cheese. However, foods derived from goat or sheep milk are only allowed in small amounts. On occasion, grass-fed butter is also acceptable.

Grain products containing gluten should be avoided at all costs.

Grain without gluten: Even gluten-free grains should be avoided. Whole grains devoid of gluten may be consumed in small quantities on occasion.

Legumes: Because of their tendency to raise blood sugar levels, the majority of legumes are discouraged. Lentils and other low-starch legumes may be allowed.

Sugar: Refined or not, adding sugar in any form is often avoided. It can be used on occasion, but only very sparingly.

Refined oils: It's best to stay away from highly processed or refined oils like canola, sunflower, soybean, and maize oil.

Food additives: It is best to stay away from artificial colorings, flavors, preservatives, and other additions.

The majority of these foodstuffs are off limits because of how your body may react to them in terms of inflammation and/or blood sugar.

1.2 Pegan Diet Makes Sense

The anthropological analysis of this diet has recently sparked a number of contentious discussions on which diet is the healthiest: Paleo or Vegan? Eaton and Konner noted the following in 1985: "Hunter-gatherers frequently consume numerous types of wild plants for food, with the exception of Eskimos & other high-latitude peoples. The most frequent primary food components are roots, nuts, beans, tubers, and fruits, although people also sometimes eat edible gums & flowers. In actuality, hunter-gatherer diets consist mostly of high-fiber foods (derived from plants), with the rest of the calories coming from meat from wild animals. The amount of fat ingested is quite modest, most of which is unsaturated and rich in omega-3 fatty acids. This diet is rich in vitamin C, potassium, trace minerals, & B vitamins and low in salt from a nutritional standpoint. It boils down to around 66 percent veggies and 33 percent meat, which places this diet in the middle of the paleo/keto and vegan eating plans".

From the perspective of eating in the twenty-first century, Dr. Hyman highlights ideas that paleo & plant-based diets have in common. He talks about how & when you eat and what you eat. Because it seems that food origins and manufacturing techniques are just as important as food categories, in terms of the timing, it is now understood that a 12-hr window between your final meal of the day & your first meal the next day can play a significant role in generating some increase in the levels of ketones in your blood (such as beta-hydroxybutyrate), which can then help tune up your metabolism. The human digestive system is longer than that of herbivores and shorter than that of carnivores when compared to other animals. Additionally, you have molars for crushing veggies and canines for shredding meat like predators (like herbivores). The physiology required to efficiently digest ultra-processed meals that include high quantities of certain partitioned components is something that humans have not evolved during evolutionary time.

Today, your understanding of phytochemicals is far greater than it was in the 19th century. For instance, it has recently been shown that plant diets contain more than 8000 phytochemicals. Additionally, it is now understood that phytochemicals play a part in the regulation of metabolism by acting as agents that influence genetic expression & intercellular communication. With the aid of this contemporary backdrop, you may better comprehend how declining phytonutrient content contributed to the alarming health trends of the 20th century, in addition to changes in dietary fat intake and a substantial rise in carbohydrate and sugar consumption. On a worldwide level, this second problem is now seen as being of vital significance.

1.3 Pillars of Pegan Diet

Nowadays, there are a plethora of different dietary philosophies to choose from, including raw, vegetarian, vegan, ketogenic, flexitarian, Paleo, pescatarian, high-fat, low-carb, Mediterranean, high-carb, low-fat, and many more. It might be daunting to search for the ideal one. Let's examine the Pegan Diet's thirteen pillars:

1. Avoid eating sugar.

That entails a diet reduced in processed carbs, sugar, and anything else that raises our insulin levels, such as flour. Consider sugar in all of its forms as a rare pleasure, something you take only on rarely and in moderation. It is advised to consider it a recreational drug. You sometimes use it for enjoyment, but it's not a necessary part of your diet.

2. Consume a lot of plants.

As you previously learned, vegetables should make up more than half of your meal. The better, the deeper the hue. The healthier, the greater the diversity. Preferably just eat non-starchy vegetables. Sweet potatoes and winter squash are fine in moderation (12 cups daily). Not too many potatoes at all! Even though potatoes are the most popular vegetable in America, French fries are not included.

3. Be gentle on fruits.

Here is where there can be some misunderstanding. Some proponents of the Paleo diet advise sticking to low-sugar fruits as berries, while other vegans advise eating all fruit equally. Avoid grapes, melons, etc., and stick to berries, kiwis, and watermelon. Keep the amount of dried fruit to a minimum and treat it like candy.

4. Avoid using hormones, antibiotics, pesticides, and GMO foods.

Additionally, there are no artificial sweeteners, colors, preservatives, additions, chemicals, or other filler ingredients. You shouldn't consume an ingredient if your kitchen does not have it for cooking.

5. Consume meals rich in beneficial fats.

Referring to healthy fats like those in seeds, nuts, olive oil, avocados, and omega-3 fatty acids. And yes, you can consume saturated fat from foods like fish, grass-fed beef, whole eggs, meat from sustainably managed farms, grass-fed ghee or butter, and virgin organic coconut butter or coconut oil.

6. Avoid most seeds, nuts, and vegetable oils.

Like soybean oil, which currently makes up roughly 10% of your calories, as well as sunflower, canola, maize, Grapeseed, and others, Macadamia, Sesame, and walnut oils, as well as other expellers- or cold-pressed nut & seed oils, are acceptable for use as seasonings or condiments. For cooking at higher temperatures, avocado oil works excellent.

7. Limit dairy intake.

Dairy doesn't work for the majority of people, so it's advised to avoid it, with the exception of the occasional yogurt, kefir, ghee, grass-fed butter, and even the cheese if it doesn't bother you. Consider using sheep or goat dairy in place of cow dairy. Go organic and grass-fed at all times.

8. Consider meat and other animal foods as condiments

The main course should be vegetables, and the side dish should be meat. 4 - 6 ounces should be the maximum serving size for each meal. 3 or 4 vegetable-side dishes should usually be on the menu.

9. Consume seafood that has been responsibly farmed or caught.

If you consume fish, go for low-mercury and low-toxin options like wild-caught salmon, herring, anchovies, and sardines (all of that have high omega-3 & low mercury levels). And they must be raised or harvested in a sustainable manner.

10. Avoid gluten.

Look for ancient forms of wheat as einkorn since Franken wheat contains the majority of gluten. If you aren't gluten-sensitive, you should only infrequently consume wheat. The world's foremost authority on gluten, Doctor Alessio Fasano of Harvard, has conducted studies demonstrating that gluten may harm the gut even in those who are not gluten sensitive and do not exhibit any symptoms.

11. Use whole grains free of gluten sparingly.

They may still cause autoimmunity and elevate blood sugar. Your blood sugar level may be raised by any cereals. Keep your quantities of low-glycemic grains, such as black rice, teff, quinoa, buckwheat, or amaranth, to minimal amounts (12 cups each meal). A diet devoid of grains and beans may be essential for treating and even curing type 2 diabetes, autoimmune disease, and digestive issues.

12. Consume beans sparingly. The best are lentils.

Avoid eating large, starchy beans. Fiber, protein, & minerals may all be found in abundance in beans. But they are the cause of stomach issues in some people, and the lectins & phytates they contain may reduce the absorption of minerals. A diet heavy in beans might cause blood sugar to rise if you have diabetes. Once again, little doses (up to 1/2 cup daily) are fine.

13. Take a test to customize your strategy.

One person's solution may not be suitable for another. This phenomenon is referred to as bio-individuality, and it is the reason it is advised for everyone to ultimately work with a functionally trained nutritionist to customize their diet with the appropriate tests further.

1.4 Pegan Food Pyramid

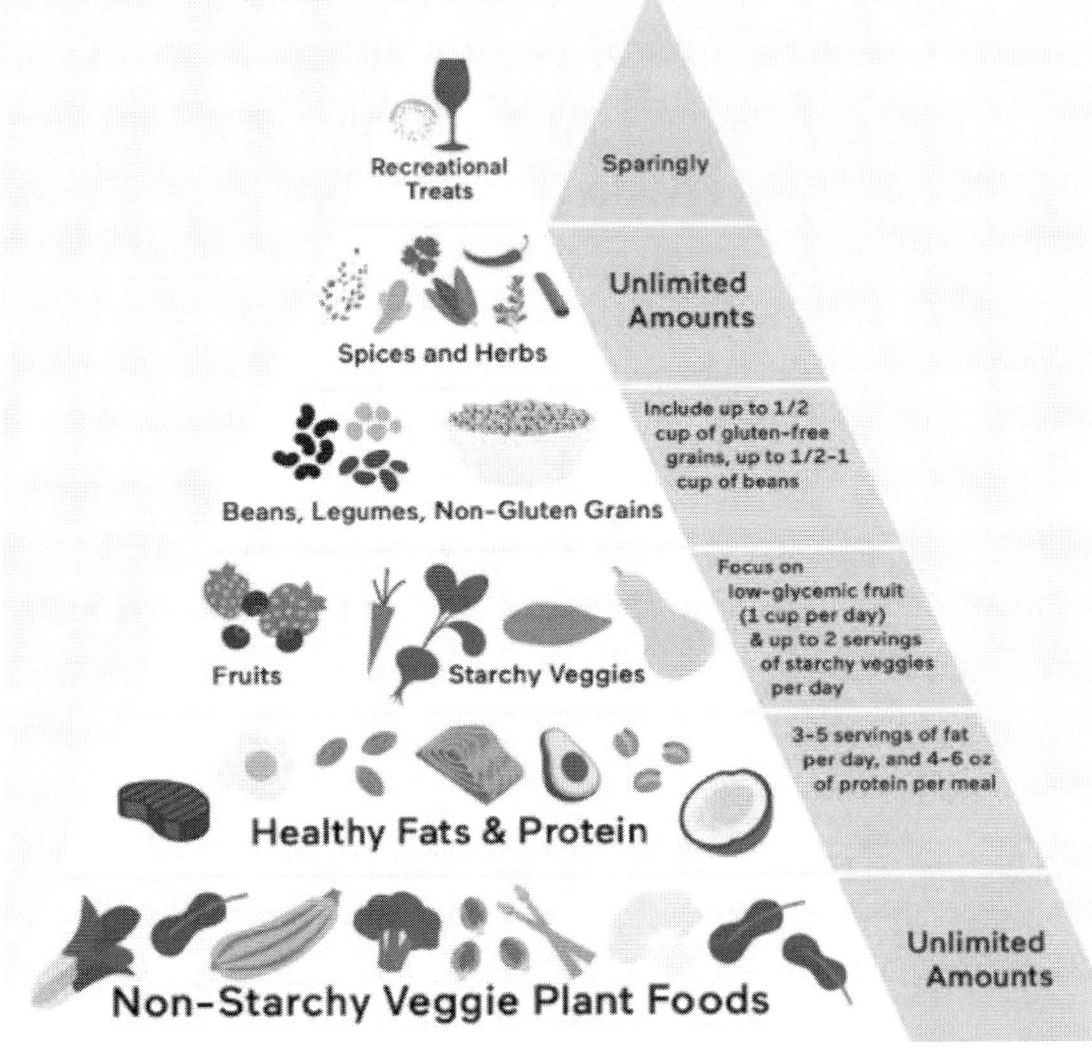

A simple to understand food pyramid that illustrates Mark Hyman made the idea. His vegan dietary pyramid has a balanced amount of healthful grains, veggies, fruit, and plant-based protein. Additionally, it includes "healthy" fats like avocado oil & omega 3s from salmon and walnuts. This diet's healthy fats work to lower blood sugar spikes that might lead to cravings for sweet foods or alcohol by slowing down digestion and absorption. It's important to consider how you ate as well as what you ate.

According to Dr. Hyman's vegetarian food pyramid, you should consume whole foods and stay away from processed foods, GMOs, sugar, gluten, and other inflammatory foods like fructose corn syrup & trans fats. The Pegan food pyramid contains organic, wild-caught fish twice a week since the goal is to promote a generally better way of eating. The cold-pressed organic olive oil, seeds, nuts, coconut butter, milk, & cream, healthful oils from avocado & coconut, grass-fed organic meats, and fatty fish such as salmon are all included in Dr. Hyman's vegetarian food pyramid.

- You are allowed to drink one glass of organic red wine each day with supper.
- When consumed in moderation, grains may be a part of a nutritious diet. The Pegan diet, for instance, contains modest quantities of whole organic grains like steel-cut oats or quinoa.
- A good Pegan meal for weight reduction and health may be seen in Dr. Mark Hyman's Pegan food pyramid.
- In addition to fatty fish in moderation, it contains non-starchy vegetables, beans, fruits and legumes, nuts, and seeds from the plant-based dietary category.
- You may consume organic, gluten-free grains like quinoa, steel-cut oats, and brown rice, according to Dr. Hyman's Pegan food pyramid.
- You may consume meat in moderation, such as the grass-fed beef that is now readily accessible in most supermarkets.
- Grass-fed butter should also be added, but dairy products like cow's milk and goat's milk should be avoided.

On Dr. Hyman's "Pegan Food Pyramid," the best foods for losing weight are cold-water fatty fish like salmon for protein, mussels, as well as vegetables, beans, fruits, and balsamic vinegar. Tempeh, blackstrap molasses, and avocado are other Pegan diet staples. While blackstrap molasses is rich in iron & calcium and is beneficial for PMS (premenstrual syndrome) and stress management, avocado is fat that may aid in weight loss. Tempeh, which is produced from fermented soybeans, provides probiotics that support good gut flora. Ingredients from the Pegan food pyramids, such as black beans, rice, and tempeh, may be used to create a healthful dish. One suggestion is to bake tempeh with red peppers after marinating it in tamari (gluten-free soy sauce), coconut oil, maple syrup, and garlic. Serve this over brown rice that has been cooked, black beans, and veggies like kale or broccoli.

1.5 Benefits of the Pegan Diet

There are several advantages to this diet that you will experience if you choose to try it.

- The main advantage of the Pegan diet is that it strongly emphasizes fruits and vegetables. You may receive most of the essential nutrients from fruits & vegetables alone since they are among the world's most varied foods. The Pegan diet places a lot of emphasis on them because of this. As per the Journal of the ADA (American

Dietetic Association), fruits and vegetables are a great source of fiber. Your gastrointestinal system needs fiber for optimal wellness. Additionally, it may reduce your body's digestion of carbs, preventing blood sugar increases. According to a study reported in the Journal of the Academy of Nutrition and Dietetics, fruits & vegetables are also rich in a variety of vitamins and minerals that work as co-factors for the enzymatic processes throughout the body. The abundance of antioxidants found in fruits and vegetables may also aid in lowering inflammation and oxidative stress throughout the body.

- The Pegan diet also advises against consuming saturated fats. This is mostly due to the fact that it urges dieters to avoid anything that can be harmful to their cardiovascular system. With this diet plan, you may avoid Trans fats that could otherwise block your blood vessels since you'll be eating a lot of whole fish, nuts, and seeds. According to Innovations in Nutrition, you may enhance the general health of the heart in this manner while following this diet. Additionally, eating plenty of fish, seeds, & nuts can increase your intake of good, unsaturated fats, which are crucial for your body's general health, without endangering your cardiovascular system.
- Finally, you will avoid processed meals since the Pegan diet promotes relying on real foods. As per Population Health Metrics, processed foods include plenty of added sugar, food coloring, preservatives, & other artificial substances that are bad for your body's health. This indicates that the Pegan diet may aid in enhancing the general quality of your dietary intake. In the end, the Pegan diet places a focus on nutrient-dense meals like fruits and vegetables. Your fat will come from very lean protein sources, and you won't be eating any Trans or saturated fats. Thus, adhering to this diet may help you both avoid the emergence of long-term health difficulties and enhance the general health of your brain, heart, lungs, and tissues.

Loss of weight

Whether or not this diet will help individuals lose weight is one of the top worries people have when deciding to start it. In the end, research is still being done since the Pegan diet is still quite new. The paleo diet & the vegan diet may both aid in weight loss, according to research published in Nutrients & the Journal of Internal Medicine. Therefore, it stands to reason that the Pegan diet will also aid in weight loss. Naturally, the majority of specialist diets aim to promote weight loss and a better lifestyle. Whether or if individuals will be able to adhere to it is the key issue. You ought to be able to reduce weight if you can adhere properly to the Pegan diet. As long as you can consume lots of fruits and vegetables while restricting your consumption of other foods to lean meat supplies and nutritious fast, the Pegan diet must help you lose weight, even if it takes some time to see benefits. Consider purchasing some mobile apps that will deliver you motivational messages all day long if you anticipate needing assistance adhering to the Pegan diet. You may also use mobile apps to identify food sources that adhere to your diet's requirements.

Last but not least, be sure to exercise often. Combining the Pegan diet with a daily exercise schedule is among the ways you may increase your chances of success. You may achieve your weight reduction objectives by walking for even only 30 minutes a day.

The Pegan diet's greatest benefit, in contrast to the abundance of healthy eating plans available, is that it enables individuals to customize it to meet their unique requirements. Hyman advises experimenting to see what actually works for you if you attempt the Pegan diet. For instance, some individuals may benefit from consuming moderate amounts of animal products, including saturated fats, whilst others benefit more from low-fat diets consisting virtually entirely of vegetables. It's not about being flawless; rather, it's about giving your body nutritious food 90% of the time while still making space for indulgences and pleasure foods. As a result, rather than upholding limitations and regulations out of principle, the eating plan encourages individuals to concentrate on what Hyman believes to be the true objective of a diet, that is, getting people healthy. He said that the true emphasis should be on getting people to switch from an obesogenic diet that causes diseases and is nutrient-depleted to one that is abundant in whole meals & protective foods that encourage weight reduction, health, and well-being. "That is the Pegan diet's objective."

1.6 Pegan is not Vegan

Contrary to what many people think, living a vegan diet does not automatically make you healthy. You could really live on potato chips, fries, & gluten-free cookies every day & still be vegan! Additionally, unhealthy fake meat items and infinite toxic processed options are readily available everywhere, concealing themselves behind "healthy" labels, thanks to the way that businesses use terms like vegan, organic, and natural as flashy marketing buzzwords. So how would you determine what is and is not healthy? The simplest way to put it is that being on a plant-based diet such as Pegan and being vegan mean two very different things. Dr. Mark Hyman prefers to consume a diet that is rich in plants rather than one that is plant-based. Dr. Hyman advises following the Pegan Diet, which is primarily a plant-based diet with the addition of high-quality meat to your diet (organic, grass-fed, local, etc.), and in quantities that differ significantly from the typical standard American diet (SAD) in which the Pegan Diet contains meat as a condiment or side to the meal rather than the main focus. Unfortunately, obtaining sufficient quantities of complete protein on a plant-based diet may still be challenging. Protein is an essential component. It's also crucial to remember that whole proteins matter and that not all proteins are created equal.

Some individuals will still want to follow a plant-based diet for a variety of reasons, and you need to understand how to become the fittest vegan you can be since it DOES need additional care to eat the right foods. It takes a lot of time and energy to lead a Pegan lifestyle, but if you are ready to put in the additional work, you can always get healthier. Here is a simple comparison between being vegan vs. being Pegan to get things started:

Vegan:

Do not take animal products, dairy, honey, eggs, or meat.

Pegan:

Similar to above, but actively seeks out and consistently consumes a variety of veggies, healthy fats, and genuine, whole foods while avoiding ultra-processed foods and refined sugar.

Consider adding lots of vegetables, selecting cashew cheese over soy cheese, making homemade organic almond milk over store-bought almond milk that has been processed, and sipping smoothies made with fruits and vegetables instead of fruit juices.

1.7 Success & Popularity of Pegan Diet

As individuals attempt to strike a balance between good nutrition and routines that adhere to their lifestyle values, various diets have recently grown in popularity due to expected advantages and alluring trade-offs. For many people interested in following lifestyle diets, food production techniques have become a significant expanding factor in the market today. And in 2022 Pegan diet has seen a rise in popularity because of assertions that it is ethical for the environment and health-promoting. According to Hyman, the Pegan diet is more like a way of life than a diet. You'll consume more nutrient-dense foods that come in all the hues of the rainbow if you stick to a Pegan diet. The Pegan diet, which combines the concepts of the Paleo and vegan diets, has recently received accolades from celebrities such as Eva Mendes and Katie Couric. Mark Hyman, M.D., initially invented the term in 2015. Thanks to Doctor Hyman's most recent book, released in February, paleo diets' popularity has recently increased once again.

The SAD (Standard American Diet) is heavily dependent on ultra-processed foods, refined carbs, red meats, saturated fat, added sugars, and excessive salt, all of which are harmful to human health, according to a registered dietitian Sheena Batura, at EverlyWell in Austin, Texas. It is unquestionably seen to be beneficial to encourage individuals to consume more vegetables and healthy fats, according to Batura. Similarly, she continues, eating less meat is better for the environment and your health. Batura understands that not everybody can afford to eat this way, even if she believes that buying local, organic, fresh, non-GMO, & pasture-raised foods is a great idea. Batura asserts that encouraging people to eat what they can afford is still preferable to not eating any fruits or vegetables because "I believe the real issue is that Americans just aren't eating sufficient fruits and vegetables." According to Batura, little scientific evidence supports the Pegan diet's restriction of nutritious grains. Hyman advises moderating of consuming gluten-containing grains, including wheat, barley, and Farro. As Dr. Hyman recommends in his book, restricting "starchy" beans like pinto or kidney beans means you're losing out on a cost-effective food source that's high in fiber, plant-based protein & vitamin B. Lessen your concentration on one particular philosophy or dietary pattern if you're trying to enhance your diet. Apply the fundamental ideas that are often emphasized among dietary patterns instead. This entails selecting meals rich in fiber, which mostly include whole grains & legumes as well as vegetables, fruits, and healthy fats; lowering dependence on meat (particularly highly processed red meats); and limiting added sugars.

A board-certified gastroenterologist in New York City named Niket Sonpal, M.D., says he agrees with the Pegan diet's emphasis on replenishing the body with foods that are high in nutrients and have anti-inflammatory characteristics rather than on weight reduction. He adds that while it may not be the simplest diet to follow, particularly if you eat out often or are cost-conscious, this diet is less restricted than the diets it is based on. He does, however, recognize the many health advantages of a Pegan diet. "The diet may be good for lowering blood pressure, heart health, and perhaps defending against some kinds of malignancies," Sonpal continues. "It encourages people to consume largely organic fruits, vegetables, and healthy fats.

1.8 A Pegan's Healthy Lifestyle - The Right Approach

People are looking for quick methods to get in shape in this particular era, and paganism is emerging as one realistic approach. Kimberly Marsh, a certified dietitian in Denver, believes that the Pegan diet is often less limiting than the vegan or paleo diets. Because there are no limits, it is simpler to follow and more nutrient-rich than other diet programs, according to Marsh. Julie Harris, a registered dietitian with a practice in Maryland, concurs, saying, "I like that the diet emphasizes eating plenty of plant foods." I like how much Peganism emphasizes getting adequate protein, eating whole grains, and ingesting healthy fats. Nutritionists generally agree that the Pegan diet's strength is its absence of restriction.

Peganism is more palatable and healthier than certain diets that exclude whole food categories, but it is still limiting, and most Pegans place a strong value on eating organically, which is fantastic but also pricey. Despite the diet's emphasis on healthy eating practices, she claims that many individuals may find it to be unsustainable or unworkable owing to the high expense of natural, organic goods. Harris concurs. Harris argues that the diet emphasizes organic, sustainably farmed foods, "It may be rather pricey."

Raw Materials to buy:

Vegetables: Any food with a GI of 55 to 69 or above that all of the following do. Hyman advises including veggies in your diet at a rate of 75%.

- Greens: collard, mustard, turnip, etc.
- Bamboo shoots
- Brussels sprouts
- Broccoli
- Cauliflower
- Tomatoes
- Eggplant
- Peppers
- Mushrooms
- Leeks

Fruits:

- Cherries
- Apples
- Dark berries
- Pears
- Citrus fruits
- Pineapple
- Mangoes

Omega-3 fats:

- Nuts
- Olive oil
- Avocados

Proteins—as long as they are sustainably sourced & grass-fed

- Turkey
- Beef
- Chicken
- Shrimp
- Eggs
- Salmon

Legumes:

- Beans, in particular, may be consumed sometimes as a protein source and fiber, although moderation is advised.

Natural sugars:

- Coconut sugar
- Maple syrup
- Honey
- Vanilla
- Dates

Foods to avoid:

- Starchy vegetables
- Dairy
- Sweet potatoes
- Gluten—which includes whole grains & alternatives
- Pumpkin

- Soy
- Most vegetable oils – such as Sunflower, Canola, etc.
- Corn
- Legumes
- Beans - Soybean
- Sugar
- processed meals, such as pizza & French fries
- food additives, such as synthetic flavors and colors

The window of time to eat:
While following the Pegan diet, integrate intermittent fasting or time-restricted eating. Fast for 12 hours every day. After supper, skip dinner, and wait 12 hours before having breakfast. And if 16-hour fast works for you, do it twice in one week or more. In particular, if you're overweight, overfat (slim on the appearance but fat on the inside), or if metabolically unsound, Dr. Hyman advises a 24-hr. fast once a month.

1.9 Sustainable Eating in a Budget

What does it mean to eat sustainably, first of all? Eat a lot of plants (enjoy vegetables & whole grains), eat a range of foods (have quite a colorful plate), waste less food, and moderate your consumption of red & white meat. You don't need to avoid red and white meat completely; instead, you can also enjoy numerous different sources of protein, such as peas, beans, & nuts. They suggest avoiding sugary beverages, limiting the intake of sweet snacks, and purchasing food that meets a trustworthy verified quality, like fair trade & free range. Theoretically, a sustainable diet might result in cost savings since it is resource-conscious, produces less waste, and has a less environmental impact, such as by substituting part of the meat and fish in your diet with beans or another less expensive source of plant protein. However, although being healthier, fresh vegetables may be more costly than highly processed commercial food.

1. Eat more plant foods

Large quantities of area, water, and feed are needed to raise animals for meat & dairy production. Only the cattle sector alone is responsible for roughly 15% of all greenhouse gas emissions caused by humans. Given the 500% increase in worldwide meat consumption between 1992 & 2016, it is obvious that you need to rebalance your diets by emphasizing vegetables and reducing your consumption of animal products.

2. Consume more variety.

Just 12 plant species and 5 animal species account for 75% of the world's food supply. A lack of options in agriculture harms the environment and jeopardizes food security. Thus, you must diversify your diets more.

3. Choose seafood responsibly.

Aquaculture does have its own problems, and around 94 percent of fish populations are either overfished (34 percent) or exploited to their maximum sustainable level (60 percent). However, when produced ethically, seafood may be good for the environment, the economy, and the climate. Eat lower on the food chain, experiment with a variety of species from well-managed sources, and choose seafood with reduced carbon emissions.

4. Eliminate waste

Food waste is one of the serious issues. Food waste accounts for 30% of total production, with severe environmental consequences. In fact, behind China and the United States, food waste would rank third in terms of greenhouse gas emissions if it were a nation. When feasible, purchase loose stuff so you can choose the precise quantity you need, and freeze whatever you can't eat while it's still fresh to reduce waste in your home.

5. Grow your very own vegetables

What could be better than farm-fresh food right from the garden? It is tasty, healthful, and has no carbon impact compared to store-bought meals.

6. Search for products, including palm oil, that has been RSPO certified.

Unsustainable palm oil contributes to greenhouse gas emissions, ups the risk of climate change, and causes extensive deforestation, endangering orangutans, tigers, and other animals. However, avoiding alternatives altogether might have unexpected repercussions since some need up to 9 times as much land to grow as alternatives, making them worse for the environment. Look for items that include RSPO-certified sustainable palm oil while you are buying.

7. Avoid using plastic

Both the natural environment and your foods now include plastic. Bring a reusable bag with you when you go shopping, choose produce that isn't packaged when you can, and urge companies that still use plastic to seek alternatives.

8. Consume what is seasonal

Try to incorporate seasonal food from your neighborhood farm store or greengrocer into your diet whenever possible. You might learn more about regional producers and get advice on cooking seasonal foods and assisting your community's economy.

9. Cooking may reduce spending and carbon

Hack your go-to meals to change things using less energy while saving money. In addition to being effective at reheating, microwaves may also be used to cook a variety of meals, such as vegetables and seafood. According to new research in Nature comparing the carbon costs of different methods of cooking meals, baking potatoes in an oven has a 60 percent environmental effect. Instead, microwave your potato for a minute before grilling it for a few mins. On each side to bring out some of the flavor and scent of baked potatoes.

10. Accessible regional

Sales of local foods increased during the first lockout as customers looked to dependable and flexible nearby providers. Purchasing directly from local farmers may save expenses by eliminating the middleman, particularly when purchasing high-welfare beef and organic veggies, since more of each retail pound proceeds to the producer. The food won't always be inexpensive, but it may support environmentally friendly farming and give your neighborhood shoppers more choices.

1.10 4-Week Meal Plan

A four-week meal plan including all the recipes already mentioned in the next chapters of this book.

1st Week

Day 1
Breakfast: 1. Coconut Strawberry Smoothie
4. Zoodles and Baked Eggs with Avocado
Lunch: 1. Taco Grilled Chicken Salad
2. Mushroom Burger
Snack: 1. Pancetta and Peas
Dinner: 1. Beef Curry Stew

Day 2
Breakfast: 2. Coconut Chocolate Smoothie
5. Vegetable Frittata
Lunch: 3. Fried Cauliflower Rice
4. Red Lentils Curry
Snack: 2. Stuffed Pico de Gallo Avocado
Dinner: 2. Shepherd's Vegan Pie

Day 3
Breakfast: 6. 1-Pan Eggs with Tomatoes and Asparagus
Lunch: 5. Zucchini Noodles in Alfredo Sauce
Snack: 3. Roasted Garlic Balsamic Brussels Sprouts & Bacon
Dinner: 3. Tempeh Lettuce Wraps & Peanut Sauce

Day 4
Breakfast: 7. Pegan Pancakes
8. Golden Milk Creamy Smoothie\
Lunch: 6. Scallion Bacon Chicken Salad
9. Chicken Scarpariello
Snack: 5. Pizza Dough Bites
Dinner: 4. Cauliflower Gnocchi

Day 5
Breakfast: 9. Baked Eggs in Tomatoes
Lunch: 7. Avocado & Salmon Poke Bowl
Snack: 6. Blueberry Muffins
Dinner: 5. Sweet Potato Pizza

Day 6
Breakfast: 11. Breakfast Salad
12. Sweet Potato Hash & Fried Eggs
Lunch: 8. Broccoli Casserole
Snack: 7. Cinnamon Apple Granola Bars
Dinner: 6. Beef Steak with Shrimp

Day 7
Breakfast: 13. Healthy Porridge
Lunch: 10. Baked Thai Pork Tenderloin
Snack: 9. Chocolate Truffles
Dinner: 7. Bbq Jackfruit Pizza with Sweet Potato Crust

2nd Week:

Day 1
Breakfast: 14. Banana Maple Pecan Breakfast Bake
Lunch: 11. Vietnamese Beef with Lettuce Wraps
Snack: 10. Sweet Potato Brownies

Dinner: 8. Spicy and Sweet Chicken Stir Fry with Broccoli

Day 2
Breakfast: 15. Sweet Potato Pegan Bowl
Lunch: 13. Thai Red Curry with Chicken & Zoodles
Snack: 11. Orange Spice Cheesecake
Dinner: 11. Sweet Potatoes with White Beans and Lemony Kale

Day 3
Breakfast: 16. Sweet Potato Hash
17. Overnight Oats with Almond Milk and Chia Seeds
Lunch: 14. Slow Cooker Delicious Chicken Mole
Snack: 12. Roasted Soy-Lime Tofu
Dinner: 12. Healthy Chicken Stir Fry

Day 4
Breakfast: 18. Breakfast Quinoa Bowl with Egg
Lunch: 15. Pumpkin Moroccan Chicken
Snack: 14. Cranberry Bliss Bars
Dinner: 13. Pumpkin Chili

Day 5
Breakfast: 19. Kale & Avocado Omelet
Lunch: 16. Oven Baked Delicious Pesto Salmon
Snack: 15. Chinese Stir-Fry Broccoli with Garlic Sauce
Dinner: 14. Short Beef Ribs
21. Mushroom Tomato Spaghetti Squash

Day 6
Breakfast: 20. Baked Eggs & Kale in Tomato Sauce
Lunch: 17. Salmon Zucchini Patties
Snack: 16. Avocado Baked Fries
Dinner: 15. Baked Salmon & Black Rice

Day 7
Breakfast: 21. Egg & Spinach Scramble with Raspberries
Lunch: 18. Lettuce Wrap Burger
Snack: 17. Sweet Potato Fries
Dinner: 16. Grilled Shrimp
20. Sweet Potato Creamy Spinach Noodles with Cashew Sauce

3rd Week:

Day 1
Breakfast: 22. Egg & Peppers with Avocado Salsa
Lunch: 19. Mexican Cauliflower Rice
Snack: 21. Poached Pears & Pomegranate Sauce
Dinner: 17. Wild Salmon & Horseradish-Mustard Sauce
19. Butternut Squash Mac & Cheese Noodles

Day 2
Breakfast: 23. Kale and Sweet Potato Skillet
Lunch: 20. Ratatouille
Snack: 23. Red Pepper & Hummus Celery Logs
Dinner: 18. Grass-Fed Steak & Parsley Pesto with Roasted Carrots

Day 3
Breakfast: 24. Chile Rellenos
Lunch: 21. Pasta Salad
Snack: 25. Roasted Corn on the Cob
Dinner: 22. Thai Chicken Coconut Curry

Day 4
Breakfast: 25. Egg Bites
26. Sausage Casserole
Lunch: 22. Zucchini Noodles with Lemon Cream Sauce
Snack: 26. Bbq Popcorn
Dinner: 23. Moroccan Lamb Stew

Day 5
Breakfast: 27. Sweet Potato Breakfast Waffles
Lunch: 23. Cauliflower Tacos
Snack: 28. Spicy Air Fried Green Beans
Dinner: 24. Grilled Flank Steak with Caprese Salad

Day 6
Breakfast: 28. Sweet Corn & Zucchini Pie
Lunch: 24. Cauliflower Tahini Steaks
Snack: 29. Dried Apple Delicious Rings
Dinner: 25. Thai Chicken Pineapple Curry

Day 7
Breakfast: 29. Sweet Potato Frittata with Spinach and Caramelized Onions
Lunch: 25. Creamy Sweet Potato Spinach Noodles & Cashew Sauce

Snack: 33. Chewy Ginger Molasses Healthy Cookies
Dinner: 26. Curried Beef & Vegetables

4th Week:

Day 1
Breakfast: 30. Breakfast Collard Green Burrito
Lunch: 26. Spicy Spaghetti Squash Peanut Ramen
Snack: 34. Gluten-Free Pizzelles
Dinner: 28. Brussels Sprout & Sweet Potato Tacos

Day 2
Breakfast: 31. Breakfast Quiche
Lunch: 27. Mexican Quinoa Lunch Salad
28. Chicken Green Chili Enchilada Casserole
Snack: 35. Corn & Cheese Vegetarian Empanadas
Dinner: 29. Mushroom Cauliflower Skillet

Day 3
Breakfast: 32. Eggs Asparagus Benedict on Portobello Mushroom
Lunch: 29. Fajita Rice Chicken Bowl with Black Beans
Snack: 36. Cauliflower Sticky Sesame Wings
Dinner: 30. Salmon-Stuffed Dinner Avocados
31. Tofu Poke

Day 4
Breakfast: 33. Papaya Strawberry Smoothie
34. Overnight Dark Chocolate Oats
Lunch: 30. Cauliflower Tabbouleh
Snack: 37. Zucchini Chicken Poppers
Dinner: 32. Roasted Rosemary Salmon with Potatoes and Asparagus

Day 5
Breakfast: 35. Flour Coconut Pumpkin Bread
42. Breakfast Potatoes
Lunch: 31. Zuppa Toscana
Snack: 38. Garlic Cauliflower Crust Breadsticks
Dinner: 33. Roasted Root Veggies on Spiced Lentils
39. Sheet-Pan Dinner Chicken Fajita Bowls

Day 6
Breakfast: 36. Almond Flour Pumpkin Pie
Lunch: 32. Chickpea Masala
Snack: 39. Corn Fritters
Dinner: 35. Tofu & Mushroom Stir-Fry

Day 7
Breakfast: 43. Breakfast Quesadillas
Lunch: 33. Chickpea and Eggplant Stew
Snack: 40. Plantain Chips
Dinner: 38. Oven-Baked Ginger-Tahini Salmon & Vegetables

Chapter 2: Pegan Diet - Breakfast Recipes

1. Coconut Strawberry Smoothie

Prep time: 5 mins.
Cook time: 0 mins.
Total time: 5 mins.
Serves: 2
Difficulty: easy
Ingredients:

- 1 banana (frozen), sliced
- 1 cup of coconut milk
- 2 cups of strawberries (frozen)
- 1 scoop of collagen peptides (optional)
- 1 tsp. Of vanilla extract

Directions:

- In the sequence specified, add each item to a high-speed blender.
- Until smooth, blend.

Nutritional values per serving:
Total Calories: 346kcal, **Fats:** 24g, **Carbohydrates:** 27g, **Protein:** 8g, **Fiber:** 4g, **Sodium:** 40mg, **Potassium:** 680mg

2. Coconut Chocolate Smoothie

Prep time: 5 mins.
Cook time: 0 mins.
Total time: 5 mins.
Serves: 2
Difficulty: easy
Ingredients:

- 1 banana (frozen), sliced
- 1 cup of coconut milk
- 1 cup of ice
- 1 scoop of collagen peptides
- ¼ cup of cacao powder (raw)

Directions:

- In the sequence specified, add each item to a high-speed blender.
- Until smooth, blend.

Nutritional values per serving:
Total Calories: 160kcal, **Fats:** 8g, **Carbohydrates:** 23g, **Protein:** 2g, **Fiber:** 5g, **Sodium:** 86mg, **Potassium:** 375mg

3. Coconut Milk Peach Smoothie

Prep time: 10 mins.
Cook time: 0 mins.
Total time: 10 mins.
Serves: 3
Difficulty: easy
Ingredients:

- 1 cup of ice
- 1 cup of chilled coconut milk
- Some lemon zest
- 2 peaches (fresh) peeled & cut into chunks

Directions:

- To a Vitamix or blender, add peaches, ice, and coconut milk. Add some grated lemon zest to taste using a Microplane.
- Blend until smooth at high speed.

Nutritional values per serving:
Total Calories: 187kcal, **Fats:** 16g, **Carbohydrates:** 12g, **Protein:** 2g, **Fiber:** 2g, **Sodium:** 10mg, **Potassium:** 356mg

4. Zoodles and Baked Eggs with Avocado

Prep time: 15 mins.
Cook time: 10 mins.
Total time: 25 mins.
Serves: 2
Difficulty: easy
Ingredients:

- 3 spiralized zucchini in noodles
- Nonstick spray
- 2 tbsp. of olive oil
- 4 eggs (large)
- Kosher salt & black pepper (freshly ground)
- Red-pepper flakes, to garnish
- 2 halved avocados, thinly sliced
- Fresh basil to garnish

Directions:

- Set the oven's temperature to 350 °F. Apply nonstick spray to a baking sheet to lightly oil it.
- Combine the olive oil and zucchini noodles in a big bowl. Add salt and pepper to taste. Make each part into a nest on the baking sheet, then divide evenly into 4 sections.
- Place a cracked egg in the middle of each nest. Bake for 9 - 11 minutes, or till the eggs are set. Add red pepper flakes & basil as a garnish after seasoning with salt & pepper. Serve with slices of avocado.

Nutritional values per serving:
Total Calories: 633kcal, **Fats:** 53g, **Carbohydrates:** 27g, **Protein:** 20g, **Fiber:** 1g, **Sodium:** 15mg, **Potassium:** 210mg

5. Vegetable Frittata

Prep time: 10 mins.
Cook time: 50 mins.
Total time: 1 hr.
Serves: 6
Difficulty: medium
Ingredients:

- 2 diced potatoes (medium), (without or with the skin)
- 1 tbsp. of olive oil or 1/4 cup of water
- 1 onion (small), diced
- 1 diced zucchini
- 1 diced bell pepper
- 2 cloves of garlic, minced
- A pinch of red pepper flakes (optional)
- A handful of grape tomatoes, quartered or halved
- Some mineral salt & pepper to taste

For the food processor/blender

- 1/4 cup of non-dairy milk, unsweetened
- 1 package of organic silken tofu (16 oz.), firm or soft, drained
- 2 heaping tsp. of cornstarch, tapioca, or arrowroot flour
- 1 tsp. of mustard (any) or 1/2 tsp. of mustard powder
- 2 – 3 tbsp. of nutritional yeast
- 1 1/2 tsp. of tarragon, basil, or thyme, dried (or a combo)
- 1/2 tsp. of salt
- 1/2 tsp. of garlic powder
- 1/8 tsp. of pepper (white or black)
- 1/4 tsp. of turmeric

Directions:

- Set oven up to 375 degrees Fahrenheit.
- In a skillet with medium heat, add the oil and the potatoes, and cook for 5 minutes. Then, add the onion and cook for 5 more minutes. When softened, add bell pepper, zucchini, and garlic. Cook for a further minute or two after adding tomatoes and red pepper flakes (optional). To taste, add salt and black pepper to the food.
- The remaining ingredients should be combined and blended into a smooth tofu egg in a food processor or blender for seasoning and taste.
- Stir the tofu mixture well into the pan in which the veggies have been cooking. Pour the mixture into a springform pan or a 9-inch round pie/quiche dish that has been gently buttered. Make sure all of the borders are filled before using a spoon or spatula to level the top flat.
- Frittata must be solid to the touch after 35 to 45 minutes of baking when placed on the center rack. Cover the top with foil or a tiny Silpat if the browning gets out of hand. Remove and let cool for ten minutes minimum. When using a pie or quiche dish, release the frittata's sides, set a plate on top, and delicately turn it over, so it falls into the plate. Then, serve.

Nutritional values per serving:
Total Calories: 139kcal, **Fats:** 3.5g, **Carbohydrates:** 17.7g, **Protein:** 9.5g, **Fiber:** 3.3g, **Sodium:** 236.5mg, **Potassium:** 12mg

6. 1-Pan Eggs with Tomatoes and Asparagus

Prep time: 10 mins.
Cook time: 20 mins.
Total time: 30 mins.
Serves: 4
Difficulty: medium
Ingredients:

- 1 pint of cherry tomatoes
- 2 pounds of asparagus
- 4 eggs
- 2 tsp. of fresh thyme, chopped
- 2 tbsp. of olive oil
- Salt and black pepper to taste

Directions:

- Set the oven up to 400°F. Use nonstick cooking spray to grease a baking sheet.
- Place the cherry tomatoes and asparagus in an equal layer onto the baking sheet. Olive oil should be drizzled over the veggies, which should then be taste-tested for salt, pepper, and thyme.
- Roast in oven for 10 to 12 minutes, or until the tomatoes are crumpled, and the asparagus is almost soft.
- Sprinkle salt and pepper on each egg before breaking it and placing it on the asparagus.
- Return it into the oven & bake for a further 7 to 8 minutes, or until the whites of egg are set, but the egg yolks are still jiggly.
- Asparagus, tomatoes, and eggs should be distributed among four dishes for serving.

Nutritional values per serving:
Total Calories: 158kcal, **Fats:** 11g, **Carbohydrates:** 13g, **Protein:** 11g, **Fiber:** 3g, **Sodium:** 200mg, **Potassium:** 20mg

7. Pegan Pancakes

Prep time: 5 mins.
Cook time: 15 mins.
Total time: 20 mins.
Serves: 4
Difficulty: easy
Ingredients:

- 3/4 cup of tapioca flour
- 1 cup of almond flour
- 1 tbsp. of baking powder
- 2/3 cup of unsweetened almond milk
- 1/4 tsp. of sea salt
- 2 tsp. of apple cider vinegar
- 1 tbsp. of coconut oil, melted
- 1 tbsp. of maple syrup
- 1 tsp. Of pure vanilla extract

Directions:

- In a blender, combine all the ingredients. After a brief period of blending, stop the blender, scrape the sides, and resume blending. However, as mentioned above, mixing does assist in making these pancakes fluffier. The batter may also be made in a bowl.
- If extra liquid or flour is required, add it gradually (1/2 Tbsp. at a time) to get the desired consistency for pancake batter.
- Pour roughly a scant 1/4 cup batter for each pancake onto an oiled skillet over medium-high heat.
- Flip pancakes when they start to bubble or when a spatula can easily slide under one. Cook the food further until both sides are golden brown.
- Before consuming pancakes, give them a little time to cool.
- Add the preferred garnishes, such as Strawberry Vanilla Roasted Bean Sauce and nut butter.

Nutritional values per serving:
Total Calories: 283kcal, **Fats:** 18g, **Carbohydrates:** 29g, **Protein:** 6g, **Fiber:** 3g, **Sodium:** 200mg, **Potassium:** 15mg

8. Golden Milk Creamy Smoothie

Prep time: 5 mins.
Cook time: 0 mins.
Total time: 5 mins.
Serves: 1
Difficulty: easy
Ingredients:

- 1 cup of light almond milk or coconut milk (store-bought), use for creamier smoothie full-fat coconut)
- 1 cup of banana (ripe, frozen, and sliced)
- 1/2 tsp. of turmeric, ground
- 1 Dash of ground cinnamon
- 1 tbsp. of ginger, fresh (plus some more to taste)
- 1 Dash of black pepper
- 1 Dash of cardamom and clove, ground
- 1 Dash of ground nutmeg

Optional:

- 1/4 cup of fresh carrot juice
- 1 tbsp. Of Hemp seeds

Directions:

- In a high-speed blender, combine the banana, turmeric, coconut milk, ginger, black pepper, cinnamon, and nutmeg. Blend on high until the mixture is creamy and smooth. If using, include clove, cardamom, & fresh carrot juice now (optional).
- If it's too thick, add extra water or coconut milk. If too thin, add ice to thicken it.
- Taste the food and make any necessary taste adjustments by adding extra cinnamon for the warmth, some black pepper for the spice, ginger for the zing, turmeric for earthiness or a deeper color, or banana for the sweetness. Carrot juice will intensify the orange/yellow color and add sweetness.
- Enjoy immediately after dividing between serving glasses. Refrigerate any leftovers for 24 hours. Use any leftovers for future smoothies by freezing them by putting them onto an ice cube tray.

Nutritional values per serving:
Total Calories: 295kcal, **Fats:** 43.7g, **Carbohydrates:** 13.9g, **Protein:** 3.5g, **Fiber:** 4.6g, **Sodium:** 23.3mg, **Potassium:** 1104mg

9. Baked Eggs in Tomatoes

Prep time: 25 mins.
Cook time: 20 mins.
Total time: 45 mins.
Serves: 4
Difficulty: easy
Ingredients:

- 8 tomatoes (medium)
- 2 tbsp. of olive oil
- 8 eggs (large)
- ¼ cup of Parmesan cheese, grated
- ¼ cup of milk
- 4 tbsp. of fresh herbs, chopped (like thyme, parsley, rosemary, or mixture)
- Salt & black pepper, freshly ground

Directions:

- Turn the oven on to 375°F. The olive oil should be used to grease a big oven-safe pan.
- Cut the tomato stems off by cutting around them with a little paring knife. Scoop out the

tomato's inside using a spoon. (Reserve the insides & incorporate them into salsa or tomato sauce.)
- Place the tomato shells in the skillet as you have prepared them. Each tomato is filled with one egg. Add 1 tbsp. Milk and 1 tbsp. Parmesan over the top of each egg. Each egg should be salted and peppered.
- Bake for 15 to 17 minutes, or until the whites of egg are set & the yolks are a bit runny, but the tomatoes are soft. After allowing it cool for five minutes, garnish with some fresh herbs. Serve right away.

Nutritional values per serving:
Total Calories: 288kcal, **Fats:** 19g, **Carbohydrates:** 12g, **Protein:** 18g, **Fiber:** 4g, **Sodium:** 100mg, **Potassium:** 55mg

10. Sheet Pan Fajitas

Prep time: 15 mins.
Cook time: 25 mins.
Total time: 40 mins.
Serves: 4
Difficulty: easy
Ingredients:

- 1 thinly sliced orange bell pepper
- 1 thinly sliced red bell pepper
- 1 thinly sliced green bell pepper
- 1 tbsp. of chili powder
- 2 tbsp. of olive oil
- 1 tbsp. of lime juice, freshly squeezed
- 1 & 1/2 tsp. of ground cumin
- 3 minced cloves of garlic
- 1 tsp. of ground paprika
- Kosher salt & black pepper (freshly ground), to taste
- 1/4 tsp. of onion powder
- 6 eggs (large)
- 1/4 cup of chopped cilantro leaves, fresh
- 1 halved avocado, peeled, seeded & sliced

Directions:

- Set oven up to 400 degrees Fahrenheit. Spray nonstick cooking spray or lightly oil the baking sheet.
- On the prepped baking sheet, spread out the bell peppers into a single layer. Add the garlic, cumin, paprika, onion powder, chili powder, and olive oil, and gently mix to blend. Add salt and pepper to taste.
- Place in oven and bake for 12 to 15 minutes or until cooked.
- After removing from the oven, make 6 wells. Add eggs, carefully breaking them all the way through while leaving the yolk undamaged. To taste, add salt and pepper.
- Place in the oven and bake for a further 8 to 12 minutes, or till the egg whites are set.
- If preferred, top with avocado & cilantro before serving.

Nutritional values per serving:
Total Calories: 261kcal, **Fats:** 19g, **Carbohydrates:** 9g, **Protein:** 12g, **Fiber:** 3g, **Sodium:** 378mg, **Potassium:** 200mg

11. Breakfast Salad

Prep time: 10 mins.
Cook time: 10 mins.
Total time: 20 mins.
Serves: 4
Difficulty: easy
Ingredients:

- 1/3 chopped shallot or red onion
- 1 1/3 cup of butternut squash, chopped and peeled
- 1 1/2 tbsp. of butter or olive oil (divided)
- 1 tbsp. of balsamic vinegar
- 12 ounces of mixture broccoli coleslaw salad
- 1 tbsp. of water
- 1/4 tsp. or more of sea salt & pepper each (to taste)
- 1/4 tsp. of garlic, minced
- 1/3 cup of blueberries
- Red pepper flakes & cilantro for garnishing
- 4 eggs
- Roasted pumpkin seeds
- 1 sliced avocado

Directions:

- Peel and cut your vegetables first. If you don't want to wait until the end, slice your avocado. Put the chopped squash and 1 tablespoon of water in a steamer over a microwave-safe plate. Steam for at least 2 and a half minutes based on the power of the microwave. Cook until mushy but still firm. Alternately, roast the squash on a baking sheet for 15 to 20 minutes at 425F.

- Eliminate, drain, and reserve. Put 1 tablespoon of butter or oil in a small skillet. Add your onions and turn the heat to medium-high.
- Fry onions for two minutes or until they begin to color slightly. Then add your slaw, garlic, salt, and pepper, along with 1 tablespoon of water and balsamic vinegar.
- Combine everything in a skillet. For two to three minutes on medium, cook covered.
- Slaw won't be entirely cooked but will be just slightly tender. Take it out and put it in a bowl.
- Toss the squash & 1/3 cup of berries into the bowl. Eggs are then cooked in same skillet. On medium-high heat, add another half tbsp of butter or oil.
- Fry until the yolk is set and the exterior is crispy. Based on how you want your yolk, cook it for 3 to 4 minutes or less. Place slaw on three to four plates or bowls.
- Fry an egg and place it on each. Add red pepper, one tablespoon of cilantro, pumpkin seeds, and any additional salt or pepper to garnish. Serve with sliced avocado.

Nutritional values per serving:
Total Calories: 235kcal, **Fats:** 15.3g, **Carbohydrates:** 18.8g, **Protein:** 9.2g, **Fiber:** 7g, **Sodium:** 213.1mg, **Potassium:** 0mg

12. Sweet Potato Hash & Fried Eggs

Prep time: 10 mins.
Cook time: 15 mins.
Total time: 25 mins.
Serves: 2
Difficulty: easy
Ingredients:
For hash:

- 1 large pinch of kosher salt
- 1 garnet yam (large)
- Black pepper, freshly ground
- Some dashes of onion powder
- Some garlic powder
- Dried herbs, a small sprinkle
- Aleppo pepper (optional)
- 2 tbsp. of fat (any)

For eggs:

- 1 tbsp. of avocado oil or ghee
- 4 eggs (large), two per serving
- Kosher salt
- Aleppo pepper (optional)
- Black pepper, freshly ground

Directions:

- Based on how many people you'll be serving, grab one or seven yams.
- In order for the yam slices to fit in your food processor, peel and chop them lengthwise. Shred the yams using the slicer blade attached to the machine. (Alternatively, you may create sweet potato "noodles" with a spiralizer.)
- Toss the shredded yams with salt, pepper, garlic powder, onion powder, and dry herbs in a large bowl. If you have fresh alliums and herbs, you can surely use them instead. To taste and season the mixture, if needed.
- In a big cast iron pan set over medium heat, melt the fat. The seasoned yams or sweet potatoes should be added when oil is shimmering.
- Stir-fry everything for a minute after tossing it all in the grease. The yams should then simmer for some more minutes with a cover on. When there are some crispy brown parts and the texture is soft & supple, the hash is prepared.
- You may divide the hash into two halves and top each with a pair of sunny-side-up eggs, or you can serve it with some Aleppo pepper and eat the hash all by yourself. This meal is made substantial and well-rounded with enough protein and fat to go with the carbohydrates, thanks to the inclusion of the eggs, which lend a delicious richness to the hash.
- A heated 8-inch cast iron pan over medium-low heat should have a tbsp. of ghee added. Two eggs should be cracked into the bowl and carefully poured into the heated pan when the fat begins to sizzle.
- Based on how gooey you prefer your yolks, season eggs with salt & pepper, and then cover them with the lid for two to three minutes.
- When they are finished, gently remove them from the pan and place them on top of a pile of hash. Repeat with the other eggs. More Aleppo pepper should be added on top.

Nutritional values per serving:
Total Calories: 574kcal, **Fats:** 31g, **Carbohydrates:** 60g, **Protein:** 14g, **Fiber:** 9g, **Sodium:** 150mg, **Potassium:** 90mg

13. Healthy Porridge

Prep time: 5 mins.
Cook time: 15 mins.
Total time: 20 mins.
Serves: 2
Difficulty: easy
Ingredients:

- 2 tbsp. of shredded coconut, unsweetened
- 2–3 tbsp. of sunflower seeds, lightly toasted (or one tbsp. of tahini)
- 1 tbsp. of flaxseed or chia seed

- 1 tsp. of ginger, ground
- 1/2 tsp. of cinnamon
- A pinch of turmeric, ground
- 1/2 cup of coconut milk or water, more if needed
- A pinch of sea salt
- 1 cup of chopped & cooked squash
- Some raw honey or pure maple syrup
- Extra toppings: cherries or berries, pomegranate seeds, coconut yogurt, or coconut cream to top.

Directions:

- In a blender or coffee grinder, combine all the dry ingredients (coconut chia, sunflower seeds, and spices) and process until the mixture resembles flour. If you're pressed for time, omit the sunflower seeds altogether and substitute tahini.
- Add the mixture of dry ingredients to some coconut milk or water in a small dish, and let it absorb the liquid and gel up. You may save a little amount of gel for topping.
- Blend the cooked squash & gel mixture until smooth in a blender.
- The porridge should only be heated on the stovetop at medium heat until it begins to boil. Stirring every so while.
- Remove from the heat, pour into your preferred bowl, and sprinkle the reserved dry mixture on top.
- **Optional:** If desired, include 1 teaspoon of ghee to assist with digestion and to offer extra nutrition. Healthy fats also aid in the absorption of nutrients.
- Add more milk, fresh berries, or other toppings.

Nutritional values per serving:

Total Calories: 331kcal, **Fats:** 17.7g, **Carbohydrates:** 43.1g, **Protein:** 7g, **Fiber:** 8.7g, **Sodium:** 180.4mg, **Potassium:** 50mg

14. Banana Maple Pecan Breakfast Bake

Prep time: 10 mins.
Cook time: 30 mins.
Total time: 40 mins.
Serves: 10
Difficulty: easy
Ingredients:

- 1/3 cup of unsweetened smooth almond butter
- 2 mashed overripe bananas (medium)
- 3 tbsp. of pure maple syrup
- 1 1/2 tsp. of pure vanilla extract
- 3 tbsp. of unsweetened applesauce
- 2 flax eggs: 5 tbsp. of water + 2 tbsp. of flaxseed, set it aside for 15 mins.
- 2 tsp. of cinnamon
- 1 1/4 cup of blanched almond flour
- 1/4 tsp. of sea salt, fine grain
- 1/2 tsp. of baking soda
- 1/2 cup of chopped pecans

Directions:

- You should either line a baking pan (square) with parchment paper or butter two little (6") or one bigger (9–10") skillets with coconut oil before preheating your oven up to 375 degrees.
- Banana puree, almond butter, applesauce, maple syrup, and vanilla should all be well combined in a big bowl. The flax eggs should then be added and combined.
- A smooth dough will develop after adding the almond flour, baking soda, cinnamon, and salt. 2 Tbsp. of the pecans are reserved for the top and are folded in.
- Bake in the oven for about 25–30 minutes if using two 6-inch skillets and 35–40 minutes if using a single 9" baking dish or pan.
- If preferred, pour with more maple syrup and serve warm. Enjoy!

Nutritional values per serving:

Total Calories: 221kcal, **Fats:** 16g, **Carbohydrates:** 16g, **Protein:** 5g, **Fiber:** 4g, **Sodium:** 123mg, **Potassium:** 199mg

15. Sweet Potato Pegan Bowl

Prep time: 5 mins.
Cook time: 0 mins.
Total time: 5 mins.
Serves: 1
Difficulty: easy
Ingredients:

- Some sliced pear
- 1 skin-on sweet potato, microwaved or baked till soft inside
- Some almond butter, pepitas, almond yogurt, dried cherries, hemp hearts, dried cranberries, cacao nibs

Directions:

- Add all of your preferred toppings to the dish with the cooked sweet potato.

Nutritional values per serving:

Total Calories: 112kcal, **Fats:** 1g, **Carbohydrates:** 26g, **Protein:** 2g, **Fiber:** 4g, **Sodium:** 72mg, **Potassium:** 438mg

16. Sweet Potato Hash

Prep time: 10 mins.
Cook time: 25 mins.
Total time: 35 mins.

Serves: 8
Difficulty: medium
Ingredients:
Spice mixture:

- 1/4 tsp. of dried thyme
- 1/2 tsp. of organic ground sage
- 1/4 tsp. of dried rosemary
- 1/2 tsp. of cinnamon
- Pinch of black pepper
- 1/8 tsp. of ground or allspice cloves
- 1/2 tsp. of onion powder
- 1/8 tsp. of nutmeg

For hash:

- 12 oz. of Brussels sprouts, in quarters or halves, based on their size
- 1 sweet potato (large), diced in 1/2" cubes
- 1 1/2 tbsp. of avocado oil or olive oil, to roast pecans and Brussels sprouts, plus some sea salt
- 2 apples (medium)
- 2 tsp. + 2 tbsp. of coconut oil, divided
- 3/4 cup of pecan halves
- 1/4 cup of cranberries (dried)
- 1/2 tsp. of sea salt

Directions:

- Set your oven's temperature to 425. In a separate bowl, combine the ingredients for the spice combination and save.
- Add 1 1/2 tbsp. of olive oil or avocado, a dash of sea salt, & 1 teaspoon of the spice combination to the Brussels sprouts before tossing. The nuts should be added to the baking sheet & gently stirred after 15 minutes of roasting in the preheated oven. Roast for a further 5-7 minutes, or until toasted.
- In the meanwhile, add 2 tablespoons of the coconut oil to a big, seasoned cast iron pan and heat it over medium heat.
- When the pan is hot, add the sweet potatoes & sprinkle with 1/2 teaspoon of sea salt equally. Stir or toss the potatoes to coat them in the salt and cooking oil. For approximately two minutes, cover the pan with any large-enough cover. If the potatoes are beginning to brown too much, remove the lid, stir them, and slightly reduce the heat. Once the potatoes are tender, cover and continue cooking for an additional 2-4 minutes.
- When the potatoes are evenly light brown, remove the lid from the pan and keep cooking while stirring. Stir in 2 tsp. of coconut oil after adding the chopped apples. Cook for a further five minutes over medium heat, turning periodically, or till the apples & potatoes are browned. To prevent burning, adjust your stovetop's heat as needed.
- Turn off the heat as soon as the apples & potatoes are toasted, then whisk in the rest of the spice mixture, cranberries, & roasted Brussels sprouts, and pecans. For the flavors to meld, let the hash remain on the heated skillet for a while. As the side dish or vegetarian dinner, serve it warm. Enjoy!

Nutritional values per serving:
Total Calories: 188kcal, **Fats:** 13g, **Carbohydrates:** 18g, **Protein:** 2g, **Fiber:** 4g, **Sodium:** 165mg, **Potassium:** 306mg

17. Overnight Oats with Almond Milk and Chia Seeds

Prep time: 10 mins.
Cook time: 0 mins.
Total time: 10 mins.
Serves: 2
Difficulty: easy
Ingredients:

- 1 cup of plain almond milk
- 1 cup of oats, gluten-free
- 1 tbsp. of honey optional
- 1 tbsp. of chia seeds

Toppings:

- 1 tbsp. of chocolate chips
- 1 tbsp. of coconut flakes
- 1 tbsp. of peanut butter

Directions:

- In a jar with a cover, combine all the ingredients. Store in the fridge overnight.
- Add your preferred toppings in the morning and enjoy.
- Increase the amount of almond milk if it's too thick.

Nutritional values per serving:
Total Calories: 335kcal, **Fats:** 14g, **Carbohydrates:** 46g, **Protein:** 9g, **Fiber:** 8g, **Sodium:** 173mg, **Potassium:** 231mg

18. Breakfast Quinoa Bowl with Egg

Prep time: 10 mins.
Cook time: 5 mins.
Total time: 15 mins.
Serves: 1
Difficulty: easy
Ingredients:

- 1 1/2 tsp. of olive oil, divided
- 1 egg (large) at room temperature
- 1/2 tsp. of minced garlic
- 1/2 cup 0f cooked quinoa
- 1 cup of roughly chopped lacinato kale
- 1/3 cup of cherry tomatoes, halved
- 1/4 tsp. of kosher salt

- 1/4 avocado, ripe
- 1/8 tsp. of black pepper, freshly ground

Directions:

- In a medium saucepan, heat 3 inches of water until it is boiling. Boil for six minutes after adding the egg. Egg into freezing water and let stand for one minute. Peel and drain.
- In a small pan over medium heat, warm 1 teaspoon of oil. 30 seconds after adding the garlic. Add the kale and simmer it for 2 - 3 minutes while frequently stirring.
- In a bowl, mix the quinoa, tomatoes, kale, and avocado. Sprinkle with salt and pepper and drizzle with the remaining 1/2 teaspoon oil. Slice the egg in half and place it on top.

Nutritional values per serving:

Total Calories: 366kcal, **Fats:** 21g, **Carbohydrates:** 33g, **Protein:** 14g, **Fiber:** 8g, **Sodium:** 592mg, **Potassium:** 62mg

19. Kale & Avocado Omelet

Prep time: 10 mins.
Cook time: 2 mins.
Total time: 12 mins.
Serves: 1
Difficulty: easy
Ingredients:

- 1 tsp. of low-fat milk
- 2 eggs (large)
- Pinch of salt
- 1 cup of chopped kale
- 2 tsp. of olive oil, divided
- 1 tbsp. of lime juice
- 1 tsp. of sunflower seeds, unsalted
- 1 tbsp. of fresh cilantro, chopped
- Pinch of red pepper, crushed
- ¼ sliced avocado

Directions:

- In a small bowl, whisk eggs, milk, and salt together in a nonstick small skillet over medium heat, and warm 1 teaspoon of oil. Add the mixture of eggs and cook for 1 to 2 minutes, or till the bottom is set & the middle is still a little runny. After approximately 30 seconds, flip the omelet over and cook it until it is set. Place on a platter.
- Combine the remaining 1 tsp of oil, cilantro, lime juice, crushed red pepper, and a sprinkle of salt with the kale. Add the avocado and kale salad to the omelet as a garnish.

Nutritional values per serving:

Total Calories: 339kcal, **Fats:** 28.1g, **Carbohydrates:** 8.6g, **Protein:** 15g, **Fiber:** 4.4g, **Sodium:** 445.5mg, **Potassium:** 506.3mg

20. Baked Eggs & Kale in Tomato Sauce

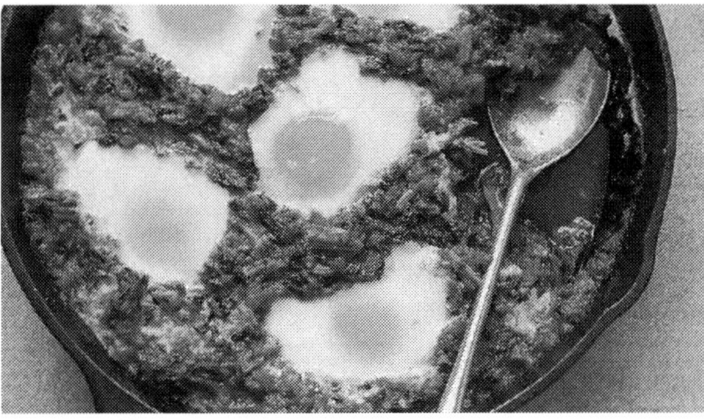

Prep time: 5 mins.
Cook time: 10 mins. (Plus 20 mins. baking)
Total time: 35 mins.
Serves: 4
Difficulty: easy
Ingredients:

- 3 packages of frozen kale, thawed & chopped (10-ounce), drained & squeezed dry
- 1 tbsp. of olive oil
- ½ tsp. of salt, divided
- 1 jar of marinara sauce, low-sodium (25-ounce) or 3 cups of canned tomato sauce, low-sodium
- ¼ tsp. of ground pepper, divided
- 8 eggs, large

Directions:

- Set oven up to 350 degrees Fahrenheit.
- A 10-inch cast-iron pan or ovenproof nonstick skillet may be heated with oil over medium heat. Add the kale and cook for 2 minutes while seasoning with 1/4 tsp. Salt and 1/8 tsp. Pepper. Add marinara sauce (or tomato sauce) & cook while stirring.
- Using the backside of a spoon, create 8 wells into the sauce. Carefully break an egg in each well. Add the remaining 1/4 tsp. Salt and 1/8 tsp. Pepper to the eggs.
- Place the pan in the oven, and bake for 20 minutes, or till the egg whites become set but yolks are still runny.

Nutritional values per serving:

Total Calories: 344kcal, **Fats:** 20.3g, **Carbohydrates:** 20.6g, **Protein:** 21.4g, **Fiber:** 5.9g, **Sodium:** 652.8mg, **Potassium:** 848mg

21. Egg & Spinach Scramble with Raspberries

Prep time: 5 mins.
Cook time: 5 mins.
Total time: 10 mins.
Serves: 1
Difficulty: easy
Ingredients:

- 1 ½ cups of baby spinach (1 and 1/2 ounces)
- 1 tsp. of canola oil
- 2 eggs (large), lightly beaten
- Pinch of ground black pepper
- Pinch of salt
- ½ cup of fresh raspberries
- 1 slice of bread (whole-grain), toasted

Directions:

- A medium nonstick skillet with medium-high heat is used to heat the oil. Add the spinach and simmer for 1 to 2 minutes, stirring often, until wilted. Onto a platter, transfer the spinach.
- Clean the pan, then add eggs and cook it up over medium-low. Cook for 1 to 2 minutes, stirring 1-2 times to achieve uniform cooking. Add the spinach, salt, and pepper, and stir. Along with bread and strawberries, serve the scramble.

Nutritional values per serving:
Total Calories: 296kcal, **Fats:** 15.7g, **Carbohydrates:** 20.9g, **Protein:** 17.8g, **Fiber:** 7g, **Sodium:** 394.2mg, **Potassium:** 292.6mg

22. Egg & Peppers with Avocado Salsa

Prep time: 25 mins.
Cook time: 10 mins.
Total time: 35 mins.
Serves: 4
Difficulty: easy
Ingredients:

- 1 diced avocado
- 2 (any color) bell peppers
- ½ cup of diced red onion
- ½ cup of chopped cilantro (fresh), plus some more for garnish
- 1 minced jalapeño pepper
- 2 seeded tomatoes, diced
- ¾ tsp. of salt, divided
- Juice of one lime
- 2 tsp. of olive oil, divided
- ¼ tsp. of ground black pepper, divided
- 8 eggs, (large)

Directions:

- Bell peppers should have the tops and bottoms cut off and diced. Remove and discard the membranes and seeds. Cut each of the peppers into four rings that are each 1/2 inch thick.
- In a medium bowl, combine the chopped pepper, avocado, onion, tomatoes, cilantro, lime juice, and 1/2 tsp. of salt.
- In a big nonstick skillet on medium heat, warm 1 teaspoon of oil. Place 1 egg in the center of each ring of 4 bell peppers. Add salt and pepper to taste, each using 1/8 teaspoon. Cook for 2 to 3 minutes, or till the whites are largely set but yolks are still runny. Flip gently and cook for a further minute for runny yolks or an additional 1 and a half to 2 minutes for firmer yolks. Repeat with the rest of the pepper rings & eggs, then transfer to serving platters.
- Serve with avocado salsa and, if preferred, top with more cilantro.

Nutritional values per serving:
Total Calories: 285kcal, **Fats:** 19.5g, **Carbohydrates:** 14.2g, **Protein:** 15.1g, **Fiber:** 5.9g, **Sodium:** 589.1mg, **Potassium:** 716.2mg

23. Kale and Sweet Potato Skillet

Prep Time: 15 mins.
Cook Time: 45 mins.
Total Time: 1 hr.
Serves: 4
Difficulty: Easy
Ingredients:

- 2 (1 & 1/2 pounds) sweet potatoes, chopped into half-inch cubes
- 2 tbsp. of avocado oil
- 1 diced onion
- 1/2 tsp. of cumin
- 1 tsp. of sea salt
- 1/2 tsp. of chili powder
- 4 cups of kale chopped
- Some black pepper, to taste
- 4 eggs
- 4 slices of bacon chopped

Directions:

- Sweet potatoes, onions, and avocado oil are added to a pan that is already heated to medium heat. Stirring periodically, season with the cumin, salt, chili powder, and black pepper. Give it 15 minutes to soften. Get rid of the heat.
- Warm up the Oven using Convection. Bake for 20 minutes at 400 °F.
- Use a fork to stir the kale into the mixture of sweet potatoes after adding it to the pan. Spread the bacon out over the surface of the pan after adding it, allowing the chunks to roast and get crisp.
- For 20 minutes, bake the skillet.

- Make four indentations all over the pan with a fork after taking it out of the oven. Place 1 egg into each depression.
- Add 5-7 minutes for medium-done eggs and up to 8-10 minutes for well-done eggs when you put the pan back in the oven and choose "additional time." Serve right away.

Nutritional Values per Serving:

Total Calories: 359kcal, **Fat:** 21g, **Carbohydrates:** 32g, **Protein:** 13 g, **Fiber:** 4g, **Sodium:** 883mg, **Potassium:** 854mg

24. Chile Rellenos

Prep Time: 30 mins.
Cook Time: 15 mins.
Total Time: 45 mins.
Serves: 4
Difficulty: Medium
Ingredients:

- 4 eggs
- 4 large poblano peppers
- 2 cups of cheese, shredded
- Chile Relleno Sauce
- 4 Pork Sausage Patties, Golden Brown
- 2 tbsp. of avocado oil
- 1 can of tomatoes, diced (14 ounces)
- 1 chopped onion
- 1 diced seeded jalapeno, if desired
- 1 tsp. of oregano
- 1 cup of water
- 1 tsp. of cumin
- 2 bay leaves
- 1 tsp. of cinnamon or 2 cinnamon sticks
- 1 tsp. of sea salt

Directions:

- The poblanos should first be blanched. The peppers should be added to a large saucepan of boiling water after approximately 10 minutes or until they are tender when poked with a fork. To prevent them from floating, it's preferred to cover your pot with the lid, but you could also just turn them over halfway through.
- Set the oven to 425°F.
- Slice the chilies lengthwise after removing them from the boiling water. You just need to be capable of filling the interior of the pepper; avoid cutting it in half. You may use a spoon to scoop out the seeds if the chiles are very hot or if you don't want them to be too spicy.
- Cook Pork Sausage patties while preparing some scrambled eggs. Half the patties and put them aside.
- In a baking dish, pour chile Relleno sauce before adding the peppers. Place one scrambled egg, a quarter of the cheese, and one sausage patty (2 halves) into each pepper. Add more cheese to the dish's surface.
- For 15 mins. or until the cheese is melted & bubbling, bake the chile Rellenos. If you prepare your chiles in advance & the sauce has chilled or cooled before baking, cover the dish using foil and bake for 15 minutes. Then remove the foil and bake for an additional 10 to 15 minutes, or until the cheese has started to bubble & brown.
- Sauce for Chile Relleno
- Add the onion and avocado oil to a large skillet. About 10 minutes of medium heat cooking will soften the onions.
- Diced tomatoes, water, bay leaves, cinnamon sticks, oregano, cumin, and the other sauce components should all be added. Once the mixture has reached a simmer, turn down the heat to medium-low. For 10 to 15 minutes, simmer the mixture.
- Blend the sauce after removing the bay leaves and cinnamon sticks. Up until the sauce becomes a smooth, process. Save the sauce until you're ready to construct your meal.

Nutritional values per serving:

Total Calories: 481kcal, **Fat:** 36g, **Carbohydrates:** 15g, **Protein:** 26g, **Fiber:** 5g, **Sodium:** 1282mg, **Potassium:** 627mg

25. Egg Bites

Prep Time: 20 mins.
Cook Time: 1 hr.
Total Time: 1 hour. 20 mins.
Serves: 9
Difficulty: Medium
Ingredients:

- 1/4 cup almond milk (unsweetened), plain not vanilla
- 8 eggs
- 1/2 tsp. of black pepper
- 1 tsp. of sea salt

Toppings:

- Pork Sausage, Little Links (No Sugar) cooked & chopped
- Feta cheese
- Chopped Bell peppers
- Bacon, crumbled, and cooked
- Chopped herbs
- Some shredded kale
- Chopped tomatoes, sun-dried
- sliced Olives
- shredded Cheddar cheese

Directions:

- Place Sous Vide inside a big pot that has water that is at least seven inches deep. Heat the water in sous vide up to 172 degrees Fahrenheit.
- In the absence of a Sous Vide, place a rack in the base of the pot & heat water on medium heat. Find the setting on a thermometer that will keep the water within +/- 5°F of 172°F. There will be air bubbles growing on the base of pot, but the water would not be boiling.
- In a big measuring cup, combine and mix the ingredients (all) for egg foundation. Use the measuring cup to make it simple to pour the mixture into the jars.
- Prepare the toppings, then add 2 to 3 tbsp. in each jar. The mixture of egg is placed on top of each jar.
- Each jar should have a tight-fitting lid on it. After the water has reached temperature, put the lids to the jars. For one hour, cook the egg bits. Check one of jars after the allotted time has passed to ensure that egg is completely set. If it's not, keep them submerged for another 10 to 15 minutes.

Nutritional Values per serving:

Total Calories: 70kcal, **Fat:** 5g, **Carbohydrates:** 1g, **Protein:** 5g, **Fiber:** 1g, **Sodium:** 324mg, **Potassium:** 68mg

26. Sausage Casserole

Prep Time: 30 mins.
Cook Time: 50 mins.
Total Time: 1hr. 20 mins.
Serves: 6
Difficulty: Easy
Ingredients:

- 2 tbsp. of avocado oil
- 1 bunch of chopped lacinato kale
- 1 thinly sliced onion
- Black pepper, to taste
- 1 tsp. of sea salt divided
- 1 Pork Sausage Roll, No Sugar (10-ounce)
- 1/4 cup of unsweetened almond milk, original (not vanilla)
- 12 eggs
- 1/4 cup of full-fat coconut milk
- 1/4 cup of tomatoes (sun-dried), sliced in thin strips
- 1 cup of shredded white cheddar cheese

Directions:

- In an 8 x 8 baking dish, place the greens.
- Next, add thinly sliced onions & avocado oil to a pan that has been heated to medium-low heat. Onions should be caramelized while the heat is low. Since it will take 15 to 20 minutes, get the other ingredients ready while you wait for onions to start turning light brown. Add black pepper and 1/2 tsp. of salt as desired. To ensure consistent browning and avoid burning, stir the onions every couple of minutes. Above the kale in the baking dish, add the onions.
- Set the oven to 350 degrees Fahrenheit as the onions are browning. This dish stays particularly moist when baked at a low temperature.
- Increase the heat up to medium to high, add the Pork Sausage Roll, & stir. As the sausage browned, shred it with a spatula. Use a fork or spatula to arrange the ingredients evenly over the surface of the baking dish after adding the kale, onions, and brown sausage to it.
- Add eggs, the remaining 1/2 tsp. of salt, the coconut and almond milk (or dairy alternative), and pepper to taste to a large bowl. If using, add half the cheese and combine the ingredients.
- Over the veggies and sausage into the baking dish, pour the egg mixture. Add more cheese and sun-dried tomatoes on top.
- Bake your casserole for 25-30 minutes with the foil covering the pan. When the center is set, remove the foil and bake for a further 20 to 25 minutes.
- Serve warm. After letting leftovers cool, keep them in the fridge for up to 3-4 days.

Nutritional Values per serving:

Total Calories: 305kcal, **Fat:** 22g, **Carbohydrates:** 9g, **Protein:** 19g, **Fiber:** 1g, **Sodium:** 674mg, **Potassium:** 565mg

27. Sweet Potato Breakfast Waffles

Prep Time: 10 mins.
Cook Time: 6 mins.
Total Time: 16 mins.
Serves: 4
Difficulty: Easy
Ingredients:

- 2 eggs
- 3 cups of shredded sweet potato (about two medium sweet potatoes)
- 2 tbsp. of coconut flour
- 1 tbsp. of arrowroot
- 1 tbsp. of avocado oil
- 1/2 tsp. of sea salt (1/4 tsp. for sweet waffles)
- Coconut sugar and cinnamon are optional, if creating a sweet waffle (use about 1/2 tsp. of cinnamon & 1 tbsp. of coconut sugar)
- Black pepper, to taste (omit it for sweet waffles)

Directions:

- Eggs, coconut flour, avocado oil, arrowroot, salt, & pepper should all be combined in a bowl. Reduce the salt, skip the pepper, and, if you want, add coconut sugar and cinnamon when creating sweet waffles.
- Stir the sweet potatoes to coat them well after adding them to the bowl.
- Waffle iron on high heat with the avocado oil spray applied. Add half the batter once it is really hot. The batter should be spread out and pressed on the waffle iron's sides using a fork. The edges should start to brown after 6-7 minutes of cooking.
- Continue by using the other half of batter.
- Serve warm or store frozen for up to three months in an airtight container. Waffles may be heated by baking them in a 400°F oven for 10–12 minutes or until they are hot & crispy around the edges. A tiny toaster oven may also be used for this.

Nutritional Values per serving:

Total Calories: 170kcal, **Fat:** 6g, **Carbohydrates:** 24g, **Protein:** 5g, **Fiber:** 4g, **Sodium:** 384mg, **Potassium:** 367mg

28. Sweet Corn & Zucchini Pie

Prep Time: 15 mins.
Cook Time: 30 mins.
Total Time: 45 mins.
Serves: 6
Difficulty: Easy

Ingredients:

- 1 tbsp. of olive oil
- 4 medium zucchini, very thinly sliced
- 1 minced onion
- 1 tsp. of sea salt
- 3 ears of sweet corn from cob
- 1 cup of shredded cheddar cheese
- 1 tsp. of sea salt

Directions:

- Slice summer squash and zucchini extremely thinly by using a mandoline.
- Add 1 teaspoon each of sea salt & black pepper to the beaten eggs.
- Over medium heat, add olive oil into a frying pan, then add the onion and sauté for approximately 7 minutes, or until it starts to turn brown. For a further 2-3 minutes, add sweet corn, salt, and pepper.
- Use parchment paper to line an 8-inch springform pan. This prevents the egg from dripping through the pan's bottom. Set your pan onto a baking tray to collect the cooked egg if you do not have anything to line your pan with.
- Add two layers of the zucchini around the springform pan's base. Add a third of corn mixture and a third of the cheese to the layer on top. About a third of the egg should be drizzled over the layer to ensure it stays together. Continue layering until you have 3 layers of corn, cheese, and egg and 4 layers of zucchini.
- Bake for 26 minutes at 400°F on Bake/Reheat in the Oven.
- If you're using a standard oven, warm it to 400 degrees Fahrenheit, then bake the dish for 40 mins, or till the top is crisp & the eggs are done.
- Before cutting pieces, let the dish sit for 20 to 30 minutes.

Nutritional Values per serving:

Total Calories: 196kcal, **Fat:** 11g, **Carbohydrates:** 14g, **Protein:** 10g, **Fiber:** 2g, **Sodium:** 553mg, **Potassium:** 538mg

29. Sweet Potato Frittata with Spinach and Caramelized Onions

Prep Time: 30 mins.
Cook Time: 1 hr. 30 mins.
Total Time: 2hr.
Serves: 8
Difficulty: Medium

Ingredients:

- 1 sweet potato (large)
- 1 tsp. of olive oil
- Sea salt & pepper to taste, freshly ground
- 1 onion
- 2 tsp. of olive oil
- Sea salt, to taste
- 1/2 cup of frozen spinach, or use four cups fresh
- 8 eggs
- 1/3 cup of parmesan cheese grated or shaved; omit if necessary
- 1/4 tsp. of sea salt
- 1/2 tsp. of Italian seasoning
- Black pepper freshly ground to taste

Directions:

- Set the oven to 425 °F. Dice the sweet potatoes. Apply 1 teaspoon of olive oil to the base of a baking dish.
- Sweet potatoes should be added after a small sprinkle of sea salt & black pepper. Bake for 25-30 minutes with a foil cover firmly.
- The onion should be finely sliced and added to the frying pan with 2 tablespoons of olive oil whilst the sweet potatoes are roasting. Until the onions are tender, cook over medium-low heat, stirring periodically. Use sea salt to season. Instead of adding extra oil if they feel dry, add a few teaspoons of water. When onions are

extremely tender and have caramelized, set aside.

- After beating the eggs, add the parmesan, seasonings, and chopped frozen or fresh spinach.
- Remove the oven dish from the sweet potatoes once they have done cooking and allow them cool for five to ten minutes.
- Loosen the foil when it has somewhat cooled. Compress sweet potatoes to make a crust while using a dish towel to shield your hands from the heat. It's difficult to do while it's really hot, so give it some extra time for cooling so it can build the crust up the edges of your baking dish as well as the bottom.
- Add the mixture of an egg after the crust has formed. Add caramelized onions to the egg mixture as a garnish. Cook the dish at 425°F for an additional 20 minutes while closely covered with foil.
- Lower the oven's temperature to 320°f after removing the foil. Based on your oven, bake for a further 10 to 15 minutes or till the eggs are set in the middle. Add additional parmesan on top.

Nutritional Values per serving:
Total Calories: 112kcal, **Fat:** 6g, **Carbohydrates:** 5g, **Protein:** 7g, **Fiber:** 4g, **Sodium:** 212mg, **Potassium:** 146mg

30. Breakfast Collard Green Burrito

Prep Time: 15 mins.
Cook Time: 25 mins.
Total Time: 40 mins.
Serves: 2
Difficulty: Medium
Ingredients:

- 1/4 peeled butternut squash, sliced
- 4 collard greens
- 1 tbsp. of olive oil
- 4 eggs, scrambled
- Salt & black pepper to taste
- 1/2 cup of black bean sauce
- 1/2 sliced avocado
- 1 tomato, sliced or chopped
- Some chopped cilantro, optional
- Black Bean Sauce
- Some hot sauce, optional
- 1 can of black beans, rinsed & drained
- 1 tsp. of cumin
- 1/2 cup of salsa
- Sea salt (optional) to taste

Directions:

- Set oven to up 450 degrees Fahrenheit.
- Thickly slice the butternut squash, place it on a baking sheet, sprinkle with olive oil, and season with black pepper and sea salt. For 25 minutes, bake the squash.
- Collard leaves should first be soaked in warm (nearly hot) water for 8-10 minutes.
- Blend all the ingredients for the black bean sauce until it is smooth, pausing occasionally to scrape down the edges.
- Add sea salt & pepper to the scrambled eggs before serving.
- Trim the stem on to the bottom of the collard greens after they have been soaked, and then the top part of the stem on the leaf's underside.
- Place two leaves side by side with their tips pointing in different directions.
- Add 1/4 cup of black bean sauce to the middle of each leaf, then top with tomatoes, butternut squash, scrambled eggs, avocados, and any extras you prefer, such as spicy sauce, lime juice, or cilantro.
- Then wrap the sides up like a burrito by first folding the top & bottom leaves over the contents. Serve with salsa after cutting diagonally.

Nutritional Values per serving:
Total Calories: 404kcal, **Fat:** 25g, **Carbohydrates:** 29g, **Protein:** 19g, **Fiber:** 10g, **Sodium:** 2319mg, **Potassium:** 884mg

31. Breakfast Quiche

Prep Time: 20 mins.
Cook Time: 1 hr. 15 mins.
Total Time: 1hr 35 mins.
Serves: 6
Difficulty: Medium
Ingredients:

- 1 tbsp. of olive oil
- 5 cups of peeled sweet potatoes & shredded
- Salt & pepper to taste
- 1/3 cup of onion minced
- 8 ounces of chopped Smoked Bacon in small pieces
- 2 cups of kale chopped
- 8 eggs
- 1 1/2 cups of mushrooms sliced
- 1/2 cup of unsweetened almond milk

- 1 tsp. of sea salt
- 1/2 cup of full-fat coconut milk, canned
- Black pepper, to taste

Directions:

- Set oven up to 425 degrees Fahrenheit.
- Olive oil should be added to a baking dish (11x7) to coat the base and sides. Add the sweet potato when it has been shredded, and season with salt and black pepper to suit.
- Bake for 30 minutes while covered with foil. Chop the bacon, put it in a big frying pan, and cook it to the desired doneness whilst the sweet potatoes are baking. Remove bacon from the skillet and equally distribute it into 2 bowls.
- After removing extra bacon fat from the frying pan, add the onion and fry it briefly for 3–4 mins in the bacon grease.
- Add the kale and mushrooms, and cook for another 5 minutes or so, or until the kale is tender.
- Add eggs, coconut milk, almond milk, salt, and pepper to a large bowl. When mixed, whisk it.
- Stir the egg mixture before adding the cooked greens, mushrooms, & half of the bacon.
- Remove the foil from the sweet potatoes after they are done cooking and let them cool for 5 to 10 minutes. To create a crust, press sweet potato firmly into the pan and against the sides with your hands.
- The bacon, egg, and vegetable combination should be placed into the sweet potato crust.
- Return to oven for a further 35 minutes with a foil cover. Bake for another 8 minutes uncovered after removing the lid.
- Serve with salsa, herbs, or your preferred spicy sauce as a garnish.

Nutritional Values per serving:

Total Calories: 417kcal, **Fat:** 27g, **Carbohydrates:** 27g, **Protein:** 16g, **Fiber:** 3g, **Sodium:** 821mg, **Potassium:** 769mg

32. Eggs Asparagus Benedict on Portobello Mushroom

Prep Time: 25 mins.
Cook Time: 25 mins.
Total Time: 50 mins.
Serves: 4
Difficulty: easy
Ingredients:

- 3 tsp. of olive oil, divided
- 12 asparagus spears (fresh)
- 1 finely chopped shallot
- 2-2/3 cups of baby Portobello mushrooms, sliced
- 2 tbsp. of butter, divided
- 2-1/2 cups of sliced shiitake mushrooms, fresh
- 1/4 cup of sherry
- 1 clove of garlic, minced
- 1/2 cup of heavy whipping cream
- 1 tbsp. of minced fresh basil
- 1/2 tsp. of salt
- 1 tbsp. of white vinegar
- 4 slices of French bread, toasted (3/4 inch in thickness)
- 4 eggs
- 2 tsp. of balsamic vinegar
- 1/4 tsp. of pepper

Directions:

- In a large pan, cook asparagus in 1 tsp. Oil until crisp-tender; remove from heat and keep warm.
- Shallots are cooked until soft in the remaining oil & 1 tbsp. Butter in same pan. Cook for a further 4 minutes after adding the mushrooms and the garlic. Stirring to remove browned pieces from the pan, add sherry. Salt and cream are combined. Bring to a boil. Cook and stir till slightly thickened, about 1 to 2 minutes. Add basil and mix well.
- White vinegar and 2-3 inches of water should be added to a big pan with high sides in the meanwhile. Bring to a boil, then decrease the heat and gently simmer. One at a time, crack a chilled egg into a custard sauce or cup, slipping each egg into the water while holding the cup just over the water's surface.
- Cook for approximately 4 minutes with the lid off until the whites are totally set and the yolks are still runny. Eggs should be lifted out of water using a slotted spoon.
- Over the bread pieces, spread the remaining butter. Add asparagus, a poached egg, and the mushroom mixture to the top of each. Balsamic vinegar should be drizzled over the pepper and spice. Serve right away.

Nutritional Values per serving:

Total Calories: 340 kcal, **Fat:** 25g, **Carbohydrate:** 19g, **Protein:** 12g, **Fiber:** 2g, **Sodium:** 533 mg, **Potassium:** 250mg

33. Papaya Strawberry Smoothie

Prep Time: 10 mins.
Cook Time: 0 mins.
Total Time: 10 mins.
Serves: 2
Difficulty: Easy
Ingredients:

- 9 oz. of strawberries
- 2 sprigs of mint
- 1 papaya (almost about 14 ounces)

- 2 kiwi

Directions:

- Dry and rinse the mint. Take a leaf and place it aside.
- Strawberries should be rinsed and dried on paper towels. Chop coarsely, then add to a tall container. Use an immersion blender to puree, then divide between two glasses.
- Peel and cut up kiwis. Use an immersion blender to puree, then spoon some into each glass.
- Slice the papaya in half, then use a spoon to scoop out the seeds. Remove the meat, then cut it up finely. Using an immersion blender, puree the meat. Put a little amount of purée in each glass, then top with mint leaves. Serve right away.

Nutritional Values per serving:

Total Calories: 340 kcal, **Fat:** 25g, **Carbohydrate:** 19g, **Protein:** 12g, **Fiber:** 2g, **Sodium:** 533 mg, **Potassium:** 250mg

34. Overnight Dark Chocolate Oats

Prep Time: 5 mins.
Cook Time: 4 hrs.
Total Time: 4 hrs. 5 mins.
Serves: 2
Difficulty: Medium
Ingredients:

- 1 cup of rolled oats
- 1 banana
- 2 tbsp. of chia seeds
- 4 tsp. of maple syrup
- 4 tsp. of cacao powder
- 1 1/3 cups of walnut milk (or any milk)
- 2 tbsp. of coconut yogurt
- 1/4 cup of chopped walnuts

Directions:

- Banana, cut in half. That should be mashed in a bowl.
- Fill the container with oats, cacao powder, chia seeds, syrup, milk, and 2 tbsp of walnuts. Combine everything, split it between two containers, and refrigerate. Allow to sit overnight or for at least four hours.
- When you're ready to serve, sprinkle your dish with 1/2 of the remaining banana, 1 tbsp. of coconut yogurt, and 1 tbsp. of chopped walnuts. Enjoy!

Nutritional Values per serving:

Total Calories: 493 kcal, **Fat:** 23g, **Carbohydrate:** 66g, **Protein:** 12g, **Fiber:** 12g, **Sodium:** 9 mg, **Potassium:** 495mg

35. Flour Coconut Pumpkin Bread

Prep Time: 10 mins.
Cook Time: 55 mins.
Total Time: 1hr. 5 mins.
Serves: 12
Difficulty: Medium
Ingredients:

- 4 eggs, large
- 1 cup of pumpkin puree
- 1/2 cup of coconut sugar
- 1 tbsp. of apple cider vinegar
- 2 tbsp. of avocado oil (or some melted coconut oil)
- 1/2 cup of coconut flour
- 2 tsp. of cinnamon
- 1/4 cup of arrowroot starch
- 3/4 tsp. of nutmeg
- 1/2 tsp. of cloves
- 3/4 tsp. of ginger
- 1/2 tsp. of salt
- 1/2 tsp. of baking soda
- 1 1/2 tsp. of baking powder
- 1/2 cup of walnuts, roughly chopped

Directions:

- Set a loaf pan on a baking sheet and preheat the oven up to 350 degrees. Spray non-stick cooking spray or use oil to coat the pan's exposed sides.
- Beat the eggs, pumpkin, sugar, oil, and vinegar together in a mixing bowl until smooth beat.
- Add dry ingredients and whisk till a smooth batter forms (don't add the walnuts yet). Toss the walnuts in. Give the batter five minutes to rest.
- Bake the batter in the middle of the oven for 45 to 50 minutes, till a cake tester placed in the center comes out clean. Transfer the batter in to the prepared pan. If the top surface is browning too soon after 40 minutes of cooking, check and cover with tinfoil.
- After 5 minutes of cooling in the pan, remove to a wire rack to finish cooling fully before slicing.
- Serve with your preferred buttery spread or nut butter after being gently warmed in the toaster oven!

Nutritional Values per serving:

Total Calories: 135 kcal, **Fat:** 8g, **Carbohydrate:** 14g, **Protein:** 4g, **Fiber:** 3g, **Sodium:** 189 mg, **Potassium:** 134mg

36. Almond Flour Pumpkin Pie

Prep Time: 10 mins.
Cook Time: 1 hr.
Total Time: 1hr. 10 mins.
Serves: 10
Difficulty: Medium
Ingredients:
For crust:

- 1/4 tsp. of fine sea salt
- 2 cups of blanched almond flour
- 1 vegan egg, either a store-bought egg replacer or flax
- 2 tbsp. of vegan butter melted

For filling:

- 1/4 cup of maple syrup
- 2 1/2 cups of pumpkin puree
- 1/3 cup of coconut milk
- 2 tbsp. of arrowroot powder
- 1/4 cup of organic cane sugar
- 1 tbsp. of coconut oil
- 1 tbsp. of a blend of cinnamon or pumpkin pie spice, ginger, nutmeg, and cloves
- 1 tsp. of vanilla extract
- 1/4 tsp. of sea salt

Directions:

- Set the oven to 350°F. A 9" pie plate should be greased and saved.
- Add the ingredients for the crust to the food processor's bowl. Process till dough begins to form. It ought to stay together when you crush it between your fingers.
- Place the "crust" on the pie plate, pressing it into the edges and bottom. You are welcome to use your fingers to soften the edges. Discard the crust.
- Reinstall the food processor's bowl on the base after washing and drying it. Blend in the filling ingredients after adding them. With a spoon or spatula, spread the filling evenly over the prepared crust.
- Bake the pie for 60 to 65 minutes, or until the filling is just jiggly and crust is golden brown. Based on heat in the oven, the crust may brown very rapidly; if this occurs, cover the sides with a pie crust protector or tin foil.
- In order to get the best results, remove the pie & let it cool for one hour at least before transferring it to the refrigerator to chill for an additional four.
- Slice & serve (with a coconut whip topping, if you want)!

Nutritional Values per serving:
Total Calories: 257 kcal, **Fat:** 18g, **Carbohydrate:** 22g, **Protein:** 6g, **Fiber:** 4g, **Sodium:** 118 mg, **Potassium:** 100mg

37. Cornbread Pumpkin French Toast

Prep Time: 25 mins.
Cook Time: 5 mins.
Total Time: 30 mins.
Serves: 12
Difficulty: Easy
Ingredients:

- 2 organic eggs (large)
- 1 batch of pumpkin cornbread, prepped in a loaf tin (9x5)
- 1/2 cup of unsweetened almond milk
- Vegan butter & maple syrup for serving
- 1 tsp. of pumpkin pie spice

Directions:

- Prepare the recipe for pumpkin cornbread. To allow for enough chilling time, this step might be completed a day beforehand. Slice the cooked bread into 1/2"-thick pieces after baking.
- In a cake or pie pan, combine the remaining ingredients, including any scrambled eggs, to form the batter.
- Griddle or skillet heated to medium heat. When the pan is hot, add a little bit of vegan butter and swirl it all around to cover the bottom.
- Slices of cornbread should be dipped into the egg mixture one at a time. Place it in the skillet with one side facing up. Then, turn it over. Cook for 2 to 3 minutes on each side, much as you would a pancake.
- Slices of cooked French toast should be placed in a hot oven to finish the batch.
- Serve with some vegan butter, warm Maple Syrup, and a dash of cinnamon.

Nutritional Values per serving:
Total Calories: 126 kcal, **Fat:** 1g, **Carbohydrate:** 29g, **Protein:** 1g, **Fiber:** 1g, **Sodium:** 449 mg, **Potassium:** 11mg

38. Apple Cinnamon Breakfast Quinoa

Prep Time: 5 mins.
Cook Time: 25 mins.
Total Time: 30 mins.
Serves: 2
Difficulty: Easy
Ingredients:

- 1 1/2 cups of water
- 1/2 cup of quinoa
- 2 apples (large)
- Honey

- 2 tsp. of cinnamon

Directions:

- Core and peel both apples. Give them a bite-sized chop.
- Apples, water, and quinoa are added to the sauce pan. Bring it to a boil, then decrease heat to a simmer for 20 to 25 minutes with a lid on. The quinoa would have absorbed the water, and the apples will be mushy.
- Add the cinnamon, then divide the mixture into two bowls.
- Honey should be drizzled over the dish before adding more cinnamon (if desired). And delight!

Nutritional Values per serving:

Total Calories: 2587 kcal, **Fat:** 2g, **Carbohydrate:** 62g, **Protein:** 6g, **Fiber:** 8g, **Sodium:** 13 mg, **Potassium:** 434mg

39. Fluffy Oatmeal Pancakes (Flourless)

Prep Time: 5 mins.
Cook Time: 10mins.
Total Time: 15 mins.
Serves: 6
Difficulty: Easy
Ingredients:

- 1 egg
- 1/2 cup of oats
- 2 1/2 tbsp. of yogurt
- 1 tbsp. of honey
- 1 tsp. of vanilla
- 1 tsp. of butter or coconut oil
- A pinch of baking soda

Directions:

- Use a food processor or a nut grinder to ground the oats.
- In a small dish, combine the egg, yogurt, vanilla, and honey.
- Oats and baking soda should be added.
- A non-stick pan has to be preheated at a low-medium temperature. Apply butter or coconut oil to the surface.
- Start preparing little pancakes with a large spoon or ladle, allowing room between each one so you can easily flip them when they are done.
- It's time to switch the sides of pancakes, gently yet quickly, after the edges of pancakes seem done and bubbles start to appear. Additionally, cook the other side.
- Serve right away with your preferred garnishes!
-

Nutritional Values per serving:

Total Calories: 233 kcal, **Fat:** 12g, **Carbohydrate:** 24g, **Protein:** 7g, **Fiber:** 2g, **Sodium:** 725 mg, **Potassium:** 540mg

4o. Pegan Breakfast Burrito

Prep Time: 15 mins.
Cook Time: 25 mins.
Total Time: 40 mins.
Serves: 5
Difficulty: Easy
Ingredients:

- 1 sliced onion
- 2 sliced red bell pepper
- 1 tbsp. of oil
- 1 tsp. of turmeric
- 1 block of extra firm tofu (8 ounces)
- 1/2 tsp. of cumin
- 1/2 cup of kidney beans
- 1/4 cup of vegetable broth
- Salt & ground black pepper
- 1 sliced avocado
- 5 tortillas
- 1/4 cup of salsa

Directions:

- For five to ten minutes, press the tofu in paper towel wrappers under a heavy object. Roughly slice into pieces measuring 1/3 inch, then put aside.
- Oil, pepper, and onion are added to a big skillet. Cook veggies in oil, tossing to coat, for 15 minutes or until tender and pepper edges start to blacken over medium-high heat.
- Take out of the skillet, then put it aside.
- Add the broth, cumin, turmeric, and tofu in to the same skillet. Cook for about 7 minutes, stirring regularly until all of the broth is absorbed. Add beans and simmer for an additional 2 to 4 minutes.
- Add 1/5 of tofu mixture to each tortilla shell before adding the pepper/onion combination, avocado, and salsa to complete the burritos.

Nutritional Values per serving:

Total Calories: 345 kcal, **Fat:** 17g, **Carbohydrate:** 34g, **Protein:** 14g, **Fiber:** 5g, **Sodium:** 485 mg, **Potassium:** 360mg

41. Potato Polenta Breakfast Bowl

Prep Time: 5 mins.
Cook Time: 25mins.
Total Time: 30 mins.
Serves: 4
Difficulty: Easy
Ingredients:

- 1 ½ tsp. of salt divided
- 4 cups of water (1 liter)
- 1 cup of yellow cornmeal, medium-grain (170 grams)
- ½ onion (medium), diced
- 1 tbsp. of oil
- 2 garlic cloves, thinly sliced
- ½ diced zucchini
- 250 grams of cherry tomatoes (9 oz.)
- 2 medium or 1 large potatoes, diced
- ½ tsp. of oregano or any other herb, dried
- ½ diced green pepper
- A jar of salsa (small)
- Some grinds of pepper

Directions:

- In a small saucepan, bring the water & 1/2 teaspoon of salt to a boil. Sprinkle into the cornmeal while you stir. Reduce the heat after whisking until the cornmeal thickens. Allow it to simmer for approximately 20 minutes, stirring occasionally, till the cornmeal is soft. You may add extra water when stirring the polenta if you like a looser consistency.
- In the meanwhile, add the oil to a big pan and heat it up over medium-high heat. Fry the garlic and onions together until they are tender and transparent. Add cherry tomatoes into the pan after removing onions to a platter. Cook them while sometimes shaking the pan until they start to split & blister. Add the zucchini on the platter after removing tomatoes from the plate (add some oil here). Cook for a couple of minutes, or until they are soft and starting to brown. Transfer zucchini to a plate.
- If the pan is really dry, add a little additional oil along with the potatoes before covering it. Fry the potatoes, tossing occasionally until they are evenly browned and cooked through. Green pepper is added when the lid is removed. Cook the pepper for a few more minutes, or until it's crisp-tender.
- Re-add the zucchini, tomatoes, onion, garlic, and leftover 1 tsp. of salt & pepper to the pan along with the potatoes. The vegetables are heated while being combined.
- Potatoes should be placed on top of the polenta in each of the four bowls. Serve with salsa to spoon on top on the side.

Nutritional Values per serving:
Total Calories: 255 kcal, **Fat:** 6g, **Carbohydrate:** 44g, **Protein:** 7g, **Fiber:** 7g, **Sodium:** 1245 mg, **Potassium:** 733mg

42. Breakfast Potatoes

Prep Time: 5 mins.
Cook Time: 15mins.
Total Time: 20 mins.
Serves: 2
Difficulty: Easy
Ingredients:

- 3 potato (medium), roughly 400g/14oz
- 2 tbsp. of olive oil
- 2 onion (medium)
- 1 tsp. of cumin, ground
- 7 oz. of firm tofu (200g)
- 2 tsp. of oregano, dried
- 1 tsp. of black pepper
- 1 tsp. of salt
- ½ cup of cherry tomatoes (4 tomatoes)

Directions:

- The potatoes should be scrubbed and then cut into cubes around the size of your tiny finger. Onions should be peeled and chopped into "half rings."
- Put a little olive oil into a pan and cook it on low to medium. Gently stir throughout the first five minutes of cooking the potatoes. Add the onions once it begins to sweat.
- Crumble the tofu in now. Salt and pepper are then added while stirring. If so, cover the pan and simmer it for 15 minutes. You may add additional oil if it seems to be needed, or you can add some hot water to reduce the amount of calories you consume.
- Add some olive oil to a second pan and stir it around. Heat is set at medium. The tomatoes should be cut in half and fried for about 5 minutes, or until some black spots emerge. If you'd like, you may also cook some drops of boiling water. Add salt and pepper to taste.
- Put the potatoes onto a platter and cover if you don't have or don't want to use a second pan (or keep it warm in oven).

- Place the tomato and potato mixture on a platter.

Nutritional Values per serving:

Total Calories: 423 kcal, **Fat:** 19g, **Carbohydrate:** 51g, **Protein:** 15g, **Fiber:** 9g, **Sodium:** 1190 mg, **Potassium:** 1141mg

43. Breakfast Quesadillas

Prep Time: 5 mins.
Cook Time: 5 mins.
Total Time: 15 mins.
Serves: 4
Difficulty: Easy
Ingredients:

- 1 red onion (small), diced
- 3 tsp. of olive oil divided
- 1 block of extra tofu firm (14-ounce), drained & pressed
- 1 tsp. of chili powder
- 2 tbsp. of nutritional yeast
- 1 tsp. of cumin
- ½ tsp. of black pepper
- ½ tsp. of sea salt
- ½ tsp. of onion powder
- ½ tsp. of red pepper flakes
- ½ tsp. of garlic powder
- ¼ tsp. of turmeric
- 1 chopped red bell pepper
- A pinch of cayenne pepper
- 1 chopped green bell pepper
- ½ cup of shredded cheese (non-dairy)
- 8 tortillas (10-inch each)
- Avocado sliced to serve
- Hot sauce to serve
- 1 cup of salsa

Directions:

- The onion should be cooked for approximately 5 minutes, until it is translucent and just beginning to brown, in a large pan with one tsp. of oil over medium heat.
- The nutritional yeast, chili powder, onion powder, cumin, garlic powder, salt, black pepper, red pepper flakes, turmeric, & cayenne are all added to the skillet with crumbled tofu and mixing everything together. Add the peppers after cooking for one or two minutes. About 5 extra minutes of cooking should soften the peppers.
- The tofu scramble should be taken out of the pan and cleaned.
- To coat the base of the pan, add an additional 1/2 teaspoon of oil and stir. Spread 2 tbsp. of the cheese over the base of the skillet with 1 of the tortillas on top. Place one tortilla on top of the first, then evenly distribute 1/4 mixture of tofu on it. Utilizing a spatula, press down.
- Using a spatula, examine the underside after approximately 5 minutes of cooking to see whether the base tortilla has started to brown a little. Suppose it hasn't; give it 1-2 mins. More to cook. If so, use a spatula to delicately turn the quesadilla over and cook it for a few more minutes until the bottom is golden. To keep it warm, take the quesadilla out of the skillet and cover it. To make four quesadillas, repeat the process with the other tortillas, tofu , and cheese mixture.
- Serve each quesadilla hot, cut into four pieces, with salsa and avocado slices.

Nutritional values per serving:

Total Calories: 290kcal, **Fats:** 10g, **Carbohydrates:** 32g, **Protein:** 15g, **Fiber:** 26g, **Sodium:** 300mg, **Potassium:** 250mg

44. Tofu Scramble Breakfast Bowl

Prep Time: 10 mins.
Cook Time: 20 mins.
Total Time: 30 mins.
Serves: 4
Difficulty: Easy
Ingredients:

- 2 small sweet potatoes (cubed)
- 1 package of Organic Firm Tofu
- 1 tbsp. of avocado oil
- 1 tsp. of paprika
- 1/2 tsp. of turmeric
- 1/2 tsp. of garlic powder
- Salt/black pepper
- 1/2 cup of diced tomatoes
- 1/2 cup of quinoa (dry)
- 1 large avocado
- 4 cups of spinach

Directions:

- Press the tofu in the fridge one night before (or some hours beforehand) using paper towels & a hefty item.
- Set the oven's temperature to 375.
- Roast the diced sweet potatoes for 20 minutes on a baking pan with 1/2 Tbsp. of oil (or until soft).
- Tofu should be cut into tiny pieces and cooked in the rest of the avocado oil over medium-high heat.
- Add the salt, paprika, pepper, garlic powder, and turmeric.
- Simmer the quinoa as directed, whereas the tofu remains cooking.
- Remove the tofu scramble from the heat after adding the chopped tomatoes.

- Each bowl should have spinach, tofu scramble, sweet potatoes, quinoa, & avocado slices.

Nutritional values per serving:

Total Calories: 289kcal, **Fats:** 13g, **Carbohydrates:** 20g, **Protein:** 14g, **Fiber:** 2g, **Sodium:** 110mg, **Potassium:** 200mg

45. Baked Sausage Patties

Prep Time: 5 mins.
Cook Time: 15 mins.
Total Time: 20 mins.
Serves: 3
Difficulty: Easy
Ingredients:

- 2 tbsp. of liquid (reserved can)
- 1 can of pinto beans (drained the reserved liquid)
- 3 tbsp. of breadcrumbs
- 2 tsp. of soy sauce
- 1 tbsp. of maple syrup
- 2 tsp. of garlic powder
- 1 tsp. of sage
- 2 tsp. of onion powder
- 1 tsp. of smoked paprika
- 1/4 tsp. of thyme
- 1/2 tsp. of rosemary
- Black pepper, to taste
- 1 pinch of chili flakes

Directions:

- Set the oven's temperature to 475 degrees. Use parchment paper to cover a baking sheet.
- The pinto beans & saved can liquid are blended together. Don't become completely mush; maintain some texture.
- Combine the other ingredients with the pinto beans.
- Shape into patties. Place the baking sheet with parchment paper inside it.
- The patties should be baked for around 16 minutes, turning them over after 7-8 minutes. Enjoy!

Nutritional values per serving:

Total Calories: 214kcal, **Fats:** 1g, **Carbohydrates:** 39.8g, **Protein:** 11g, **Fiber:** 17g, **Sodium:** 250mg, **Potassium:** 180mg

46. Crumbled Breakfast Tempeh Sausage

Prep Time: 5 mins.
Cook Time: 10 mins.
Total Time: 15 mins.
Serves: 6
Difficulty: Easy
Ingredients:

- 1 & ½ cup of water
- one package of tempeh (8 oz.), plain & unflavored
- 2 tbsp. of soy sauce
- 1 tsp. of paprika
- 1 tsp. of Worcestershire sauce
- 1 tsp. onion powder
- Half tsp. of oregano
- 1 tsp. garlic powder
- Half tsp. of sage
- ¼ tsp. of black pepper
- ¼ tsp. of thyme
- 1 tbsp. of oil
- A pinch or 2 of chili flakes

Directions:

- In a pan, crumble the tempeh.
- Stir well after adding the water and the additional ingredients, except the oil.
- Medium-low heat is used to bring to a simmer. Let simmer until all of the water has been absorbed by the tempeh.
- Add the oil, stir, and cook for a further 5 mins or so over medium heat. (If you have eliminated oil from your diet, you may skip this step; the sausage would still taste great).

Nutritional values per serving:

Total Calories: 30kcal, **Fats:** 2g, **Carbohydrates:** 2g, **Protein:** 1g, **Fiber:** 1g, **Sodium:** 349 mg, **Potassium:** 36mg

47. Breakfast Hash with Beans and Veggies

Prep Time: 10 mins.
Cook Time: 40 mins.
Total Time: 50 mins.
Serves: 4
Difficulty: Medium
Ingredients:

- 2 tsp. of oil
- 3 russet potatoes (large)- peeled & cubed
- ½ tsp. of salt
- 1 can of beans, drained & rinsed
- ¼ tsp. of black pepper
- 2 cups of loosely packed baby spinach
- 1 squash (medium), chopped
- 1 zucchini (medium), chopped
- 1 chopped red bell pepper
- 1½ tsp. of garlic powder
- ½ cup of mushrooms, sliced
- 1½ tsp. of onion powder
- A pinch of chili flakes
- ½ tsp. of paprika

Directions:

- On medium heat, add the potatoes & oil in to a large skillet. Add salt and pepper and toss.

- The potatoes should be caramelized and cooked until soft (about 25 minutes.) About every five minutes, toss.
- With the exception of the spinach and beans, add the other ingredients to the pan. Sauté the veggies until they are soft (about 10 minutes.)
- Add the spinach and beans. The spinach should be wilted after a further 3–4 minutes of sautéing.

Nutritional values per serving:
Total Calories: 332.8kcal, **Fats:** 16.4g, **Carbohydrates:** 33.1g, **Protein:** 17.4g, **Fiber:** 3.4g, **Sodium:** 1,431.4 mg, **Potassium:** 1,367.1 mg

48. Eggy Breakfast Sandwiches

Prep Time: 20 mins.
Cook Time: 15 mins.
Total Time: 4hrs. 40mins. (soak time 4hrs.)
Serves: 6
Difficulty: Medium
Ingredients:

- 2 tbsp. of hot sauce, vinegar-based (like Cholula), plus some more to taste
- 1 cup of cashews (raw), soaked in the water for 4 - 8 hrs., drained & rinsed
- ½ tsp. of salt
- 2 tbsp. of unflavored and unsweetened milk (non-dairy), plus some more as needed

For Eggy Chickpea Patties:

- 2 tbsp. of nutritional yeast flakes
- ⅔ cup of chickpea flour
- ½ tsp. of baking powder
- ½ tsp. of paprika
- ½ tsp. of ground cumin
- ¼ tsp. of turmeric
- ¼ tsp. of black pepper
- ¼ tsp. of Kala namak (for the eggy flavor, can replace table salt)
- ½ cup of water
- 1 tbsp. of olive oil
- 1 tbsp. of soy sauce

For Sandwiches:

- ½ batch of tempeh bacon (optional)
- 4 English muffins (vegan), split & toasted
- ½ cup of baby spinach
- Additional sauces or fillings of choice, like salsa, vegan sliced cheese, ketchup, avocado, etc.

Directions:

- Put each item into the s-blade-equipped food processor's bowl, until smooth, blend.
- Test the mixture's flavor and tweak the ingredients to your preference. If the mixture looks too thick, add more milk to thin it down. Blend once more.
- In a small bowl, combine the chickpea flour, baking soda, nutritional yeast, cumin, turmeric, paprika, Kala namak, and black pepper.
- Soy sauce and water are whisked in.
- Put a medium skillet over medium heat and coat the bottom with olive oil.
- Give the oil 1 minute to warm up before adding about 1/4 cup of the batter to the skillet to form an about 3-inch patty. Repeat for as many as you can comfortably put in the skillet.
- The patties should be cooked for a further 3 - 4 minutes until bubbles appear in the middle and the patties are firm and gently browned.
- The patties should be taken out of the pan and placed on a platter. Continue till all the batter has been consumed.

To put the sandwiches together:

- Spread spicy cashew cheese on the interior of one or both muffin half, then stack and stuff the bottom halves with eggy patties, spinach, tempeh bacon (if you're using), and any other contents you choose. Serve.

Nutritional values per serving:
Total Calories: 468kcal, **Fats:** 17g, **Carbohydrates:** 55 g, **Protein:** 21g, **Fiber:** 9g, **Sodium:** 1189mg, **Potassium:** 751mg

49. Scrambled Eggs with Cauliflower and Chickpeas

Prep Time: 10 mins.
Cook Time: 15 mins.
Total Time: 25 mins.
Serves: 2
Difficulty: Easy
Ingredients:

- 1 can of chickpeas drained
- 1 tbsp. of olive oil
- 1 head of chopped cauliflower, in small pieces or run it through a food processor for some seconds
- 1 tsp. of smoked paprika
- 2 chopped tomatoes (whole)
- 1/4 tsp. of garlic powder
- Salt/black pepper, to taste
- 1 tsp. of herbs de Provence

Directions:

- Olive oil is heated at medium heat. Add cauliflower for a few minutes, and cook. Mix in all the spices and chickpeas.
- Turn up the heat. Cook for a little while, pounding chickpeas as you go. Add tomatoes. For a few minutes, cook

- Serve the food simply, on toast, in tortillas, rice crackers, etc.

Nutritional values per serving:

Total Calories: 171kcal, **Fats:** 8g, **Carbohydrates:** 22g, **Protein:** 7g, **Fiber:** 8g, **Sodium:** 96mg, **Potassium:** 1313mg

50. Protein Baked Oats

Prep time: 30 mins.
Cook time: 30 mins. (Baking)
Total time: 1 hr.
Serves: 6
Difficulty: easy

Ingredients:

- 4 eggs (large)
- 2 cups of rolled oats
- 1/4 cup of vanilla protein powder
- 2 cups of unsweetened coconut or almond milk
- 1/4 cup of pure maple syrup or raw honey
- 1 tsp. of vanilla extract
- 1/4 cup of nuts of choice, chopped like almonds
- 1 tsp. of fresh lemon zest
- 1 banana (large), sliced
- Coconut oil to greasing pan
- 1 cup of mixed frozen or fresh berries

Directions:

- Set the oven up to 350 degrees Fahrenheit and use coconut oil to butter a 9x13 baking dish.
- Eggs, honey, protein powder, vanilla, zest, and milk should be whisked together in a large mixing dish until frothy.
- Your oats should now be added. Stir thoroughly to mix everything.
- Allow mixture to soak the oats up for 30 minutes if time permits.
- After that, incorporate the berries, banana slices, and chopped almonds.
- Place the oat mixture into the baking dish that has been prepared.
- Bake for 30-35 minutes at 350 degrees Fahrenheit, or until the center is set and the top & edges are golden browns.
- Remove the oats from the oven after they are a lovely golden brown.
- Make 6 evenly spaced squares or bars.
- These squares are simple to keep in a sealed container in the refrigerator for up to a week, sandwiched between layers of wax paper. They heat up well!

Nutritional values per serving:

Total Calories: 176kcal, **Fats:** 4g, **Carbohydrates:** 32g, **Protein:** 4g, **Fiber:** 4g, **Sodium:** 132mg, **Potassium:** 48mg

Chapter 3: Pegan Diet - Lunch Recipes

1. Taco Grilled Chicken Salad

Prep time: 30 mins.
Cook time: 20 mins.
Total time: 50 mins.
Serves: 4
Difficulty: easy
Ingredients:

- ¾ cup of medium-hot salsa
- 1 can of black beans (15 ounces), rinsed & drained
- ½ cup of chopped fresh cilantro
- 2 tbsp. of chili powder
- 1 tbsp. of lime juice
- 1 tsp. of ground cumin
- 1 tsp. of brown sugar
- 1 tsp. of ground coriander
- ¼ tsp. of cayenne pepper
- 1 pound of boneless, skinless chicken breast halves
- 1 tbsp. of olive oil
- 4 corn tortillas (7 inches)
- ½ cup of chopped fresh cilantro
- 4 cups of shredded lettuce
- 1 peeled avocado, pitted & sliced (Optional)
- ¼ cup of sour cream (Optional)
- 1 lime, cut in wedges (Optional)

Directions:

- Set an outside grill over medium-high heat and give the grates quick oiling.
- In a bowl, combine the black beans, salsa, half the cilantro, and lime juice.
- Rub the mixture on chicken breasts by combining chili powder, coriander, cumin, brown sugar, olive oil , and cayenne pepper in a bowl.
- Cook the chicken breasts on a hot grill for 10 to 12 minutes on each side or until juices run clear and the center is no longer pink. In the middle, an instant-read thermometer should register at least 165 degrees Fahrenheit (74 degrees C). Place the tortillas on the grill and cook them for 3 to 5 minutes, or until they are just beginning to gently brown on both sides.
- Slice the chicken into long, thin strips after transferring it to a chopping board. On top of the tortillas, distribute the chicken strips, the bean mixture, the lettuce, and the last 1/2 cup of cilantro. Serve with avocado, sour cream, and lime wedges.

Nutritional values per serving:
Total Calories: 470kcal, **Fats:** 18.7g, **Carbohydrates:** 44.4g, **Protein:** 35.2g, **Fiber:** 15.9g, **Sodium:** 831.8mg, **Potassium:** 1215.1mg

2. Mushroom Burgers

Prep time: 15 mins.
Cook time: 50 mins.
Total time: 1 hr. 10 mins.
Serves: 6
Difficulty: medium
Ingredients:

- 1 peeled sweet potato (medium), about 9 ounces, sliced thinly
- 2 tsp. of olive oil, divided
- 16 ounces of mushrooms, cleaned & sliced
- 1/4 cup of walnuts
- 1 red onion (medium), sliced
- 1/4 tsp. of red pepper flakes
- 1/4 tsp. of onion powder
- 1/2 tsp. of Italian seasoning
- 1/4 tsp. of garlic powder
- 1/4 tsp. of sea salt, some more to taste
- 1/2 tsp. of ginger powder
- 1/4 tsp. of black pepper, some more to taste
- 1 egg
- 3/4 cup of almond flour
- 1 tsp. of chia seeds

Directions:

- Heat the oven up to 400 °F.
- Put the sweet potato onto a parchment paper–covered sheet tray. Add 1 teaspoon of sea salt, 1 teaspoon of pepper, and 1 teaspoon of olive oil. To become tender when forked, roast for 15-20 minutes.
- Cook the mushrooms & onions for approximately 10 minutes over high heat, or until they are tender and the liquid has completely evaporated.
- Let the mushrooms and sweet potatoes cool until they are not hot to the touch.

- Add the combination of mushrooms, sweet potatoes, walnuts, herbs, salt, and pepper. Also, include the egg & chia seeds. Don't over-process the mixture; simply pulse a few times to blend. The sweet potato pieces should be the size of peas.
- Lower the oven's temperature to 350 °F and line a sheet pan with parchment paper.
- Create six 1-inch patties out of the sweet potato & mushroom mixture.
- Cook the burgers for a further 5 minutes after flipping them after baking for 30 minutes. Serve warm with your preferred toppings after 5 minutes of cooling.

Nutritional values per serving:
Total Calories: 129kcal, **Fats:** 8.1g, **Carbohydrates:** 10g, **Protein:** 6.5g, **Fiber:** 3.8g, **Sodium:** 102mg, **Potassium:** 200mg

3. Fried Cauliflower Rice

Prep time: 5 mins.
Cook time: 20 mins.
Total time: 25 mins.
Serves: 4
Difficulty: easy
Ingredients:

- 2 tbsp. of neutral oil (like coconut, vegetable, or peanut)
- 1 head of cauliflower, cut in florets
- 1 bunch of scallions, thinly sliced
- 1 tbsp. of minced fresh ginger
- 3 cloves of garlic, minced
- 2 peeled carrots, diced
- 1 diced red bell pepper
- 2 diced celery stalks
- 1 cup of frozen peas
- 3 tbsp. of soy sauce
- 2 tbsp. of rice vinegar
- 2 tsp. of Sriracha, or some more to taste

Garnishes:

- 4 eggs
- 1 tbsp. of neutral oil (like coconut, vegetable, or peanut)
- Salt & black pepper, freshly ground
- 4 tbsp. of scallions, thinly sliced
- 4 tbsp. of chopped cilantro (fresh)
- 4 tbsp. of sesame seeds

Directions:

- In a bowl of a food processor, pulse cauliflower for two to three minutes, or till the mixture resembles rice. Place aside.
- Over medium heat, warm the oil in a large skillet. Stir-fry the scallions, ginger, and garlic for approximately a minute or until aromatic.
- Stir-fry the celery, carrots, and red bell pepper after adding them for 9 to 11 minutes, or until the veggies are soft.
- Add cauliflower rice & stir-fry for an additional 3 to 5 minutes, or until it starts to turn golden. The frozen peas are added, and they are well mixed up.
- Stir in the soy sauce, Sriracha, and rice vinegar after adding them. Place aside.
- Heat the oil into a medium pan over medium to high heat. Directly into the pan, crack the eggs, and cook for 3 to 4 minutes, or till the whites are set the yolks yet are still runny. Add salt and pepper to each.
- Four plates with cauliflower rice and fried eggs should be used for serving. Add one tsp. of sesame seeds, one tbsp. of cilantro, and one tbsp. of scallions to each dish. Serve right away.

Nutritional values per serving:
Total Calories: 291kcal, **Fats:** 7g, **Carbohydrates:** 23g, **Protein:** 13g, **Fiber:** 4g, **Sodium:** 100mg, **Potassium:** 95mg

4. Red Lentils Curry

Prep time: 15 mins.
Cook time: 30 mins.
Total time: 45 mins.
Serves: 6
Difficulty: easy
Ingredients:

- 1/2 onion (large), diced
- 1 1/2 cups of lentils, rinsed & picked over
- 2 tbsp. of butter
- 1/2 tbsp. of garam masala
- 2 tbsp. of red curry paste
- 1 tsp. of curry powder
- 1 tsp. of sugar
- 1/2 tsp. of turmeric
- 1 tsp. of garlic, minced
- Some sprinkles of cayenne pepper
- 1 tsp. of minced ginger
- 1 can of tomato puree (14-ounce)
- Some cilantro to garnish
- 1/4 cup of coconut cream or milk
- Some rice to serve

Directions:

- The lentils should be prepared as directed. Drain then set apart.
- In a big pan over medium-high heat, melt the butter. When aromatic and golden, add onion and continue to cook for a few minutes. Stir-fry for 1-2 minutes after adding all the spices (garam masala, curry paste, curry powder, cayenne, turmeric, garlic, sugar, and ginger).

When smooth, whisk in the tomato puree and continue to boil.

- Add the cream & lentils. Simmer for a further 15 to 20 minutes (the more, the better) and stir to blend! Garnish with cilantro & serve with rice.

Nutritional values per serving:

Total Calories: 249kcal, **Fats:** 6.5g, **Carbohydrates:** 35.1g, **Protein:** 12.5g, **Fiber:** 14.5g, **Sodium:** 181.9mg, **Potassium:** 650.3mg

5. Zucchini Noodles in Alfredo Sauce

Prep time: 15 mins.
Cook time: 5 mins.
Total time: 20 mins.
Serves: 2
Difficulty: easy
Ingredients:

- 1-2 tbsp. of Parmesan (optional)
- 2 zucchinis spiralized (medium)

Alfredo Sauce:

- 2 tbsp. of lemon juice
- ½ cup of cashews (raw), soaked for some hours or in the boiling water for 8-10 minutes
- 3 tbsp. of nutritional yeast
- 1 tsp. of onion powder
- 2 tsp. of white miso (can substitute soy sauce, tamari, or coconut aminos)
- ¼-1/2 cup of water
- ½ tsp. of garlic powder

Directions:

- Slice zucchini into noodles, then pat them dry.
- Starting with 1/4 cup of water, combine all the Alfredo ingredients in a high-speed blender and process until smooth. If the sauce is very thick, add a tablespoon of water at a time till you reach the desired consistency.
- The zucchini may either be left raw or heated for two to three minutes in a skillet with some olive oil. Note: Avoid overcooking the zoodles as they will get mushy.
- Alfredo sauce and optional vegan parmesan are served on top of zucchini noodles.

Nutritional values per serving:

Total Calories: 225kcal, **Fats:** 16g, **Carbohydrates:** 19g, **Protein:** 14g, **Fiber:** 6g, **Sodium:** 200mg, **Potassium:** 350mg

6. Scallion Bacon Chicken Salad

Prep time: 15 mins.
Cook time: 20 mins.
Total time: 35 mins.
Serves: 5
Difficulty: easy
Ingredients:

- 1/2 tsp. of garlic powder
- 1 lb. of skinless, boneless chicken breasts
- 1/2 tsp. of onion powder
- 8 slices of bacon (uncured), sugar-free
- Sea salt & black pepper, to taste
- 3 scallions, thinly sliced (green onions)
- 1/2 cup of homemade vegan mayo

Directions:

- Slice the bacon into bite-sized pieces and cook it in a large pan over medium-high heat until it is crisp.
- While keeping the reduced fat in the pan, remove the bacon from the skillet and put it aside to drain it on paper towels.
- The chicken breasts should be pounded to a thickness of 1/2 inch or sliced in half so that each piece is half inch thick.
- Reduce the heat to medium. Place the chicken breasts in the bacon fat-coated skillet after liberally seasoning them with salt, pepper, garlic powder, and onion powder. If you would like, use refined coconut oil or ghee. Cook for two to three minutes on each side, or till the inside is not pink anymore.
- Place the chicken into a large bowl, cover, and chill in the fridge. Now is the perfect time to make mayo if you haven't already.
- Once the chicken has cooled, shred or roughly cut it into bite-sized pieces and combine with the scallions, bacon, and mayonnaise in a large bowl. Mix everything well.
- If necessary, taste & add salt or pepper. Immediately serve, or cover and store for later. In a container that is well closed, the chicken salad may be stored in the fridge for 3–4 days. Enjoy!

Nutritional values per serving:

Total Calories: 420kcal, **Fats:** 34g, **Carbohydrates:** 0g, **Protein:** 25g, **Fiber:** 0g, **Sodium:** 420mg, **Potassium:** 422mg

7. Avocado & Salmon Poke Bowl

Prep time: 20 mins.
Cook time: 0 mins.
Total time: 20 mins.
Serves: 4
Difficulty: easy
Ingredients:
For Poke:

- ½ cup of yellow onion, thinly sliced
- 1 ripe avocado (medium), diced
- ½ cup of scallion greens, thinly sliced
- ¼ cup of caviar
- ½ cup of fresh cilantro, chopped

- 3 tbsp. of tamari (reduced-sodium)
- ½ tsp. of Sriracha
- 2 tsp. of toasted sesame oil (dark)

Brown Rice Salad:

- 2 cups of spicy greens (packed), like watercress, arugula, or mizuna
- 2 cups of cooked brown rice (short-grain), warmed
- 2 tbsp. of rice vinegar
- 1 tbsp. of Dijon mustard or Chinese-style
- 2 tbsp. of olive oil

Directions:

- Salmon, onion, avocado, scallion greens, caviar, cilantro, tamari, sesame oil, & Sriracha should all be gently mixed together in a medium bowl.
- In a big bowl, mix the greens and the rice. In a small bowl, combine the oil, mustard, and vinegar. Add to rice salad and well combine. Serve the rice salad with the poke.

Nutritional values per serving:

Total Calories: 442kcal, **Fats:** 21.9g, **Carbohydrates:** 34.3g, **Protein:** 29.5g, **Fiber:** 7g, **Sodium:** 791.7mg, **Potassium:** 828mg

8. Broccoli Casserole

Prep Time: 10 mins.
Cook Time: 45 mins.
Total Time: 55 mins.
Serves: 6
Difficulty: Easy
Ingredients:

- 1/3 cup of heavy whipping cream
- 3 whisked eggs
- 1/2 cup of grated parmesan cheese
- Some pepper, to taste
- 1 tsp. of sea salt
- 6 cups of cauliflower rice
- 4 cups of broccoli florets
- 2 packages of Smoked Canadian Bacon
- 2 cups of cheddar cheese

Directions:

- Set the oven to 425°F.
- Combine the eggs, parmesan, heavy whipping cream, cheese, salt, and pepper in a medium mixing bowl.
- Cauliflower rice, broccoli, ham, and the egg mixture should all be placed in a 9-by-9-inch casserole dish. Mix the items together with a fork.
- Cheddar cheese shreds should be placed on top of the dish.
- Bake the casserole for 35 minutes with the foil covering. To give the cheese brown color on top, uncover the dish and bake it for an additional 10 minutes.

Nutritional Values per serving:

Total Calories: 431kcal, **Fat:** 26g, **Carbohydrates:** 18g, **Protein:** 33g, **Fiber:** 6g, **Sodium:** 1396mg, **Potassium:** 1189mg

9. Chicken Scarpariello

Prep Time: 30 mins.
Cook Time: 50 mins.
Total Time: 1hr. 20 mins.
Serves: 8
Difficulty: Medium
Ingredients:

- 1 tbsp. of olive oil, plus 2 tbsp.
- 1 1/2 pounds cocktail potatoes
- Sea salt, to taste
- Black pepper, to taste
- 8 thighs of chicken
- 1 yellow onion, in strips
- 3 sweet pre-cooked Italian sausages, sliced
- 1 red bell pepper, in strips
- 1 cup of white wine
- 3 cloves of garlic, minced
- 1/4 cup of white wine vinegar
- 1/2 cup of sweet pickled peppers or Peppadew peppers
- 1 cup of chicken broth
- 3 sprigs of rosemary (fresh)

Directions:

- Set the Oven to Bake Mode on 450° F for 25 minutes for 1 tray.
- Bake some tiny potatoes on a baking sheet. Season the potatoes with Salt and pepper after drizzling them with olive oil. To uniformly coat the potatoes, use your hands.
- While the braised chicken dish is cooking, bake the potatoes.
- Sprinkle sea salt & pepper liberally on the chicken thighs.
- A large Dutch oven should be heated to medium heat. Place chicken thighs in the saucepan skin side down after adding the olive oil. Give the chicken skin 5-7 minutes to brown. Chicken thighs should be taken out of the pan and placed aside.
- Sausage should be added to the heated pan and browned for approximately five minutes. Remove and set aside the sausage.
- Add the onions to the heated pan and lower the heat to medium-low. For approximately 5-7 minutes, as the onions start to soften, stir them. Add red bell peppers, garlic, and salt & pepper

to taste. Stirring to avoid burning, soften for a further 7 to 10 minutes.

- White wine & white wine vinegar are then added, and the mixture is simmered until it has been reduced by half.
- Put the sausage, peppadew peppers, and chicken broth in the saucepan. The sausage is stirred into a combination of onion and pepper.
- Place the chicken into the sausage and vegetable mixture, and then garnish with rosemary sprigs.
- After the potatoes have been taken from the oven, set the oven to bake for 30 minutes at 350 degrees Fahrenheit.
- Put the Dutch oven onto a tray and set the Steam Oven on the lower shelf.
- A chicken thigh, a little pepper & onion mixture, and a teaspoon of white wine sauce should be added on top of the potatoes.

Nutritional Values per serving:

Total Calories: 386kcal, **Fat:** 24g, **Carbohydrates:** 15g, **Protein:** 21g, **Fiber:** 3g, **Sodium:** 210mg, **Potassium:** 703mg

10. Baked Thai Pork Tenderloin

Prep Time: 15 mins.
Cook Time: 15 mins.
Total Time: 30 mins.
Serves: 6
Difficulty: Easy
Ingredients:

- 3 tbsp. of rice wine vinegar
- 2 tbsp. of soy sauce or 1/4 cup of coconut aminos + 2 tbsp. of water
- 3 tbsp. of lime juice
- 2 tbsp. of coconut sugar
- 2 tbsp. of sesame oil
- 2 tbsp. of grated ginger fresh
- 1 tbsp. of paleo Sriracha
- 1 tbsp. of garlic, minced
- 2 pounds of pork tenderloin
- 1 tsp. of sea salt

Directions:

- In a bowl, mix all the ingredients with the exception of the pork.
- Put the pork tenderloin with the marinade in an airtight container. Turning tenderloin over periodically will help ensure even marinating. Marinate for two hours overnight.
- The oven should be preheated to 485°.
- Turn the oven's broil setting on if using a standard oven.
- Put the remaining marinade into a small saucepan, then pour it over the pork in the baking dish.
- For a medium-cooked pork tenderloin, bake the meat for 15 minutes, or till the internal temperature reads 145°F. .
- Turn over the tenderloin halfway through baking and check the internal temperature then and every three to four minutes after that, if using a regular oven set to broil.
- The marinade should be heated to a simmer over low heat, stirring regularly, and simmering until it has reduced by half.
- To get rid of the ginger and garlic pieces, pour the marinade using a mesh strainer.
- Prior to slicing, let the meat 10 minutes to rest. Serve along with the sauce or drizzle it with the reduced sauce.

Nutritional Values per serving:

Total Calories: 253kcal, **Fat:** 10g, **Carbohydrates:** 7g, **Protein:** 31g, **Fiber:** 1g, **Sodium:** 701mg, **Potassium:** 613mg

11. Vietnamese Beef with Lettuce Wraps

Prep Time: 30 mins.
Cook Time: 10 mins.
Total Time: 40 mins.
Serves: 4
Difficulty: Medium
Ingredients:

- 1 tsp. of sea salt
- 12 ounces of sirloin steaks (grass-fed)
- 3 tbsp. of coconut aminos
- 3 tbsp. of minced lemongrass finely
- 3 tbsp. of lime juice
- 2 cloves of garlic, finely minced
- 1 finely minced shallot

Peanut Vietnamese Sauce:

- 1/4 cup of coconut milk
- 1/4 cup of Butter (No Sugar Added)
- 1/4 cup of coconut aminos
- 2 tbsp. of lime juice
- 2 tbsp. of rice wine vinegar
- 1-3 tbsp. of paleo sriracha
- 1 tbsp. of sesame oil

Lettuce Beef Wraps:

- 1 cup of carrots julienned
- 1 head of butter lettuce
- 1 cup of thinly sliced purple cabbage
- 1/2 cup of fresh mint
- 1 cup of fresh basil
- 2 tbsp. of sesame seeds to garnish (optional)

Directions:

- To coat the steaks, combine the marinade ingredients with the steaks in an airtight container. For up to 24 hours, marinate. The steak may be thinly sliced and marinated for an hour if you do not have the time to prepare them a day in advance.

Peanut Sauce

- Blend the sauce ingredients in a blender until completely smooth. Until you are ready to use, set away, or chill. The remaining sauce is excellent as a salad dressing or vegetable dip and keeps well in the fridge for about a week.

Beef Lettuce Wraps:

- On a dish, arrange lettuce leaves and then garnish with herbs and veggies.
- If at all feasible, cook the steak outside to the desired doneness. If grilling outside isn't an option, sear the steak on both sides in a cast iron skillet that has been oiled with avocado oil over high heat. Cook at a lower temperature as desired until desired doneness.
- Before slicing, let the steak rest for 8-10 minutes with the foil covering it. Divide the thinly sliced meat among the lettuce leaves. If desired, top with sesame seeds.

Nutritional values per serving:

Total Calories: 364kcal, **Fat:** 21g, **Carbohydrates:** 22g, **Protein:** 25g. **Fiber:** 3g, **Sodium:** 1260mg, **Potassium:** 717mg

12. Lettuce Thai Chicken Wraps

Prep Time: 30 mins.
Cook Time: 15 mins.
Total Time: 45 mins.
Serves: 4
Difficulty: Medium
Ingredients:

- 1 cup of red cabbage shredded
- 1 head of romaine lettuce
- 1 sliced mango
- 1/2 cup of roasted sunflower seeds, almonds, or cashews
- red chillis (optional)
- cilantro & Thai basil for garnishing

Ginger Chicken:

- 1 pound of chicken (ground) can substitute for ground turkey
- 1 tbsp. of sesame oil
- 1/4 cup of ginger, grated (fresh)
- 2 tbsp. of coconut aminos (can substitute soy or Tamari sauce)
- 1/4 cup of minced Thai shallots
- 1/2 tbsp. of chili sauce (or some more, to taste)
- 1/4 tsp. of sea salt (or some more, to taste)

Thai Almond Sauce

- 1/4 cup of full fat coconut milk (from can)
- 1/4 cup of sunflower seed butter or almond butter, no sugar added
- 1 tbsp. of rice wine vinegar
- 1/2 tbsp. of lime juice, fresh (1/2 large lime)
- 1 1/2 tbsp. of coconut aminos
- 1/2 tsp. of chilli sauce
- A pinch salt, to taste
- 1 tsp. of sesame oil

Directions:

- Sesame oil is heated in a pan over medium-high heat, then ginger and shallots are added to prepare the chicken. Cook until extremely soft and aromatic, 7 to 10 minutes.
- Brown the ground chicken after adding it. To taste, add coconut aminos, sea salt, and chilli sauce.
- Blend all the ingredients together to create the SunButter sauce. While a blender may make it more quickly, you can also make it using a bowl & a little whisk. The SunButter sauce should be refrigerated until used.
- Add the chicken, mango, and cabbage to the wraps before adding the toasted nuts and herbs.
- Serve with a side of hot SunButter sauce or drizzle some over.

Nutritional Values per serving:

Total Calories: 497kcal, **Fat:** 33g, **Carbohydrates:** 26g, **Protein:** 28g, **Fiber:** 6g, **Sodium:** 559mg, **Potassium:** 1381mg

13. Thai Red Curry with Chicken & Zoodles

Prep Time: 20 mins.
Cook Time: 30 mins.
Total Time: 50 mins.
Serves: 6
Difficulty: Easy
Ingredients:

- 3 cloves of garlic minced
- 1 tbsp. of avocado oil or substitute olive oil
- 3 tbsp. of ginger, grated
- 2 cups of vegetable or chicken broth
- 1/2 tsp. of turmeric

- 1/4 cup of SunButter (No Added Sugar)
- 1 pound of chicken breasts, thinly sliced or cubed
- 2 tbsp. of paste of Thai red curry, add less if needed
- 1 sweet potato (large), peeled & cubed
- 1 red bell pepper, in thin strips
- 1 can of full-fat coconut milk (14 ounces)
- 1 cup of thinly sliced red onion
- 2 tbsp. of fresh lime juice
- 3 tbsp. of coconut aminos or 1 & 1/2 tbsp. of soy sauce or tamari
- 1 zucchini (large) zoodles, about 6 cups
- Some chopped green onions for garnishing, optional
- Chopped cilantro for garnishing, optional

Directions:

- Add the garlic, ginger, turmeric, and avocado oil to a big Dutch oven or soup pot and heat over medium heat. The aromatics should be softened after around 5 minutes of sautéing.
- Add SunButter, red curry paste, and a little amount of vegetable broth to the saucepan. Add the sweet potatoes, chicken, and remaining vegetable broth after whisking to make a creamy paste. Allow it to boil for approximately 15 minutes, or till the chicken is cooked & the sweet potatoes become tender.
- Regain a simmer after adding the onions, red peppers, and coconut milk. Lime juice and coconut aminos are used to season the soup. If required, taste the soup and add sea salt as desired. Give the veggies five minutes or so to soften.
- Make zoodles using a spiralizer whilst the soup is simmering. If you do not have a spiralizer, you may just cut the zucchini or make long strands of it using a vegetable peeler.
- To serve, top bowls with hot soup and add zoodles. If desired, add cilantro & green onions as a garnish.

Nutritional values per serving:

Total Calories: 265kcal, **Fat:** 10g, **Carbohydrates:** 24g, **Protein:** 20g, **Fiber:** 3g, **Sodium:** 607mg, **Potassium:** 665mg

14. Slow Cooker Delicious Chicken Mole

Prep Time: 30 mins.
Cook Time: 4 hr.
Total Time: 4 hr. 30 mins.
Serves: 8
Difficulty: Medium
Ingredients:

- Some salt, to taste
- 2 pounds of boneless chicken breasts
- Black pepper, to taste
- 1/2 minced yellow onion
- 2 tbsp. of avocado oil
- 4 cloves of garlic, peeled & minced
- 1/4 cup of chili powder
- 1 minced jalapeno (optional)
- 1 tsp. of cinnamon
- 2 1/2 cups of chicken broth
- 1 tsp. of cumin
- 3 tbsp. of Organic SunButter
- 1 tbsp. of arrowroot powder mix with 2 tbsp. of water
- 2 tbsp. of tomato paste
- 1 tsp. of sea salt
- 1 tbsp. of cocoa powder

Directions:

- Add the chicken to the slow cooker and season it with salt and pepper.
- When translucent and aromatic, for approximately 6 minutes, add the minced onion, garlic, and jalapeño (if used) to a large pan with the avocado oil.
- Stir in the salt, cumin, cinnamon, and chili powder before adding the veggies.
- Add SunButter and tomato paste after adding the chicken broth. Blend and smooth with a whisk. Simmer for a little while.
- Stir in the arrowroot while continuously swirling the sauce after combining it with 2 tbsp of water.
- Chili powder & salt should be taste-tested before being added, along with the cocoa powder.
- The sauce may now be ultra-smoothened using either an immersion or a regular blender. Even if you neglect this step, the sauce will still taste fantastic.
- The chicken should be covered with half the sauce. Turn the crockpot to low and simmer for 4-5 hours. For serving, save the remaining sauce.
- Take out the chicken breasts and chop or shred them.
- To sprinkle on the chicken, reheat the remaining sauce. It may also be simply added into the slow cooker along with the chicken that has been shredded.
- For up to three days, keep leftovers in the refrigerator. This frozen mole with shredded chicken is fantastic. For up to three months, keep in an airtight container in the freezer.

Nutritional Values per serving:

Total Calories: 214kcal, **Fat:** 10g, **Carbohydrates:** 6g, **Protein:** 26g, **Fiber:** 1g, **Sodium:** 724mg, **Potassium:** 549mg

15. Pumpkin Moroccan Chicken

Prep Time: 20 mins.
Cook Time: 4 hr.
Total Time: 4 hr. 20 mins.
Serves: 8
Difficulty: Medium
Ingredients:

- 1 tbsp. of olive oil
- 2 pounds of chicken breasts, in chunks
- 1 chopped onion
- 2 tsp. of cumin
- 2 tsp. of ginger powder
- 1 tsp. of sea salt
- 1/2 tsp. of turmeric
- 1 tsp. of cinnamon
- 1/4 tsp. of cayenne
- 1 cup of vegetable or chicken broth
- 1 cup of fresh pumpkin, canned also works
- toasted almonds, for garnishing, optional
- chopped cilantro to garnish

Directions:

- Add 1/2 tbsp. of olive oil to a frying pan on high heat. Sauté the onion till transparent after adding it.
- Add the chicken pieces and heat until browned but not fully cooked.
- Add salt & spices after the chicken has begun to brown, then stir to coat the chicken and onions in a uniform layer.
- Pumpkin puree & vegetable broth should be added to the crockpot after the chicken & onions have been added. The pumpkin puree should be mixed into the chicken mixture while stirring.
- For four hours, cook on low heat. This may also be cooked for two hours on high, but the texture won't be as excellent.

Nutritional values per serving:
Total Calories: 167kcal, **Fat:** 5g, **Carbohydrates:** 5g, **Protein:** 25g, **Fiber:** 1g, **Sodium:** 543mg, **Potassium:** 518mg

16. Oven Baked Delicious Pesto Salmon

Prep Time: 15 mins.
Cook Time: 14 mins.
Total Time: 29 mins.
Serves: 2
Difficulty: Easy
Ingredients:

- 2 tbsp. of walnuts
- 2 (4-6 ounces each) salmon fillets
- 1 tbsp. of parmesan cheese
- 2 cups of broccoli, chopped
- sea salt & black pepper, to taste
- 1 sliced bell pepper
- 1 tbsp. of olive oil
- 1 cup of cherry tomatoes
- 2 tbsp. of basil pesto

Directions:

- Heat to 450° F. Put parchment paper on a baking sheet and put it aside.
- In a food processor bowl, combine the parmesan cheese, salt, and pepper with the walnuts. Process till a fine crumb develops.
- Put the walnut mixture on a shallow plate, and then cover the salmon pieces' tops with it. Include in a baking pan.
- Olive oil should be drizzled over the broccoli, peppers, and tomatoes (or any chosen veggies) in the bowl. Add salt and pepper to taste.
- Around the salmon, add the vegetables to the baking sheet. Avoid packing the pan too full to prevent uneven roasting. With just two pieces of salmon, use a half-sheet pan so you can add several veggies and give them room to roast.
- For 14 minutes, bake the salmon and veggies.
- Serve the salmon with vegetables and a pesto topping.

Nutritional values per serving:
Total Calories: 499kcal, **Fat:** 31g, **Carbohydrates:** 15g, **Protein:** 40g, **Fiber:** 5g, **Sodium:** 296mg, **Potassium:** 1452mg

17. Salmon Zucchini Patties

Prep Time: 20 mins.
Cook Time: 20 mins.
Total Time: 40 mins.
Serves: 18
Difficulty: Easy
Ingredients:

- 2 cups of zucchini shredded
- 1 1/2 pounds of salmon cooked
- 2 eggs
- 2 tbsp. of finely minced onion
- 1/4 cup of cilantro, chopped
- 2 tbsp. of finely minced jalapeno (or to taste)
- 2 tsp. of salt
- 3 tbsp. of lime juice
- olive oil, to fry (about 1/4 cup)
- 3/4 cup of almond flour

Directions:

- In a food processor, combine the salmon, eggs, zucchini, onion, jalapenos, cilantro, lime juice, and salt. Pulse until the salmon and veggies are blended but still have some texture.
- Fill a bowl with almond flour.

- In a large skillet, heat the oil over medium-high heat. Go to the following step after the oil is heated.
- Scoop out 1/4 cup of the salmon mixture, then use your hands to make patties. Use a heaping spoonful and follow the very same directions to produce salmon patties the size of an appetizer.
- Add the patties to the heated pan after coating them on both sides with the almond flour. If they are frying too rapidly or too slowly, lower the heat. Each side should take almost about 5 minutes to become golden.
- Take the patties out of the pan and place them on a platter covered with paper towels.
- Serve immediately or keep chilled for up to 2-3 days or frozen for up to 1 month.
- Allow frozen patties to defrost before baking at 425° F for 15-20 minutes to restore their crispness.

Nutritional Values per serving:

Total Calories: 91kcal, **Fat:** 5g, **Carbohydrates:** 2g, **Protein:** 9g, **Fiber:** 1g, **Sodium:** 154mg, **Potassium:** 232mg

18. Lettuce Wrap Burger

Prep Time: 10 mins.
Cook Time: 15 mins.
Total Time: 25 mins.
Serves: 4
Difficulty: Easy
Ingredients:

- 2 tbsp. of sesame oil divided
- 1 pound of ground chicken
- 1/2 cup of cilantro, finely chopped
- 2-4 tsp. of sriracha
- 1 tsp. of ginger powder
- 1/2 tsp. of salt
- 4 slices of pineapple
- 6 tbsp. of Teriyaki Sauce (Soy Free)
- 4 slices of Canadian Bacon

To Serve: (optional)

- lettuce
- Gluten-Free Buns
- tomatoes
- cheddar cheese
- onions
- Dijon mustard

Directions:

- Add 1 tbsp. of sesame oil, ginger, salt , and ground chicken to a bowl. Mix well, then include the cilantro. Create patties by dividing the chicken into 4 pieces.
- Apply the rest of the sesame oil to the grill pan or grill and turn the heat up high.
- Place the chicken burgers on the grill and cook for 7 minutes. Burgers should be flipped and brushed with teriyaki sauce. Allow cooking for a further 7 minutes or so.
- Additionally, cook pineapple & Canadian bacon for around five minutes on high heat.
- Burgers can be served with lettuce wraps or buns and a ton of toppings!

Nutritional Values per serving:

Total Calories: 337kcal, **Fat:** 18g, **Carbohydrates:** 16g, **Protein:** 27g, **Fiber:** 1g, **Sodium:** 1706mg, **Potassium:** 852mg

19. Mexican Cauliflower Rice

Prep Time: 15 mins.
Cook Time: 15 mins.
Total Time: 30 mins.
Serves: 3
Difficulty: Easy
Ingredients:

- 1 tbsp. of Olive oil
- 3 cups of (stems removed & washed) Cauliflower Florets
- 1 finely chopped Onion (small)
- 1 finely chopped Jalapeno
- 3-4 Cloves of Garlic, minced
- 2 finely chopped Tomatoes
- 1 tsp. of Cumin Powder
- ¾ cup of Bell Peppers, diced
- ½ tsp. of red chili or Paprika Powder
- Salt to taste
- 1 tbsp. of Cilantro / Coriander, chopped
- More cilantro, jalapenos, sliced avocados, lime juice, etc. for the topping

Directions:

- In a chopper or food processor, add the cauliflower florets and pulse several times until the cauliflower resembles tiny chunks (like rice). Avoid going too far, or it can get mushy.
- Onions, garlic, and jalapenos are added to hot oil in a pan. The onion should be transparent, and the garlic should be aromatic after a few minutes of stir-frying.
- Salt, tomatoes, cumin, and paprika powder should all be added to the pan. The tomatoes should be cooked for 4-5 minutes or until they are tender.
- Mix thoroughly after adding the cauliflower rice and diced bell peppers to the pan. The cauliflower should be stir-fried for 3–4 minutes or until soft.
- Add your preferred topping & serve hot.

Nutritional values per serving:
Total Calories: 114kcal, **Fat:** 5g, **Carbohydrates:** 15g, **Protein:** 4g, **Fiber:** 5g, **Sodium:** 39mg, **Potassium:** 637mg

20. Ratatouille

Prep Time: 20 mins.
Cook Time: 1 hr.
Total Time: 1 hr. 20 mins.
Serves: 4
Difficulty: Medium
Ingredients:

- 1 tbsp. of olive oil
- 1 cup of crushed tomatoes
- 1/4 tsp. of apple cider vinegar
- One tbsp. of fresh basil, almost about 4 large sliced leaves, plus some more for garnish
- 1/4 tsp. of black pepper
- 1 tsp. of minced garlic
- 1 tsp. of herbs de Provence
- 1 red or sweet onion (medium), sliced
- 1/4 tsp. of salt
- 1/4 tsp. of chili powder
- 1-2 zucchini (large), about 1 & 1/2 cups of slices)
- 3 fresh tomatoes (large), about 3 cups of slices
- 1 Japanese eggplant (large), about 3 cups of slices

Directions:

- Set the oven to 350°F. A baking dish (6"x9") should be lightly greased and left aside.
- Crushed tomatoes, vinegar , and oil should all be combined in a mixing dish. Add the salt, pepper, chili powder, garlic, basil, and herbs de Provence.
- The tomato mixture should be poured into the prepped baking dish and spread evenly around the bottom of the dish.
- Place the vegetable slices in the pan on their side, resting against the pan's edge, in alternate patterns (e.g., onion, eggplant, zucchini, tomato; repeat). Repeat this process until you've made a few rows of vegetables, filled your pan, and consumed all of the vegetable slices.
- Optionally, apply oil with a brush or spray to the uncovered tops of the vegetables to promote browning inside the oven. You are welcome to omit this only step if you choose since it is mostly for aesthetics.
- Bake for approximately an hour, or until the vegetables are soft and the tomato sauce is boiling at the bottom.
- Before serving, garnish with more finely chopped fresh basil (optional). Serve warm or cool.

Nutritional Values Per serving:
Total Calories: 109kcal, **Fat:** 10g, **Carbohydrates:** 17g, **Protein:** 4g, **Fiber:** 3g, **Sodium:** 241mg, **Potassium:** 350mg

21. Pasta Salad

Prep Time: 10 mins.
Cook Time: 20 mins.
Total Time: 30 mins.
Serves: 8
Difficulty: Easy
Ingredients:

- 1 cup of diced red pepper
- 1 pound of pasta (gluten-free)
- 1 cup of diced purple onion
- 1 small diced zucchini
- 1 cup of black olives
- 1/3 cup of Evo
- 1/4 cup of red wine vinegar
- 4 tbsp. of dried oregano
- 1/2 tsp. of pink sea salt

Optional:

- 1/2 tsp. of red pepper flakes

Directions:

- Follow the directions on the pasta package while cooking it. In a bowl, combine each item. For about 1 week, you can keep the pasta salad in an airtight container.

Nutritional Values per serving:
Total Calories: 122kcal, **Fat:** 12g, **Carbohydrates:** 4g, **Protein:** 1g, **Fiber:** 1g, **Sodium:** 413mg, **Potassium:** 108 mg

22. Zucchini Noodles with Lemon Cream Sauce

Prep Time: 10 mins.
Cook Time: 10 mins.
Total Time: 20 mins.
Serves: 4
Difficulty: Easy
Ingredients:

- 1/3 cup of nutritional yeast
- 1/2 cup of cashews (raw), soaked for 2 hours, at least
- 2 cloves of garlic
- 1 tsp. of miso paste

- 3 tbsp. of lemon juice (fresh)
- 1 tsp. of tahini
- 1/4 tsp. of nutmeg
- 1/4 tsp. of smoked paprika
- 1/4 tsp. of sea salt
- 1/3 cup to 1/2 cup of filtered water
- 1/4 tsp. of pepper
- 3 - 4 zucchinis (medium)

Directions:

- The cashews should be rinsed and drained before being combined with the rest ingredients, beginning with only 1/3 cup of water, in a blender.
- Add additional water, 1 tbsp. At a time, till the sauce is pourable and continue blending on high till smooth and creamy.
- The zucchini should be spiralized and put in a big basin. Add sauce to the noodles and mix.
- If preferred, garnish immediately with chopped herbs, fresh cracked pepper, and hot sauce.

Nutritional values per serving:

Total Calories: 144kcal, **Fat:** 8g, **Carbohydrates:** 13g, **Protein:** 7g, **Fiber:** 3g, **Sodium:** 215mg, **Potassium:** 575 mg

23. Cauliflower Tacos

Prep Time: 20 mins.
Cook Time: 30 mins.
Total Time: 50 mins.
Serves: 8
Difficulty: Medium
Ingredients:

- ¾ cup of flour
- 1 head of cauliflower in florets
- 3 tbsp. of corn starch
- 1 tsp. of white pepper
- ½ tsp. of salt
- 5 tbsp. of sriracha, separated
- ¼ cup of water
- ½ cup of milk (non-dairy), unsweetened
- panko bread crumbs
- 2 tbsp. of rice vinegar
- ½ cup of vegan mayo
- black sesame seeds (optional)

For tacos:

- 1 cup of shredded green cabbage
- 1 cup shredded purple cabbage
- juice of 1 lime
- 2 sliced avocados
- salt to taste
- 8 tortillas, flour, or corn
- cilantro, sriracha, and lime wedges for serving

Directions:

- Put parchment paper on a baking pan and preheat the oven to 425 degrees.
- In a dish, mix the nondairy milk, water, non-dairy milk powder, corn starch, white pepper, salt, and 1 tablespoon of Sriracha. Combine by whisking. Spread some panko in a different bowl.
- Cauliflower should be dredged in the liquid mixture, letting extra drop off. The place there and completely covered with panko. Repeat with the other cauliflower florets after placing the final one on the baking sheet. 15 minutes of baking will take place in the oven. Cook for a further five minutes after flipping.
- Make the slaw and cook the cauliflower at the same time. In a bowl, mix the cabbage, lime juice, and a little salt. Combine by stirring, then put aside.
- Combine the rice vinegar, vegan mayo, and remaining sriracha (you may use 2-4 tablespoons depending on your spice taste) in a bowl to make the sauce as well. Combine by whisking.
- After taking the cauliflower out of the oven, dip the florets into the sauce with a fork. Reposition the florets on the baking pan. 5 more minutes of baking are needed in the oven. Turn oven to broil & cook the cauliflower for an additional two to three minutes for even more crunch. Add sesame seeds after taking the dish out of the oven.
- Tacos are put together after the tortillas have been heated in a pan or over an open flame. Slaw, cauliflower, avocado, cilantro, and sriracha should be layered on top of the tortillas. Slices of lime are optional.

Nutritional Values per serving:

Total Calories: 301kcal, **Fat:** 14g, **Carbohydrates:** 37g, **Protein:** 6g, **Fiber:** 4g, **Sodium:** 698mg, **Potassium:** 429mg

24. Cauliflower Tahini Steaks

Prep Time: 15 mins.
Cook Time: 20 mins.
Total Time: 35 mins.
Serves: 4
Difficulty: Easy
Ingredients:

- ⅔ cup of tahini (150g)
- 1 whole cauliflower (large)
- ⅓ cup of water
- 3 cloves of garlic
- ⅓ cup of lemon juice
- ½ tsp. of sea salt, to taste
- ¼ tsp. of smoked paprika
- ½ tsp. of dried dill

Directions:

- Heat the oven to 400 degrees. A baking sheet may be lined with a silicone liner or parchment paper, or it can simply be gently greased with oil.
- Cut the cauliflower into roughly four 1-inch-thick "steaks" using a broad, sharp knife. There will be some cauliflower on the side that will probably break up into florets, but that's good. Keep them, to bake them as well.
- Use a small food processor or blender to mix all the ingredients to produce the sauce until smooth, and blend. It should be rather liquid and thin. If it isn't, you may need to add extra water; if the tahini is thick, this is frequently the case. Alternately, grate or dice the garlic finely before combining it with the other ingredients in a bowl. 1/4 cup of sauce should be set aside for the final drizzle. Fill your cauliflower steaks with the remaining mixture in a big, shallow bowl.
- Slices of cauliflower should be coated on both sides with sauce before shaking off the extra. Put them on the baking sheet you've prepared.
- Place the remaining florets in the sauce and combine with the sauce after coating all the cauliflower steaks.
- Once golden brown, bake for another 20 minutes.
- You may use it as a side or a main meal. Add some of the tahini sauce you set aside.

Nutritional Values per serving: Total Calories: 580kcal, **Fat:** 18g, **Carbohydrates:** 84g, **Protein:** 31g, **Fiber:** 4g, **Sodium:** 250mg, **Potassium:** 110mg

25. Creamy Sweet Potato Spinach Noodles & Cashew Sauce

Prep Time: 2o mins.
Cook Time: 5 min.
Total Time: 25 mins.
Serves: 4-6
Difficulty: Easy
Ingredients:

- 3/4 cup of water (some more for soaking)
- 1 cup of cashews
- 1/2 tsp. of salt
- 1 tbsp. of oil
- 1 clove of garlic
- 4 sweet potatoes (large), spiralized
- a handful of basil leaves (fresh), chives, or any other herbs
- 2 cups of baby spinach
- olive oil, to drizzle
- salt & pepper, to taste

Directions:

- In a dish, cover cashews with water and let them soak for about two hours.
- Drain and thoroughly rinse. Add the ingredients to a blender or food processor, along with the 3/4 cup of water, salt, & garlic, until very smooth and pureed.
- Over high heat, warm the oil in the big skillet. Add sweet potatoes and stir with tongs for 6-7 minutes, until they are soft and crisp. After taking it off the heat, add the spinach; it should start to wilt fast.
- Stir together half of the sauce and half the herbs in the pan. If the batter is just too sticky, add water. Add the rest of the fresh herbs on top after liberally seasoning with salt & pepper and drizzling with olive oil.

Nutritional Values per serving:
Total Calories: 203kcal, **Fat:** 10g, **Carbohydrates:** 23g, **Protein:** 5g, **Fiber:** 3g, **Sodium:** 253mg, **Potassium:** 480mg

26. Spicy Spaghetti Squash Peanut Ramen

Prep Time: 15 mins.
Cook Time: 5 mins.
Total Time: 20 mins.
Serves: 4
Difficulty: Easy
Ingredients:

- 8 oz. of sliced crimini mushrooms
- 1 spaghetti squash (large), cooked
- 2-3 tsp. of olive oil to cook mushrooms
- 1/4 cup of chopped cashews or peanuts
- 1/2 cup of cilantro
- 2 sliced limes in wedges
- red peppers flakes, as per taste
- black sesame seeds, as per taste
- 4 cups of chicken broth or vegetable broth

Directions:

- Sliced mushrooms & a drizzle of some olive oil should be added to a frying pan. Stir occasionally while sautéing until golden, then put away.
- Blend or process the sauce's components until they are completely smooth. After that, mix with the vegetable broth in a pot and boil over medium heat for a little while before removing and setting aside.
- Ramen noodles, spaghetti squash, and sautéed mushrooms should all be added to the skillet and heated until it is ready to eat. Add sesame seeds, chopped peanuts, cilantro, red pepper flakes, fresh lime juice, or lime wedges to taste as a garnish.

Nutritional Values per serving:

Total Calories: 613kcal, **Fat:** 46g, **Carbohydrates:** 43g, **Protein:** 16g, **Fiber:** 12g, **Sodium:** 1439g, **Potassium:** 940mg

27. Mexican Quinoa Lunch Salad

Prep Time: 10 mins.
Cook Time: 20 mins.
Total Time: 30 mins.
Serves: 4
Difficulty: Easy
Ingredients:

- 2 cups of vegetable broth
- 1 cup of pre-rinsed organic quinoa (uncooked)
- 2 limes, juiced and zested
- 2 corn ears off the cob
- 15 oz. of black beans (1 can), rinsed & drained.
- 1 bunch of chopped cilantro
- 1 tsp. of cumin
- 2 tbsp. of red wine vinegar
- , salt & black pepper, to taste
- 3 tbsp. of olive oil

Directions:

- In a saucepan, mix the quinoa and the broth. Boil for a few minutes, then turn heat down to low and simmer covered for 12 to 15 minutes. After taking it off the heat, cover it and let it rest for an additional five minutes. Once again, fluff with a fork.
- Over medium heat, cook the corn in 1 tbsp. oil until just starting to faintly caramelize.

Nutritional Values per serving:
Total Calories: 447kcal, **Fat:** 14g, **Carbohydrates:** 66g, **Protein:** 17g, **Fiber:** 14g, **Sodium:** 482g, **Potassium:** 781mg

28. Chicken Green Chili Enchilada Casserole

Prep Time: 15 mins.
Cook Time: 30 mins.
Total Time: 45 mins.
Serves: 8
Difficulty: Medium
Ingredients:

- 2 cups of shredded cheddar
- 2 cups of cooked chicken, diced or shredded
- 1/3 cup of sour cream
- 15 ounces of green chili (canned) enchilada sauce
- 4 ounces of canned green chillis (diced), drained if needed
- 12 corn tortillas (6-inch)
- Salt & pepper to taste
- 10.5 ounces of cream of chicken soup

Topping Options:

- Salsa
- Sour cream
- Shredded lettuce
- Jalapeños
- Tomatoes

Directions:

- Set oven up to 350 degrees Fahrenheit.
- Combine the cream of the chicken soup, 1/3 cup of enchilada sauce, sour cream, salt, and black pepper in a large bowl. Add chicken and green chilies, diced. Mix everything up completely.
- On an 8-inch by 8-inch baking sheet, spread 1/4 cup of enchilada sauce till the bottom is completely covered. To cover the pan's bottom, use 3 tortillas. To fill up spaces, cut them in half.
- Over the tortillas, spread 1/3 of the chicken mixture. Add 1/3 cup of enchilada sauce on top of the chicken mixture. Cover the top layer with three additional tortillas.
- Spread out the remaining third of the mixture of chicken over the tortillas. Over the chicken mixture, sprinkle 1 cup of shredded cheese and 1/3 cup of enchilada sauce. Cover the 2nd layer with three additional tortillas.
- Spread tortillas with the leftover chicken mixture after adding it. Over the chicken mixture, spread another third cup of enchilada sauce. More tortillas should be used to cover the third layer.
- Pour the remaining sauce over the casserole's whole top. To prevent the tortillas from drying out as the casserole bakes, try to cover as much of them as you can. Over the sauce, sprinkle the leftover cup of cheese.
- Bake the casserole for 25-30 minutes, or till the cheese, is melted & it is bubbling nicely.
- For servings that are simple to serve, take the baking sheet out of the oven and let it rest for 5-10 minutes.

Nutritional Values per serving:
Total Calories: 275kcal, **Fat:** 15g, **Carbohydrates:** 26g, **Protein:** 11g, **Fiber:** 4g, **Sodium:** 979g, **Potassium:** 148mg

29. Fajita Rice Chicken Bowl with Black Beans

Prep Time: 15 mins.
Cook Time: 30 mins.
Total Time: 45 mins.
Serves: 4-6
Difficulty: Medium
Ingredients:

- Salt & black pepper, freshly ground
- 1 1/4 lbs. of skinless, boneless diced chicken breasts, 1-inch pieces
- 2 1/2 tbsp. of olive oil
- 3 cups of bell pepper, chopped (about 2 medium)
- 1 cup of yellow onion, diced
- 3 cloves of garlic, minced
- 1 can of fire-roasted tomatoes (15 oz.)
- 1 2/3 cups of chicken broth, low-sodium
- 1 can of black beans (15 oz.), drained & rinsed
- 1 1/2 tsp. of ground cumin
- 2 1/2 tsp. of chili powder
- 2 cups of instant brown rice
- 3/4 cup of Mexican cheese, shredded
- 1 1/2 tbsp. of fresh lime juice
- 1/3 cup of chopped cilantro

Directions:

- In a 12-inch deep skillet or nonstick sauté pan, heat 1 tablespoon of olive oil over high heat.
- Add the chicken and season with salt, pepper, 1 1/2 teaspoons chili powder, and 1 teaspoon cumin. Cook for approximately 7 minutes, sometimes stirring, until well cooked.
- Wrap the chicken in foil to keep it warm by transferring it there.
- Heat the skillet again over medium-high. Add onions and cook for three minutes in the rest of 1 1/2 Tbsp. of olive oil.
- After another three minutes, add the bell peppers, and after another minute, add the garlic.
- Add the remaining 1 teaspoon of chili powder, 1/2 teaspoon of cumin, tomatoes, black beans, chicken stock, and salt and black pepper to taste & bring to a boil (liquid must bubble up in the center of pan, not just edges).
- Reduce heat to medium, add rice, and stir well to coat and fully immerse in liquid. For 6 to 7 minutes, cover and simmer.
- Remove from heat and give a five-minute break. Chicken, lime juice, cheese, and cilantro are all stirred in. Serve hot.

Nutritional Values per serving:

Total Calories: 650 kcal, **Fat:** 18 g, **Carbohydrates:** 66 g, **Protein:** 55 g, **Fiber:** 9g, **Sodium:** 990g, **Potassium:** 1460mg

30. Cauliflower Tabbouleh

Prep Time: 40 mins.
Cook Time: 0 mins.
Total Time: 40 mins.
Serves: 6
Difficulty: Easy
Ingredients:

- 1/4 cup of packed mint leaves
- 1 cup of packed parsley leaves
- 1 head of cauliflower (small), or 16-oz. of cauliflower rice (frozen), leaves & stem removed
- 2 tbsp. of olive oil
- 2 Roma tomatoes (plum), seeded & diced
- 3 tbsp. of freshly squeezed lemon juice
- 1/4 tsp. of black pepper
- 1/4 tsp. of salt

Directions:

- Parsley & mint leaves should be minced or processed into a food processor before being added to a big bowl.
- Use a box grater to shred the cauliflower, then combine it with the parsley & mint.
- Toss the salad with the diced tomato after adding it.
- Add salt (optional) & black pepper to the salad along with olive oil & lemon juice. To coat, stir.
- Before serving, let the Tabbouleh for 30 minutes to marinade undercover.

Nutritional Values per serving:

Total Calories: 70 kcal, **Fat:** 5 g, **Carbohydrates:** 6 g, **Protein:** 2 g, **Fiber:** 2g, **Sodium:** 130g, **Potassium:** 360mg

31. Zuppa Toscana

Prep Time: 5 mins.
Cook Time: 45 mins.
Total Time: 50 mins.
Serves: 6
Difficulty: Easy
Ingredients:

- 2 tsp. of olive oil

- 3 red potatoes, thinly sliced (whole), about 6 oz. each, 1/8 inch)
- 4 cloves of garlic, minced
- 1 can (15oz.) of cannellini beans, drained & rinsed
- 1 yellow onion (whole), medium & minced
- 8 cups of vegetable broth (low sodium)
- 1/2 tsp. of salt
- 1 tsp. of Italian seasoning
- 1/4 tsp. of black pepper
- 1/2 cup of cashews (raw)
- 1 bunch of kale (about 1 lb. of destemmed & chopped)
- 12 oz. of Ground Vegan Meat Substitute

Directions:

- In a big saucepan, warm the oil over medium heat. Add the ground beef sub, and cook for 6-7 minutes, stirring regularly, until it is browned and crumbly.
- Cook the onion and garlic in the saucepan for three to four minutes, stirring periodically, until tender.
- Add salt, pepper, Italian seasoning, black pepper, and beans to the pot. Put a lid on it and simmer it.
- Add the potatoes and greens once it has simmered. Potatoes should be fork-tender after 10 to 15 minutes of simmering on low heat.
- Pour 1 cup boiling water over the cashews whilst the soup is cooking. Give it 15 minutes to sit. Blend the cashews & water until they are completely smooth.
- After removing the soup from the heat, mix in the cashew cream.

Nutritional Values per serving:

Total Calories: 320 kcal, **Fat:** 9 g, **Carbohydrates:** 42 g, **Protein:** 20 g, **Fiber:** 11g, **Sodium:** 670g, **Potassium:** 1590mg

32. Chickpea Masala

Prep Time: 15 mins.
Cook Time: 40 mins.
Total Time: 55 mins.
Serves: 3
Difficulty: Medium
Ingredients:

- 1/2 tsp. of cumin seeds
- 2 tbsp. of sunflower oil
- 1-inch piece of ginger, fresh (peeled & grated)
- 1 red onion, medium (finely diced)
- 2 cloves of garlic (grated)
- 2 tsp. of smoked paprika
- 1/4 tsp. of ground turmeric
- 2 tsp. of amchoor (mango) powder
- 1 tsp. of ground coriander
- 1 tbsp. of tomato paste
- 1 tomato, medium (finely diced)
- 1 cup of water
- Juice of 1/2 lemon
- 1 can of chickpeas (garbanzo beans) (15-oz), drained & rinsed
- 1 tbsp. of cilantro leaves, finely minced
- 1/4 tsp. of salt

Directions:

- Cumin seeds are added to hot oil in a heavy-bottomed pan on medium-high heat. Ginger and garlic are added and sautéed for one minute after the seeds begin to spatter. Add the onion and cook for approximately 2 minutes, or till the onion is golden brown.
- To the onion mixture, add the amchoor powder, paprika, turmeric, tomato, coriander, and tomato paste. Reduce heat to medium and continue to swirl regularly while cooking for 2 minutes or till the masala comes together.
- Stir the chickpeas into the masala after adding them. Mix thoroughly before adding 1 cup (240 mL) of water. For 20 minutes, simmer.
- Remove the sauce from the heat after it has thickened, then stir in the cilantro, salt, & lemon juice. Serve warm.

Nutritional Values per serving:

Total Calories: 220 kcal, **Fat:** 11 g, **Carbohydrates:** 26g, **Protein:** 7 g, **Fiber:** 6g, **Sodium:** 670g, **Potassium:** 220mg

33. Chickpea and Eggplant Stew

Prep Time: 15 mins.
Cook Time: 1 hr.
Total Time: 1 hr. 15 mins.
Serves: 4
Difficulty: Medium
Ingredients:

- 2 yellow onions (medium), 1 diced & 1 sliced
- 4 tsp. of Olive Oil (divided)
- 3 cloves of garlic (minced)
- 2 cups of chickpeas, canned (no-salt-added)
- 1 lb. of eggplant (cubed)
- 1 tsp. of ground cumin
- 1 tsp. of coriander
- 1 tsp. of ground cinnamon
- 1 can ((28-ounce) of tomatoes, no-salt-added, chopped or diced
- 1/4 tsp. of black pepper, freshly ground
- 1/4 tsp. of salt
- 1/4 cup of freshly chopped cilantro

Directions:

- In a big saucepan set over medium heat, warm 2 tablespoons of olive oil. Add garlic and onion

& Cook them until the onions are tender. Add the tomatoes, salt, pepper, cumin, cinnamon, coriander, eggplant, and chickpeas to the mixture. Heat up to a boil on a high setting. Turn down the heat, then cover the saucepan. Cook your stew for 45 mins.–1 hour, or until the eggplant is really soft.

- Meanwhile, add onion slices to the heated 2 tablespoons of olive oil. Cook till golden and then turn off the heat. When the stew is done, transfer it to serving dishes and garnish it with cilantro and fried onions.

Nutritional values per serving:
Total Calories: 270 kcal, **Fat:** 7 g, **Carbohydrates:** 46g, **Protein:** 11 g, **Fiber:** 12g, **Sodium:** 240g, **Potassium:** 150mg

34. Vegetable Fresh Rolls

Prep Time: 25 mins.
Cook Time: 0 mins.
Total Time: 25 mins.
Serves: 12
Difficulty: Medium
Ingredients:

- 1 lb. of tofu, extra firm (drained & cut lengthwise in 12 half-inch-thick planks)
- 12 leaves of Boston or bib lettuce
- 1 carrot, large (peeled & cut in 2-inch matchsticks lengthwise)
- 2 cups of clover sprouts or mung bean (blanched)
- 1/2 hothouse or English cucumber (seeded, peeled, and cut in 2-inch matchsticks lengthwise)
- 24 leaves of fresh mint

Directions:

- Water should be put in a flat, circular cake pan. On your work table, spread out a smooth, clean (not fuzzy) kitchen towel. Create separate stacks of lettuce, carrots, tofu, sprouts, cucumber, and mint on a platter.
- In the water, submerge 1 rice paper. Infuse until pliable. Over the kitchen towel lay the rice paper. Blot to dry. The paper ought to be tacky rather than slick. On the side of the paper nearest to you, arrange the components in the following order, above the other: One lettuce leaf, one tofu cube, a few carrots, cucumber, and sprouts as well as two mint leaves placed next to one another.
- The furthest edge of the paper should be folded securely over the filling. Take care not to rip it. Roll it all the way towards the finish while folding the sides in. With the remaining components, repeat this procedure.

Nutritional values per serving:
Total Calories: 85 kcal, **Fat:** 2 g, **Carbohydrates:** 13g, **Protein:** 5 g, **Fiber:** 1g, **Sodium:** 55g, **Potassium:** 155mg

35. Ginger Garlicky Eggplant

Prep Time: 10 mins.
Cook Time: 10 mins.
Total Time: 20 mins.
Serves: 4
Difficulty: Easy
Ingredients:

- 2 Japanese eggplants (in 1-inch pieces)
- 2 tbsp. of sesame oil
- 2 tsp. of fresh ginger, minced
- 1/2 cup of chopped mushrooms
- 2 cloves of garlic (minced)
- 1 cup of mung bean sprouts, fresh
- 1/4 tsp. of red pepper flakes, crushed
- 1/4 cup of fresh basil (chopped)
- 1 tbsp. of hoisin sauce

Directions:

- In a large skillet, warm the sesame oil. Add bean sprouts, mushrooms, ginger, & garlic. Stir-fry eggplant for 4-6 minutes at medium-high heat, or until it starts to soften.
- Hoisin sauce, basil, and chili flakes should all be added to the eggplant. Cook for a further 1-2 minutes. Serve after removing from heat.

Nutritional values per serving:
Total Calories: 90 kcal, **Fat:** 7 g, **Carbohydrates:** 6g, **Protein:** 2 g, **Fiber:** 2g, **Sodium:** 80g, **Potassium:** 190mg

36. Tofu with Broccoli

Prep Time: 35 mins.
Cook Time: 30 mins.
Total Time: 1 hr. 5 mins.
Serves: 4
Difficulty: Medium
Ingredients:

- 16oz. of tofu, extra firm (drained & cut in 1-inch chunks)
- 1 cooking spray (nonstick)
- 1 tbsp. of soy sauce (lower sodium), plus 1 tsp. (divided use)
- 3 tsp. of vegetable oil (divided use)
- 1 tbsp. of rice vinegar, plus 2 tsp. (divided use)
- 2 cloves of garlic (minced & divided use)
- 1 tbsp. of Cornstarch, plus 2 tsp. (divided use)
- 1 tsp. of grated ginger (divided use)
- 1/2 cup of vegetable broth (low sodium)
- 1 1/2 tsp. of tomato paste

- 1 tbsp. of honey or 1-2 packets of artificial sweetener
- 2 tsp. of sesame oil
- 2 green onions, thinly sliced (scallion)
- 1/2 tsp. of hot sauce, Asian-style (like sambal oelek)
- 2 cups of broccoli (steamed)

Directions:

- Spray cooking spray on a baking sheet and preheat the oven to 350° F. Place aside.
- With a paper towel, pat the tofu dry.
- Make the tofu marinade: Half minced garlic, half grated ginger, 1 tsp. of soy sauce, 2 tsp. of rice vinegar, 1 tsp. of oil, and 1 tsp. Are combined in a bowl. Add the tofu and coat well. 30 minutes of marinating
- Over the tofu, add 1 tbsp. of cornstarch and turn it to coat well. On the baking pan, evenly distribute the tofu. Turning often, bake for 30 minutes or until golden brown on both sides.
- In a separate bowl, combine the broth, remaining one tbsp. of soy sauce, honey, remaining two tbsp. of cornstarch, remaining 1 tbsp. of vinegar, remaining 2 tbsp. Tomato paste, sesame oil, and spicy sauce whilst the tofu is baking. Place aside.
- Over medium-high heat, add the last 2 tablespoons of vegetable oil into a large wok or sauté pan. Stir-fry for a minute before adding scallions and the remaining garlic and ginger. Cook the sauce mixture for two to three minutes, or until it thickens.
- Serve the sauce after stirring in the baked tofu & broccoli.

Nutritional values per serving:

Total Calories: 315 kcal, **Fat:** 19 g, **Carbohydrates:** 24g, **Protein:** 12 g, **Fiber:** 4g, **Sodium:** 890g, **Potassium:** 690mg

37. Grilled Portabellas with Tuscan Herbs and Tomato

Prep Time: 25 mins.
Cook Time: 10 mins.
Total Time: 35 mins.
Serves: 6
Difficulty: Easy
Ingredients:

- 2 tbsp. of lemon juice
- 1/4 cup of Olive Oil
- 2 tbsp. of balsamic vinegar
- 1 sprig of rosemary, fresh (minced)
- 1 tbsp. of fresh oregano (minced)
- 2 tbsp. of basil (minced)
- 1/2 cup of tomatoes (chopped)
- 2 cloves of garlic (minced)
- 6 portabello mushrooms (stem removed & wiped clean)
- 1/2 tsp. of black pepper

Directions:

- Put all marinade ingredients in a big, firmly closed plastic bag after mixing them all together in a medium bowl. For optimal results, marinate the mushroom caps for at least 15 to 30 mins at room temperature.
- Place the mushroom caps on the grill grates and preheat the grill to medium-high. Cook for five minutes on each side over direct heat until tender. While cooking, baste periodically with more marinade. Any marinade that is left over may be poured over the mushrooms before serving.

Nutritional values per serving:

Total Calories: 105 kcal, **Fat:** 9 g, **Carbohydrates:** 5g, **Protein:** 2 g, **Fiber:** 1g, **Sodium:** 5mg, **Potassium:** 315mg

38. Coconut Curry Veggie Rice Bowls

Prep Time: 10 mins.
Cook Time: 30 mins.
Total Time: 40 mins.
Serves: 6
Difficulty: Easy
Ingredients:

- 1 cup of water
- 2/3 cup of brown rice
- 1 tsp. of curry powder
- green onion (chopped)
- 3/4 tsp. of salt
- 1 cup of sliced yellow or red bell pepper
- 1 cup of chopped red cabbage
- 1 cup of matchstick carrots
- 1 can of sliced water chestnuts (8 oz)
- 1 can of coconut milk (13 oz)
- 1 can of chickpeas (15 oz), no-salt-added (rinsed & drained)
- 1 1/2 tbsp. of sugar
- 1 tbsp. of grated fresh ginger

Directions:

- In the Instant Pot, mix the curry powder, rice, water, and 1/4 tsp. of salt. Close the valve, secure the lid, and choose 15 minutes for the Manual/Pressure Cook timer.
- Utilize a 12-minute natural pressure release. Carefully remove the cover and add the additional ingredients when the valve has dropped.
- Sauté is selected after pressing the Cancel button. Press "More" or "High" on the Adjust button after that. Stirring periodically, bring to a

boil for two minutes, or till all the ingredients are well heated.

Nutritional values per serving:

Total Calories: 240 kcal, **Fat:** 6g, **Carbohydrates:** 42g, **Protein:** 8 g, **Fiber:** 7g, **Sodium:** 330mg, **Potassium:** 540mg

39. Lentil Healthy Sloppy Joes

Prep Time: 15 mins.
Cook Time: 30 mins.
Total Time: 45 mins.
Serves: 6
Difficulty: Easy
Ingredients:

- 1/4 tsp. of salt
- 1 sliced white onion (in 12 onion slices, thin)
- 6 leaves of lettuce
- 6 hamburger bun, whole wheat s (1 1/2 oz. of each)
- 1/2 tsp. of chili powder
- 1/2 tsp. of smoked paprika
- 1 tbsp. of brown sugar
- 1 tbsp. of Worcestershire sauce
- 2 oz. of tomato sauce (1/4 cup)
- 1 cup of lentils (green & rinsed)
- 1 tbsp. of Olive Oil
- 1 yellow onion, small (diced)
- 2 cloves of garlic (minced)
- 2 cups of vegetable broth (low sodium)

Directions:

- Set a pot on a moderate heat source. Add the onion, garlic, and oil. Cook for 3 to 4 minutes, stirring periodically, or until the onion starts to soften.
- Lentils and broth are added. Until lentils are cooked, bring to boil, then lower heat to simmer & cover for approximately 20 minutes.
- Add the spices, Worcestershire sauce, brown sugar, and tomato sauce after stirring.
- Lentils are served by dividing them among buns. Add lettuce & onion rings on top.

Nutritional values per serving:

Total Calories: 270 kcal, **Fat:** 5g, **Carbohydrates:** 48g, **Protein:** 12 g, **Fiber:** 12g, **Sodium:** 450mg, **Potassium:** 620mg

40. Moroccan Lentils & Stewed Tomatoes

Prep Time: 5 mins.
Cook Time: 40 mins.
Total Time: 45 mins.
Serves: 8
Difficulty: Easy
Ingredients:

- 1 cup of canned no-salt-added chopped tomatoes
- 1 cup of brown lentils, uncooked (sorted & rinsed)
- 1 yellow onion, medium (chopped)
- 1/2 tsp. of salt
- 1 tsp. of ground coriander
- 1/4 cup of chopped fresh cilantro
- 1/4 tsp. of black pepper

Directions:

- Add water to immerse the lentils into a medium saucepan. Over high heat, bring to a boil, lower the heat, cover, and simmer for 30-35 minutes or till soft. Drain then set apart. (This step might be completed a day beforehand.)
- In a big pot, mix lentils, onion, tomatoes, salt, coriander, and pepper. Over high heat, add 1 cup of water and bring it to a boil. Simmer for 10 minutes with the lid on, on low heat.
- Mix in the cilantro. Serve warm.

Nutritional values per serving:

Total Calories: 90 kcal, **Fat:** 0g, **Carbohydrates:** 16g, **Protein:** 6 g, **Fiber:** 6g, **Sodium:** 125mg, **Potassium:** 330mg

41. Red Quinoa & Farro

Prep Time: 15 mins.
Cook Time: 40 mins.
Total Time: 55 mins.
Serves: 4
Difficulty: Medium
Ingredients:

- 2 cups of vegetable broth, low sodium (divided)

- 1/2 cup of Farro
- 1/4 cup of red quinoa
- 1 tbsp. of lime juice
- 1 tbsp. of olive oil
- 1 tsp. of white wine vinegar
- 1/2 tsp. of garlic powder
- 1 tsp. of dried oregano
- 1/4 tsp. of stevia brown sugar blend (such as Truvia)
- 1/8 tsp. of black pepper
- 1/4 tsp. of salt
- 1/8 tsp. of red pepper flakes, crushed

Directions:

- The Farro & 1 1/2 cups of broth should be brought to a boil in a saucepan on high heat. When the Farro is ready, cook it for approximately 25 minutes on medium-low heat. Farro should be placed in a big basin and let 10 minutes to chill.
- The remaining 1/2 cup of broth & the quinoa should be added to the same medium pot and heated over high heat. The quinoa should be soft after approximately 15 minutes of simmering at medium-low heat. Before putting it in the big bowl of Farro, fluff using a fork and let cool for 10 minutes.
- Combine the olive oil, vinegar, lime juice, oregano, brown sugar mixture, garlic powder, salt, black pepper, & red pepper flakes in a small bowl. Whisk to combine.
- Toss the quinoa and Farro together in a large bowl. Mix the grains one more after drizzling the combination of olive oils over them.

Nutritional values per serving:
Total Calories: 180 kcal, **Fat:** 5g, **Carbohydrates:** 28g, **Protein:** 5 g, **Fiber:** 5g, **Sodium:** 220mg, **Potassium:** 240mg

42. Brown Rice & Scallions

Prep Time: 5 mins.
Cook Time: 40 mins.
Total Time: 45 mins.
Serves: 6
Difficulty: Medium
Ingredients:

- 1/4 tsp. of ground ginger
- 5 thinly sliced scallions
- 2 cups of vegetable broth (low sodium) or water
- 2 tbsp. of soy sauce (lower sodium)
- 1 cup of brown rice
- 1 tbsp. of rice vinegar
- 1 tbsp. of olive oil

Directions:

- Combine the soy sauce, rice vinegar, olive oil, and ginger in a small bowl. To uniformly cover the rice, drizzle the mixture of soy sauce over it and stir. Toss in the scallions after adding them.
- Bring the rice & broth to boil in a saucepan on high heat. After lowering the heat to medium-low, let the rice simmer for approximately 40 minutes or until it is cooked. (Alternatively, you may cook the rice in a rice cooker.) With a fork, fluff the rice and put it in a big bowl.

Nutritional values per serving:
Total Calories: 140 kcal, **Fat:** 3g, **Carbohydrates:** 25g, **Protein:** 3 g, **Fiber:** 2g, **Sodium:** 230mg, **Potassium:** 310mg

43. White Beans Ratatouille

Prep Time: 15 mins.
Cook Time: 6 hrs.
Total Time: 6hrs. 15 mins.
Serves: 6
Difficulty: Medium
Ingredients:

- 2 cans (15-oz) of cannellini beans, low-sodium (drained & rinsed)
- 1 tbsp. of olive oil
- 1 can of fire-roasted tomatoes (diced), no-added-salt (14.5-oz)
- 1 1/2 cup of vegetable broth, low sodium
- 1 cup of tomato sauce, low-sodium
- 1/2 diced med eggplant (with skin on)
- 1 sliced red bell pepper (in 1-inch strips)
- 2 cups of green cabbage, shredded
- 3 cloves of garlic (minced)
- 1 tsp. of dried oregano
- 2 tbsp. of Apple Cider Vinegar
- 3 bay leaves
- 1/4 tsp. of black pepper
- 1/4 tsp. of salt, plus 1/8 tsp.

Directions:

- Olive oil should be used to brush inside the slow cooker. Stir all of the remaining ingredients into the slow cooker.
- For six hours on low heat, with the lid on, simmer the veggies and beans until tender. Before serving, take out and throw away the bay leaves.

Nutritional Values per serving:
Total Calories: 180 kcal, **Fat:** 3g, **Carbohydrates:** 30g, **Protein:** 10 g, **Fiber:** 10g, **Sodium:** 230mg, **Potassium:** 970mg

44. Freekeh & Vegetable "Fried Rice" with Peanuts and Shishito Peppers

Prep Time: 15 mins.
Cook Time: 30 mins.
Total Time: 45 mins.

Serves: 2
Difficulty: Easy
Ingredients:

- 6 oz. of fresh green beans
- 1/2 cup of cracked freekeh
- 6 oz. of carrots (3 whole)
- 1 piece of fresh ginger (1-inch)
- 2 cloves of garlic
- 2 scallions
- 3 tbsp. of roasted peanuts, unsalted
- 2 eggs
- 3 oz. of shishito peppers
- Some red pepper flakes (crushed) to taste
- 3 tsp. of olive oil
- 1 tbsp. of rice vinegar
- 1 tbsp. of soy sauce, lower sodium

Directions:

- To prepare the freekeh, fill up a medium pot with salted water until it is 3/4 full, cover it, and cook it on high until it boils. Freekeh should be added and cooked for 25 to 30 minutes, uncovered after the water has boiled. Drain completely.
- Get the ingredients ready: Wash & dry the fresh vegetables in the meanwhile. Green beans should have their stem ends removed and discarded before being cut in half. Slice the carrots thinly at an angle after peeling. Peel and coarsely chop two garlic cloves. Ginger should be peeled and chopped coarsely. Slice the scallions very thinly, removing the hollow green tops from the white bottoms. The white ends of the scallions should be cut, along with the ginger and garlic. Pour the cracked eggs in a separate basin. Beat until smooth after seasoning with salt and pepper. Chop the peanuts roughly. The peppers' stems should be removed and discarded before cutting into 1-inch chunks. After handling, immediately wash your hands thoroughly.
- Cook the eggs and vegetables: Heat 1 tsp. of olive oil to a hot temperature in a big pan (preferably nonstick). Add the pepper pieces and green beans in an equal layer and season with salt (if desired) and pepper. Without stirring, cook for 3 - 4 minutes, or until softened and gently browned. The carrots, cut into slices, should be added. Cook for 3 to 4 minutes, stirring regularly, or till slightly softened. Based on how spicy you want the meal to be, add as many pepper flakes as you wish, along with the minced garlic, ginger, & white bottoms slices of the scallions. Cook for 2 to 3 minutes, stirring regularly, or until softened. Move the veggies to 1 side of the pan using a spoon. Then add beaten eggs and 1 tsp. of olive oil to the other side. Cook the eggs for 30 sec to 1 minute, stirring often, or until fully done. Eggs and veggies should be properly mixed. Place in a large bowl. To stay warm, wrap the area with foil. Clean the pan.
- Complete and plate your dish: One tsp. Olive oil should be heated to a hot temperature in the same pan. A layer of the cooked freekeh should be added. Cook for 3 to 4 minutes without stirring or until just beginning to get crispy. After removing the pan from the heat, mix the soy sauce & vinegar. Transfer to the dish with the scrambled eggs and cooked veggies. Serve the prepared freekeh and veggies with chopped peanuts and thinly cut scallion green tips as a garnish. Enjoy!

Nutritional Values per serving:
Total Calories: 490 kcal, **Fat:** 23g, **Carbohydrates:** 49g, **Protein:** 24 g, **Fiber:** 11g, **Sodium:** 650mg, **Potassium:** 770mg

45. Spinach Whole-Wheat Parathas

Prep Time: 1 hr.
Cook Time: 1 hr. 40 mins.
Total Time: 2hr. 40 mins.
Serves: 8
Difficulty: Medium
Ingredients:

- 1 tsp. of ground cumin
- 2/3 cup of water
- 2 cups of pastry flour, whole wheat (divided), plus 1 tbsp.
- 1 cup chopped baby spinach (tightly packed)
- 1/2 tsp. of amchoor (mango) powder
- 3 tsp. of sunflower oil (divided use)
- 1/2 tsp. of sea salt, fine (divided use)
- 1 tbsp. of fresh ginger, grated
- 1 green chile, finely minced (seeds discarded)
- 1 tsp. of ajwain seeds

Directions:

- 2 cups of flour and 1/4 tsp. of salt should be combined into a shallow dish to produce the dough for paratha. To the flour mixture, stir in the spinach mixture. The addition of water gradually can help you create a smooth dough (the consistency of pizza dough). Till the dough is smooth, knead it. Incorporate into a glass bowl. Wrap with a wet towel. Place aside for 30 to 60 minutes at room temperature.
- Heat one tablespoon of oil over medium to high heat in a heavy-bottomed pan. The ajwain

seeds, ginger, and chile should be added. Stirring constantly, cook for about one minute.

- Add 1/4 tsp. of salt and spinach. Cook for 3-4 minutes, or until the spinach's liquid has been absorbed & the base has dried up. Stir thoroughly before adding the cumin and amchoor powder. Take it off the heat. Set apart for cooling.
- Knead the dough again after the waiting period. Form into eight balls. Dust your work area with the last tablespoon of flour. Each dough ball should be flattened with a rolling pin until it is 6" in diameter.
- Over medium-high heat, preheat a flat skillet or griddle made of cast iron. One dough piece should be placed in the skillet. Cook for around one minute, till it bubbles.
- Switch the sides of paratha. Apply 1/4 tsp. of the rest of the oil on the brush. Once the edges are browned on both sides, cook for a further 3–4 minutes on each side, flipping as necessary. To ensure that the paratha cooks evenly, push the center with a flat spatula while it cooks.
- Take out of the skillet. With the rest of the pieces of dough and oil, repeat the cooking procedure. Serve warm.

Nutritional Values per serving:
Total Calories: 130 kcal, **Fat:** 2g, **Carbohydrates:** 25g, **Protein:** 3 g, **Fiber:** 150 g, **Sodium:** 180mg, **Potassium:** 793mg

46. Grilled Fish Packets

Prep Time: 35 mins.
Cook Time: 15 mins.
Total Time: 50mins.
Serves: 4
Difficulty: Easy
Ingredients:

- 3 carrots
- 11 oz. of button mushroom
- ½ cup of vegetable broth
- Some peppers
- Salt, to taste
- 4 fillets of cod (about 5 ounces each)
- 2 stalks of lemongrass

Directions:

- Mushrooms should be cleaned and sliced into pieces.
- Clean the carrots. Slice thinly lengthwise then cut into thin strips.
- 5 tbsp. of broth, and the carrot, strips should be combined in a saucepan. Bring it to a boil before adding the mushroom slices. For approximately five minutes, cook with a cover over medium heat. Add salt and pepper to taste.
- Place four big (12 × 12 inches) foil pieces on a work area after cutting them out. To prevent juices from dripping out, slightly fold the sides up.
- Among the foil packages, distribute the veggies. Fish fillets should be rinsed, dried off, and placed on the veggies. Add salt and pepper to taste.
- Peel the lemongrass's rough outer skin after rinsing it. Roughen up the root end. Sprinkle the finely chopped, soft interior over fish fillets.
- Over each package, add 2 tablespoons of vegetable broth. Cook the fish on a hot grill for 12 to 15 minutes, or until it is completely opaque, folding the foil closely to seal the contents. Open with care to serve.

Nutritional values per serving:
Total Calories: 167 kcal, **Fat:** 1g, **Carbohydrates:** 3g, **Protein:** 35g, **Fiber:** 4g, **Sodium:** 950mg, **Potassium:** 793mg

47. Mushroom and Chicken Skewers

Prep Time: 20 mins.
Cook Time: 5 mins.
Total Time: 25mins.
Serves: 1
Difficulty: Easy
Ingredients:

- ½ tsp. of olive oil
- 1 red chili pepper (small)
- Some salt, to taste
- 3 oz. of chicken breasts
- 4 oz. of small button mushroom
- ½ bunch of cilantro

Directions:

- Wooden skewers should be soaked in warm water.
- Remove the seeds, cut the chili pepper in half lengthwise, and then finely chop.
- In a small bowl, combine the chile pepper, oil, and some salt to taste.
- Remove the skewers from the water. Trim and rinse the mushrooms.
- The chicken breast should be washed, dried with paper towels, and then cut into pieces. Thread chunks of chicken & mushrooms on skewers alternately.

Nutritional values per serving:
Total Calories: 100 kcal, **Fat:** 2g, **Carbohydrates:** 20g, **Protein:** 1g, **Fiber:** 3g, **Sodium:** 800mg, **Potassium:** 656mg

48. Pork Rolls

Prep Time: 30 mins.
Cook Time: 15 mins.
Total Time: 45mins.
Serves: 4
Difficulty: Medium
Ingredients:

- 6 tbsp. of olive oil
- 2 red onions
- 12 oz. of pork
- 2 tsp. of smoked ground paprika

Directions:

- Warm up a nonstick pan. Over medium heat, add chile oil to the pan and cook the skewers until they are golden brown on both sides.
- Pull cilantro leaves off stems after rinsing and drying. After serving, top the skewers with cilantro leaves.
- Peel the onion, then cut it in half and make extremely thin rings. Combine the oil and paprika in a little bowl.
- Pork should be rinsed, dried, and sliced into 15-16 thin slices.
- The slices should be placed on a big sheet of plastic wrap, which should then be covered with more plastic wrap.
- Use a heavy pan or a meat mallet to flatten. Slices of meat should be covered with half of the paprika oil after removing the plastic wrap.
- Place onion rings onto the meat and firmly coil each piece. Each skewer should include 4 rolls.
- Spread the remaining paprika oil over the rolls before placing them on an aluminum grill plate. Grill each side for 6 to 8 minutes.

Nutritional values per serving:
Total Calories: 243 kcal, **Fat:** 14g, **Carbohydrates:** 1g, **Protein:** 27g, **Fiber:** 3g, **Sodium:** 300mg, **Potassium:** 263mg

49. Braised Mackerel with Fresh Garlic and Peppers

Prep Time: 45 mins.
Cook Time: 15 mins.
Total Time: 1 hr.
Serves: 4
Difficulty: Medium
Ingredients:

- 1 white onion (large)
- 8 red Hungarian wax peppers (large), about 100 grams each
- 1 big garlic clove (fresh)
- 1 (600 grams) mackerel, fresh (ready to cook)
- 2 ⅕ lbs. of fully ripe tomatoes
- Salt and black pepper to taste
- 2 tbsp. of olive oil

Directions:

- Wax peppers should be cleaned, trimmed, and split in half lengthwise. Place onto a baking sheet with the cut side up & broil under the oven's broiler till the skin is black & blistered.
- Peel and finely slice one onion in the meanwhile. Take the garlic out of its covering.
- Trim the stem ends off tomatoes after rinsing them.
- In a bowl, cover the tomatoes with boiling water, and let them soak for two minutes. Rinse in the cold water after draining. Slice tomatoes in half, remove the seeds, and then finely dice them.
- Take the wax pepper halves out from the oven. Place the peppers onto a damp towel and let them cool a little. Crosswise slice the peppers into strips after removing the peel.
- Take the mackerel's head and tail off. Slice the fish into inch-thick pieces after rinsing it and drying it with paper towels. Add salt and pepper to taste.
- In a big sauté pan, heat the olive oil. Cook mackerel chunks for roughly five minutes over medium heat, flipping to ensure equal browning.
- Spread the fish out in a large baking dish that can withstand the heat. In the leftover olive oil, add the onion, garlic, & peppers to the pan & sauté for approximately 2 minutes.
- Cook the mixture for a further 5 mins. on medium heat before adding the diced tomatoes and seasoning to taste.
- In a preheated oven set at 180°C, or around 350°F/convection 325°F, spread & roast the mackerel pieces over vegetables for 15 minutes.

Nutritional values per serving:
Total Calories: 326 kcal, **Fat:** 20g, **Carbohydrates:** 18g, **Protein:** 29g, **Fiber:** 7g, **Sodium:** 800mg, **Potassium:** 1319mg

50. Thyme Schnitzel

Prep Time: 10 mins.
Cook Time: 5 mins.
Total Time: 15 mins.
Serves: 4
Difficulty: Easy
Ingredients:

- Some salt, to taste
- 4 pork cutlets (about 150 grams each)
- Peppers, freshly ground
- 2 tbsp. of fresh thyme
- 2 tbsp. of olive oil
- Some lemon juice

Directions:

- The cutlets should be rinsed, dried off, and pounded if required to an equal thickness. Add salt and pepper, and cook for one minute on each side until browned in heated olive oil.
- Add lemon juice and fresh thyme, then simmer for an additional 1-2 minutes, or until done. Serve right after removing it from the pan.

Nutritional values per serving:
Total Calories: 500kcal, **Fat:** 26.9g, **Carbohydrates:** 70.1g, **Protein:** 48.2g, **Fiber:** 0g, **Sodium:** 1240mg, **Potassium:** 880mg

Chapter 4: Pegan Diet - Dinner Recipes

1. Beef Curry Stew

Prep time: 15 mins.
Cook time: 8 hr. 10 mins.
Total time: 8 hr. 25 mins.
Serves: 4
Difficulty: easy
Ingredients:

- 1 pound of beef stew meat
- 1 tbsp. of olive oil
- salt & pepper to taste
- 1 tsp. of chopped fresh ginger
- 2 cloves of garlic, minced
- 1 jalapeno pepper (fresh), diced
- 1 can of diced tomatoes (14.5 ounces) with juice
- 1 tbsp. of curry powder
- 1 cup of beef broth
- 1 sliced onion, quartered

Directions:

- The steak should be browned evenly in a pan over medium heat with olive oil. Season with salt & pepper after removing from the pan and conserving the juices. Curry powder is added after cooking and stirring the ginger, garlic, and jalapeño in the pan for 2 minutes, or until they are soft. Add the juice and chopped tomatoes together.
- The browned meat should be layered on top of the onion into the bottom of the slow cooker. Add the beef broth after transferring the skillet mixture to the slow cooker.
- Cook for 6-8 hours on Low with a cover.

Nutritional values per serving:
Total Calories: 291kcal, **Fats:** 19.1g, **Carbohydrates:** 7.6g, **Protein:** 20.6g, **Fiber:** 2g, **Sodium:** 441.7mg, **Potassium:** 460.7mg

2. Shepherd's Vegan Pie

Prep time: 15 mins.
Cook time: 45 mins.
Total time: 1 hr.
Serves: 6
Difficulty: medium
Ingredients:
Mashed potatoes:

- 3-4 tbsp. of vegan butter
- 3 pounds of Yukon gold potatoes, thoroughly washed & partially peeled
- Sea salt & black pepper (to taste)

Filling:

- 1 onion, medium (diced)
- 1 tbsp. of olive oil
- 2 cloves of garlic (minced)
- 1 pinch of sea salt & black pepper each
- 2 tbsp. of tomato paste (optional)
- 1 1/2 cups of uncooked green or brown lentils (rinsed & drained)
- 2 tsp. of thyme, fresh (or substitute 1 tsp. of dried thyme per two tsp., fresh)
- 4 cups of vegetable stock
- 1 bag of mixed veggies, frozen (10-ounce): peas, green beans, carrots, and corn

Directions:

- Any large potatoes should be cut in half, put in a big saucepan, and just filled with water. Add salt liberally, bring to a boil over medium-high heat, cover, and simmer for 20 to 30 minutes, or until they easily come off a knife.
- When done, drain, add to the pot again to help evaporate any water left, and then transfer them to a mixing bowl. Mash the ingredients until smooth using a fork, pastry cutter, or masher. Add the required quantity of vegan butter (original recipe calls for 3–4 Tbsp.; adjust if the batch size is changed), then season with salt & pepper to taste. Set aside and loosely cover.
- Pre-heat the oven up to 425 degrees F (218 degrees C) while the potatoes are cooking, and gently butter a baking dish (2-quart) (or a dish of a similar size, such as a 9-by-13-inch pan). Adjust the number of dishes used or the size of the dish if the batch size is changed; an 8 by 8 won't quite fit it all.
- It takes around 5 minutes to softly brown and caramelize the garlic and onions in olive oil in a big pot on medium heat.

- Add a dash of each salt and pepper, along with the optional tomato paste. Then whisk in the stock, lentils, and thyme. Achieve a low boil. After that, put a lid on it and simmer it. Continue to boil the lentils until they are soft (35-40 minutes). When the food is cooked, take off the top and boil it uncovered for another few minutes, stirring periodically to cook out any extra liquid.
- Add the frozen vegetables, stir, and cover for the last 10-12 minutes of simmering to combine the flavors.
- If necessary, taste and adjust the spices. After that, move to the oven-safe baking dish you've prepared and gently add the mashed potatoes on top. With a fork or spoon, smooth down the surface and season with more sea salt and pepper.
- Place the mashers onto a baking sheet to collect spillover and bake for 10 to 15 minutes, or until the tops are just starting to brown.
- Let cool momentarily before serving. It will thicken more the longer it sits. Before covering and storing in the refrigerator for up to some days, let it cool fully.

Nutritional values per serving:
Total Calories: 396kcal, **Fats:** 5.3g, **Carbohydrates:** 72g, **Protein:** 17.7g, **Fiber:** 19g, **Sodium:** 109mg, **Potassium:** 50mg

3. Tempeh Lettuce Wraps & Peanut Sauce

Prep time: 20 mins.
Cook time: 10 mins.
Total time: 30 mins.
Serves: 2
Difficulty: medium
Ingredients:

- 1 cup of vegetable broth
- 8-ounce tempeh block
- 1 tsp. of soy sauce
- 1/4 tsp. of ground coriander
- 1 tsp. of maple syrup
- 1/8 tsp. of garlic powder
- 1 carrot, (medium) peeled & julienned
- 8 leaves of butter lettuce
- 1 red bell pepper (medium), sliced
- 1 to 1 1/4 cups of red cabbage, thinly sliced
- Some peanut sauce

Garnish: (optional)

- red pepper flakes
- 1 stalk of sliced scallions

Directions:

- Transfer the tempeh cubes to the food processor after cutting them into 1/2-inch pieces. For approximately 5 seconds, blend the tempeh until it is broken up into very little bits. You will notice the smell of fermented soybeans when you open the food processor's cover, and that is quite normal.
- Vegetable broth, maple syrup, soy sauce, garlic powder, & powdered coriander should all be combined in a bowl.
- A nonstick sauté pan or skillet should be heated to medium. Add the broth mixture and the tempeh. Cook the tempeh for about 8-9 minutes, stirring regularly, or until the liquids are entirely absorbed. Although the tempeh may seem to be ready to be taken off the heat in 5 minutes, resist the desire to do so. The tempeh isn't yet ready if, while tapping it with the back side of a spatula, you hear a sound like that of walking through rain puddles. You're probably off by a few minutes. Take the pan off the heat when the liquid is absorbed.
- Put the lettuce wrappers together. Include part of the tempeh as well as the carrots, red bell pepper, cabbage, and lettuce leaves. If desired, top the filling with peanut sauce and garnish with red pepper flakes and sliced scallions. Serve right away.

Nutritional values per serving:
Total Calories: 201kcal, **Fats:** 7.2g, **Carbohydrates:** 23.6g, **Protein:** 14.1g, **Fiber:** 8.3g, **Sodium:** 539mg, **Potassium:** 250mg

4. Cauliflower Gnocchi

Prep time: 20 mins.
Cook time: 40 mins.
Total time: 1 hr.
Serves: 4
Difficulty: medium
Ingredients:
Gnocchi:

- 3/4 cup of cassava flour
- 4 cups of cauliflower minced
- 1/2 tsp. of sea salt optional

Sauce:

- 4 cups of spinach
- 1 can of full-fat coconut milk, canned
- 2 garlic cloves (large)
- salt & pepper to taste
- 2 tbsp. of tapioca flour

Directions:

- Heat the oven to 425F.
- For approximately five minutes, steam the cauliflower until it's tender. Put the cauliflower into a dish towel and squeeze the extra water

out to remove the water. About 1 1/2 cups of the leftover cauliflower should be measured.

- Blend the gnocchi ingredients into a food processor until they are smooth.
- Roll out the dough in four equal pieces and divide it into "on a board lightly dusted with cassava flour, diameter tubes. Cut the dough tubes into 1 "pieces.
- Gnocchi is added to boiling water in a big saucepan. Remove them after they have reached the top and spritz with a little olive oil.
- Gnocchi should be placed on a baking sheet covered with parchment paper & gently greased. After 20 minutes of baking at 425°F, flip the gnocchi over & bake for a further 20 minutes, or until golden.
- Except for the spinach, combine all of the sauce's components in a saucepan and whisk constantly until the mixture is smooth & the sauce starts to thicken. The flour will make it overly thick and sticky if you overcook it. Keep stirring to prevent clumps. Then turn the heat off, add the spinach, let it wilt, and toss in the gnocchi.

Nutritional values per serving:
Total Calories: 298kcal, **Fats:** 14g, **Carbohydrates:** 39g, **Protein:** 7g, **Fiber:** 8g, **Sodium:** 129mg, **Potassium:** 1062mg

5. Sweet Potato Pizza

Prep time: 20 mins.
Cook time: 40 mins.
Total time: 1 hr.
Serves: 2
Difficulty: easy
Ingredients:

- 2/3 cup of rolled oats
- 1 sweet potato (medium), peeled
- 1 egg
- a pinch of garlic powder
- 1/2 tsp. of salt
- 1 tbsp. of olive oil

Directions:

- Preheat the oven up to 400 degrees. The sweet potato & oats should be processed in the food processor till very fine. Salt, garlic powder, and egg have been added. Pulse one more to combine. The ingredients ought to resemble a thick batter or loose dough.
- Transfer to a circular pizza pan or baking sheet coated with parchment paper. You may either form two smaller crusts (you'll obtain more crispy side surface area) or one bigger crust by pressing into and shaping them with your hands. The ideal crust thickness is between 1/4 and 1/2 inch.
- The top should feel dry when touched after baking for 25 to 30 minutes. Remove from the oven, let to cool, then flip back over onto the pan with dry side up. Olive oil should be brushed on after very carefully peeling the top layer off of paper. To obtain a lovely crispy top, bake for an additional 5 to 10 minutes.
- Add your preferred pizza toppings, then reheat the pan in the oven to melt the cheese.

Nutritional values per serving:
Total Calories: 258kcal, **Fats:** 9.4g, **Carbohydrates:** 32.7g, **Protein:** 7.8g, **Fiber:** 4.8g, **Sodium:** 654.4mg, **Potassium:** 627.8mg

6. Beef Steak with Shrimps

Prep time: 15 mins.
Cook time: 30 mins.
Total time: 45 mins.
Serves: 2
Difficulty: medium
Ingredients:

- 1 tbsp. of butter, melted
- 1 tbsp. of olive oil
- 1 tbsp. of finely minced onion
- 1 tsp. of Worcestershire sauce
- 1 tbsp. of white wine
- 1 tsp. of lemon juice
- 1 tsp. of seafood seasoning
- 1 tsp. of dried parsley
- 1 clove of garlic, minced
- 12 shrimp (medium), peeled & deveined
- $\frac{1}{8}$ tsp. of black pepper, freshly ground
- 2 filet of mignon steaks (4 ounce)
- 1 tsp. of steak seasoning
- 2 tsp. of olive oil

Directions:

- In a bowl, combine shrimp with 1 tbsp. oil, onion, butter, wine, lemon juice, Worcestershire sauce, parsley, garlic, seafood seasoning, and black pepper. Evenly coat by tossing. Refrigerate for at least 15-20 minutes to let flavors meld before removing plastic wrap from the bowl.
- Set an outside grill over medium-high heat and give the grates quick oiling. Two teaspoons of olive oil and steak seasoning should be applied to the steaks.
- Cook steaks for 5 to 7 minutes on each side, or until they are starting to firm up and are the appropriate degree of doneness. The inside temperature should register 140 degrees Fahrenheit on an instant-read thermometer (60

- degrees C). Place the steaks on a plate and cover them loosely with a sheet of aluminum foil.
- Remove shrimp from the marinade and grill for two to three minutes on each side, or until the shrimp are brilliant pink on the exterior and the flesh is no longer translucent.

Nutritional values per serving:
Total Calories: 444kcal, **Fats:** 35.2g, **Carbohydrates:** 2.7g, **Protein:** 26.9g, **Fiber:** 0.3g, **Sodium:** 925.6mg, **Potassium:** 385.3mg

7. Bbq Jackfruit Pizza with Sweet Potato Crust

Prep time: 15 mins.
Cook time: 15 mins.
Total time: 30 mins.
Serves: 8
Difficulty: medium
Ingredients:
Pizza Crust:

- 1 pizza crust made with sweet potato

BBQ Sauce:

- 1 tbsp. of tomato paste
- 1/2 cup of passata/tomato sauce
- 2 tbsp. of coconut sugar
- 1 tbsp. of apple cider vinegar
- 1 tbsp. of molasses
- 1 tbsp. of chili powder
- 1 tsp. of salt
- 1 tsp. of onion powder
- 1 tsp. of garlic powder
- 1/2 tsp. of mustard powder
- 3/4 tsp. of paprika
- 1 tbsp. of chipotle paste, optional

Toppings:

- 1/4 cup of red onion, sliced
- 1 cup of jackfruit can, in water
- fresh cilantro

Directions:

- Get the crust (sweet potato) ready.

Jackfruit & BBQ sauce:

- In a medium or small sauce saucepan, combine all the ingredients and cook them while whisking. Allow to boil for five minutes. Jackfruit should be rinsed and drained before being cut into smaller pieces. Here, you can mash everything together with a fork or a potato masher, but it is simpler to take apart bigger bits with your fingers.
- The leftover BBQ sauce should be stirred into it before the jackfruit is cooked for a short time on low heat.
- Pizza may be topped with red onions and jackfruit marinated in BBQ sauce. Bake for 10 minutes at 205°C/400°F.
- Serve garnished with fresh cilantro!

Nutritional values per serving:
Total Calories: 146kcal, **Fats:** 1g, **Carbohydrates:** 25g, **Protein:** 2g, **Fiber:** 3g, **Sodium:** 589mg, **Potassium:** 250mg

8. Spicy and Sweet Chicken Stir Fry with Broccoli

Prep time: 10 mins.
Cook time: 20 mins.
Total time: 30 mins.
Serves: 4
Difficulty: easy
Ingredients:

- 1 tbsp. of olive oil
- 3 cups of broccoli florets
- 2 boneless & skinless halves of chicken breast, cut in 1-inch strips
- 4 cloves of garlic, thinly sliced
- ¼ cup of sliced green onions
- 1 tbsp. of hoisin sauce
- 1 tbsp. of low sodium soy sauce
- 1 tbsp. of chile paste
- ½ tsp. of ground ginger
- ½ tsp. of salt
- ¼ tsp. of crushed red pepper
- ⅛ cup of chicken stock
- ½ tsp. of black pepper

Directions:

- In a steamer with 1" of boiling water, add the broccoli and close the lid. Cook for approximately 5 minutes, or until fork-tender but firm.
- Chicken, garlic, and green onions should be sautéed in oil over medium heat till the chicken is not pink anymore and the juices flow clear.
- Add the ginger, salt, red pepper, and black pepper to the pan along with the hoisin sauce, chili paste, and soy sauce. Add the chicken stock & stir, then simmer for approximately two minutes. Add the steamed broccoli and combine until the broccoli is evenly covered.

Nutritional values per serving:
Total Calories: 156kcal, **Fats:** 6.2g, **Carbohydrates:** 10.9g, **Protein:** 15.9g, **Fiber:** 2.3g, **Sodium:** 606.4mg, **Potassium:** 379.1mg

9. Vegetable Ratatouille

Prep time: 10 mins.
Cook time: 25 mins.
Total time: 35 mins.
Serves: 4
Difficulty: easy
Ingredients:

- 1 onion (large), diced
- 2 tbsp. of olive oil
- 1 tsp. of red pepper flakes
- 3 (any color) bell peppers
- 1 eggplant (large), about 2 & 1/2 lbs.
- 2 (about 1 lb.) zucchini
- 8 oz. of mushrooms
- 1 (about 1/2 lb.) yellow squash
- 1 tbsp. of garlic, minced
- 2 cans of diced tomatoes (no-salt-added)
- 1 tbsp. of tomato paste
- 2 tbsp. of fresh thyme
- 1/4 cup of fresh parsley
- 1/4 cup of fresh basil
- salt & pepper, to taste
- 1/2 tbsp. of balsamic vinegar

Directions:

- While preparing the other ingredients, toss the diced eggplant with 1 tbsp. Salt and put aside in a colander. Any bitter fluids will be drawn out by this.
- Peppers may be roasted until the skin is browned over a gas burner or under a broiler. Remove the peel and seeds after 10 minutes of letting the fruit rest in a plastic bag. Dice.
- In the meanwhile, warm 2 tablespoons of olive oil into a Dutch oven. In approximately 5 minutes, add the onion & red pepper & cook until barely transparent. Add the salt-free eggplant to the saucepan after giving it a good washing. For approximately 5 minutes, sauté the eggplant, often turning, until it is halfway cooked.
- Include mushrooms, zucchini, and squash. Add salt & pepper to taste and simmer the mushrooms for 10 minutes or until they start to juice.
- Add tomato paste & garlic, and simmer for an additional one to two minutes, or until aromatic. 5 more minutes of simmering after adding tomatoes and stirring in roasted peppers.
- Adjust salt and stir in some fresh herbs, saving some for garnish. Serve either hot or at normal temperature after adding a dash of vinegar to brighten.

Nutritional values per serving:
Total Calories: 175kcal, **Fats:** 5.5g, **Carbohydrates:** 27.3g, **Protein:** 6.7g, **Fiber:** 7.8g, **Sodium:** 71mg, **Potassium:** 198mg

10. Mediterranean Cauliflower Rice

Prep time: 10 mins.
Cook time: 10 mins.
Total time: 20 mins.
Serves: 4
Difficulty: easy
Ingredients:

- 1 tbsp. of olive oil
- 1 head of cauliflower (medium), about 3 cups
- 1/4 cup of onion, chopped
- 1 tbsp. of lemon juice
- 2 cloves of garlic, minced
- zest from 1/2 a lemon
- 1/4 tsp. of red chili flakes
- 2 tbsp. of pine nuts
- chopped fresh parsley

Directions:

- Prepare the cauliflower by removing the leaves and stalks and chopping it into florets of various sizes. Cauliflower florets should be pushed into a food processor that is running with a grating attachment.
- Alternately, use a box grater to rice the cauliflower.
- In a big skillet, heat the olive oil. The onion should be added to the heated oil and cooked for 4 to 5 minutes on medium heat or until tender and transparent. For one more minute, add the garlic.
- Cauliflower should be added to the skillet. To thoroughly combine everything, stir.
- Then add the pine nuts, chile flakes, lemon zest, and high heat. One more minute of cooking. The cauliflower won't get too mushy because of the high heat's ability to remove extra moisture.

- Add the parsley after turning the heat off. Serve warm and take a sip after tasting; add additional salt if necessary.

Nutritional values per serving:
Total Calories: 71kcal, **Fats:** 2g, **Carbohydrates:** 8g, **Protein:** 3g, **Fiber:** 2g, **Sodium:** 38mg, **Potassium:** 50mg

11. Sweet Potatoes with White Beans and Lemony Kale

Prep time: 15 mins.
Cook time: 55 mins.
Total time: 1 hr. 10 mins.
Serves: 4
Difficulty: medium
Ingredients:

- 1 tbsp. of olive oil, optional
- 4 large/ medium sweet potatoes
- 1 chopped shallot or any other onion
- 1 tsp. of lemon zest
- 1 - 2 cloves of garlic, minced
- ½ to 1 tsp. of sea salt, to taste
- 1 can of Cannellini beans, 15 oz. (about almost 2 cups of cooked beans)
- 1 bunch of kale (chopped), remove thick stems (can substitute baby kale, collards, spinach, chard, etc.)
- ½ to 1 tsp. of red pepper flakes (crushed), optional
- Some tamari pumpkin seeds, toasted
- juice from 1/2 a lemon

Directions:

- Turn the oven on to 350 degrees. Dry and wash the sweet potatoes. With a fork, prick the tops many times. Place onto a baking sheet, and depending on size, bake for 45 to 60 minutes, or until tender.
- A sauté pan should be heated to medium. Including oil, add it now. Stirring sporadically throughout the next two minutes, add the shallot. Cook for one minute after adding the salt, garlic, and lemon zest. When the kale is reduced and attains a deep green color, add the beans and red pepper flakes, and continue to simmer, stirring periodically, for another 2 to 3 minutes, including the lemon juice Season to taste and make any adjustments. Get rid of the heat.
- Let the sweet potatoes cool a little. Add the kale & bean combination, followed by the pumpkin seeds, to each. Or, if you're preparing food, let everything cool. For up to 3-4 days, keep the potato and bean combination separate in the fridge.

Nutritional values per serving:
Total Calories: 295kcal, **Fats:** 8.5g, **Carbohydrates:** 46g, **Protein:** 12g, **Fiber:** 11g, **Sodium:** 529mg, **Potassium:** 150mg

12. Healthy Chicken Stir Fry

Prep time: 5 mins.
Cook time: 20 mins.
Total time: 25 mins.
Serves: 4
Difficulty: easy
Ingredients:

- 2 chicken breasts (large), diced
- 1 tbsp. of sesame oil
- 1 package (16 oz.) of frozen vegetables
- salt & pepper

For stir fry sauce:

- 1 tbsp. of sesame oil
- 3 tbsp. of tamari
- 2 cloves of garlic, chopped
- ¼ tsp. of ginger
- 1 tbsp. of fish sauce
- 2 tbsp. of water or chicken broth
- 1 tsp. of sriracha
- 1 tbsp. of corn starch

Directions:

- Chicken should be diced and salted, and peppered. Place aside.
- In a small bowl, whisk the sauce.
- Add 1 tablespoon of sesame oil to the Instant Pot and set it to sauté. Chicken is added and cooked until it begins to brown. In the instant pot, it won't brown it that much, but some minutes should start the process.
- Stir the sauce in the pan. Cook for 4 minutes on the manual setting of the instant pot. Turn the valve slowly to perform a rapid release when it is finished. After that, add the frozen veggies and switch the instant pot to sauté. Cook and stir until well heated.
- Quickly serve with cauliflower rice.

Nutritional values per serving:
Total Calories: 210kcal, **Fats:** 9g, **Carbohydrates:** 3g, **Protein:** 25g, **Fiber:** 4g, **Sodium:** 1239mg, **Potassium:** 459mg

13. Pumpkin Chili

Prep time: 10 mins.
Cook time: 30 mins.
Total time: 40 mins.
Serves: 8

Difficulty: easy
Ingredients:

- 1/2 lb. of beef or ground pork (organic), if preferred
- 1 lb. of ground beef, grass-fed
- Sea salt & black pepper
- 1 onion (medium), diced
- 1/2 tbsp. of olive oil or avocado oil for browning of the meat
- 1 green bell pepper (large), diced
- 1 minced jalapeno pepper
- 4 cloves of garlic minced
- 3/4 - 1 tsp. of sea salt, adjust it to taste
- 1 can of diced tomatoes (14.5 oz.), no salt added & not drained
- 1 can of crushed tomatoes (28 oz.)
- 1 can of pumpkin puree (15 oz.)
- 3/4 tsp. of smoked paprika
- 2 tsp. of chili powder
- 1/4 tsp. of chipotle powder
- 1 1/2 tsp. of cinnamon or pumpkin spice, if preferred
- 1 tsp. of cumin
- Chopped cilantro (fresh) for garnish

Directions:

- Coconut oil is added to a Dutch oven that is already hot to the touch. Use a spoon or fork to break up lumps as the meat and pork are added, then season with sea salt & black pepper and brown evenly.
- When it is halfway done, add the onions & peppers and, if desired, drain some of the fat (but not all). Stir and heat for another 2 minutes, or until the meat is browned and the pepper and onions are beginning to soften. No further fat should be drained. Stir in the garlic and jalapeno, then simmer for an additional minute.
- Reduce the heat before adding the pumpkin, diced tomatoes, crushed tomatoes, 1/2 teaspoon salt, and all the spices. Stir well, then turn up the heat to bring it to a boil. As soon as it begins to bubble, reduce heat to a moderate simmer, cover, and let the mixture simmer for 15 minutes at least (and as long as 45) to blend the flavors. This chili is excellent as leftovers since the taste just gets stronger as it simmers.
- To serve, garnish with cilantro, diced avocado, red onion, and sour cream. For up to 4 days, keep leftovers sealed in the refrigerator.

Nutritional values per serving:
Total Calories: 218kcal, **Fats:** 15g, **Carbohydrates:** 3g, **Protein:** 15g, **Fiber:** 1g, **Sodium:** 211mg, **Potassium:** 313mg

14. Short Beef Ribs

Prep time: 5 mins.
Cook time: 45 mins.
Total time: 50 mins.
Serves: 6
Difficulty: easy
Ingredients:

- 1 chopped onion
- 6 short ribs of beef (about 3 to 3 ½ pounds)
- 3 garlic cloves, diced
- ½ tsp. of dried thyme
- 2 tbsp. of tomato paste
- ½ tsp. of dried rosemary
- 1 ½ cups of beef broth
- 1 tbsp. of avocado oil or olive oil
- 1 ½ tbsp. of cornstarch (or almond flour)
- ½ tsp. of pepper
- ¾ tsp. of Kosher salt

Directions:

- Salt and pepper the short ribs liberally.
- Add 1 tablespoon of olive oil to the sauté setting on the Instant Pot. Brown Ribs. Allow them to remain still on each side so they would have time to brown. Around 8-10 minutes.
- Remove the ribs. If the pan is dry, add some more oil. Sauté the onions, garlic, and other delicious ingredients at the bottom of the pan. Add all ingredients but cornstarch after sautéing for around 5 minutes. Reposition the ribs in the sauce.
- Set the Instant Pot to stew setting and secure the cover. Organize a 30-minute timer. Allow the pot to naturally release once the timer whistles; do not open. The ribs get sensitive at this point. You must add 15-20 minutes to the preparation time if you use bone-in ribs.
- Turn the pot to sauté after removing the meat into a platter. In a small dish, combine the cornstarch with 2-3 tablespoons of water and stir thoroughly. Add to the sauce in the pan's bottom and stir thoroughly. Remove all of the brown residues from the pan's bottom. Cook food until the desired thickness.
- Serve with rice, mashed potatoes, or cauliflower mash. To taste, add salt and pepper.

Nutritional values per serving:

Total Calories: 49kcal, **Fats:** 2g, **Carbohydrates:** 5g, **Protein:** 1g, **Fiber:** 2g, **Sodium:** 558mg, **Potassium:** 119mg

15. Baked Salmon & Black Rice

Prep time: 10 mins.
Cook time: 50 mins.
Total time: 1 hr.
Serves: 3
Difficulty: easy
Ingredients:

- 1 cup of black rice
- 3 salmon fillets (4 oz. each)
- 2 cups of water
- 3 tbsp. of dried cranberries
- ½ cup of sugar snap peas
- 1 tsp. of garlic powder
- ¼ tsp. of pepper
- ½ tsp. of salt
- 1 tbsp. of orange zest

Directions:

- To make rice, combine 1 cup of black rice with 2 cups of water in a rice cooker. OR cook the rice and salt in 2 cups of water on the stovetop. Cook rice on low for 30 to 35 minutes, or until it is soft.
- Turn the oven on to 400 degrees. Add salt, pepper, and garlic to the fish. Put the item onto a baking sheet and bake for 15 to 20 minutes.
- As soon as the rice is finished cooking, stir in the snap peas, salt, cranberries, and pepper. Add salmon and orange zest to the top. To taste, add salt and pepper. Rosemary is a nice garnish. (optional)

Nutritional values per serving:
Total Calories: 288kcal, **Fats:** 2g, **Carbohydrates:** 62g, **Protein:** 5g, **Fiber:** 3g, **Sodium:** 402mg, **Potassium:** 182mg

16. Grilled Shrimps

Prep time: 20 mins.
Cook time: 5 mins.
Total time: 25 mins.
Serves: 3
Difficulty: easy
Ingredients:

- 2 tbsp. of olive oil
- 1 lb. of shrimp (extra-large), shelled & deveined (about 18-20 shrimp)
- 1/2 tbsp. of fresh lemon juice
- 1/4 tsp. of red pepper
- 1 clove of garlic, minced
- 1/4 tsp. of paprika
- 1/2 tsp. of honey
- 1/8 tsp. of cayenne pepper
- 1/2 tsp. of salt

Directions:

- The shrimp should be skewered. Skewing them apart will result in crispier shrimp while skewing them closely together will result in juicier shrimp. Put six shrimp on each skewer. Make sure the shrimp are big enough to go between the grill's grates if you're not using a skewer and just to put them straight on the grill.
- The crooked shrimp should be oiled. Coat the shrimp equally with the other ingredients, which should be combined in a separate dish. Prior to grilling, marinate shrimp for 15 to 20 minutes. Longer marinating times may cause the lemon to begin to "cook" shrimp. Simply combine all the ingredients and cover the shrimp equally if you aren't skewering them.
- Grill at a high temperature. Prior to placing the shrimp on the grill or rack, they should be hot. On each side, they would cook for around two minutes. Lay shrimps all out if you are directly cooking them on the grill; you'll probably need to start flipping the 1st ones over if you have them all spread out.
- When the shrimp have just begun to completely turn opaque throughout, they are prepared.

Nutritional values per serving:
Total Calories: 288kcal, **Fats:** 20g, **Carbohydrates:** 6g, **Protein:** 23g, **Fiber:** 0g, **Sodium:** 273mg, **Potassium:** 1612mg

17. Wild Salmon & Horseradish-Mustard Sauce

Prep time: 15 mins.
Cook time: 5 mins.
Total time: 20 mins.
Serves: 4
Difficulty: easy
Ingredients:

- 4 wild salmon fillets (6-oz., about 1-inch thick)
- 2 tbsp. of olive oil, divided
- 1 tbsp. of fresh thyme (chopped), divided
- 3/4 tsp. of black pepper, divided
- 3/4 tsp. of kosher salt, divided
- 1/2 cup of sour cream (whole milk)
- 1 1/2 tsp. of grainy Dijon mustard
- 1 1/2 tsp. of prepared horseradish

Directions:

- Sprinkle 1 tsp. Thyme, 1/2 tsp. Salt, and 1/4 tsp. Pepper equally over the tops of the fillets after applying 1 tbsp. oil. A nonstick large skillet is preheated on medium-high. Swirl the remaining 1 tbsp. oil in the pan to coat. Skin-side down, add the fillets to the pan, and cook for 3 minutes, or until the skin starts to brown. Cook the fillets for 2 to 3 minutes, depending on the desired level of doneness.
- Stir well to include the remaining 2 tablespoons of thyme, horseradish, mustard, and remaining 1/4 tsp. salt, and remaining 1/2 tsp. Pepper. Serve alongside salmon.

Nutritional values per serving:
Total Calories: 314kcal, **Fats:** 18g, **Carbohydrates:** 1g, **Protein:** 35g, **Fiber:** 0g, **Sodium:** 512mg, **Potassium:** 660mg

18. Grass-Fed Steak & Parsley Pesto with Roasted Carrots

Prep time: 40 mins.
Cook time: 30 mins.
Total time: 1 hr. 10 mins.
Serves: 4
Difficulty: easy
Ingredients:

- 3/4 tsp. of sea salt (fine), divided
- 1 pound of flank steak (grass-fed)
- 1/2 tsp. of black pepper, freshly ground
- 1 pound of rainbow carrots
- 1/2 tsp. of light brown sugar
- 1 tbsp. of canola oil, divided
- 1/2 tsp. of ground coriander
- 1/2 tsp. of cumin
- 1 cup of fresh parsley leaves (flat-leaf)
- 1/4 cup of olive oil
- 1/2 cup of chopped fresh mint
- 1 tbsp. of apple cider vinegar
- One tsp. of salted butter
- 1/2 tsp. of crushed red pepper

Directions:

- Steak should be uniformly sprinkled with 1/4 teaspoon each of sugar, black pepper, and salt before being chilled overnight, and uncovered.
- Set the oven to 400 °F. While the oven is heating, let the steak rest at room temperature.
- Toss carrots with 1/4 teaspoon salt, 1 tsp. Canola oil, cumin, and coriander. Carrots should be spread out onto a baking sheet and roasted for 40 minutes at 400°F or until just soft.
- In a food processor, combine parsley, olive oil, mint, vinegar, and red pepper. Process until finely chopped. Place in a compact bowl. Add the last 1/4 teaspoon of salt and mix well.
- Big cast-iron skillet heated to high. Add the remaining 2 teaspoons of canola oil and the butter. Add the steak to the pan and cook it for 3 - 4 minutes on each side, depending on how done you want it.
- On each serve, place 2 teaspoons of pesto. Distribute the steak and carrots equally among the four plates.

Nutritional values per serving:
Total Calories: 376kcal, **Fats:** 25g, **Carbohydrates:** 13g, **Protein:** 26g, **Fiber:** 4g, **Sodium:** 574mg, **Potassium:** 86.48mg

19. Butternut Squash Mac & Cheese Noodles

Prep time: 10 mins.
Cook time: 15 mins.
Total time: 25 mins.
Serves: 4
Difficulty: easy
Ingredients:

- 1/2 Cup of Onion diced
- 1 tbsp. of olive oil, divided plus 1 tsp.
- 2 lbs. of peeled Butternut squash (Small), seeded & spiralized using Blade
- 6-7 tbsp. of Nutritional yeast, to taste
- 1 Cup of Roasted cashews (salted), soaked overnight in water (140g)
- 6 tbsp. of almond milk, unsweetened
- Generous amount of pepper
- 1 - 1 1/4 tsp. of salt

Directions:

- A very big pan with medium-high heat should be used to heat 2 tablespoons of the olive oil; save the remaining oil for another use.
- When the onions are tender and golden brown, add them and cook them while stirring often. Put them in a powerful blender
- Reduce the heat to medium-low and add the last 2 teaspoons of oil to the pan. Butternut squash that has been spiralized should be added. Cook for 7 to 10 minutes, stirring regularly, or till the noodles are soft to the fork.
- Drain the cashews of their water, and then add them to the blender with the almond milk, yeast, salt, and pepper while the noodles are cooking.
- Mix everything together until it's creamy and smooth, stopping to scrape the edges as necessary. The sauce needs to be rather thick!
- After adding the sauce, add the cooked noodles to the saucepan and toss to coat the noodles completely.

Nutritional values per serving:
Total Calories: 353kcal, **Fats:** 21.1g, **Carbohydrates:** 35.3g, **Protein:** 11.8g, **Fiber:** 8.3g, **Sodium:** 242mg, **Potassium:** 756mg

20. Sweet Potato Creamy Spinach Noodles with Cashew Sauce

Prep time: 15 mins.
Cook time: 10 mins.
Total time: 25 mins.
Serves: 6
Difficulty: easy
Ingredients:

- 3/4 cup of water (some more for soaking)
- 1 cup of cashews
- 1/2 tsp. of salt
- 1 tbsp. of oil
- 1 clove of garlic
- 4 sweet potatoes (large), spiralized
- a handful of basil leaves (fresh), chives, or any other herbs
- 2 cups of baby spinach
- olive oil to drizzle
- salt & pepper to taste

Directions:

- In a dish, cover cashews with water and let them soak for about two hours.
- Drain and thoroughly rinse. Add the ingredients to a blender or food processor, along with the 3/4 cup of water, salt, & garlic , until very smooth, and puree.
- Over high heat, warm the oil into a big skillet. Add sweet potatoes and stir with tongs for 6-7 minutes, until they are soft and crisp. After taking it off the heat, add the spinach; it should start to wilt fast.
- Stir together half the sauce and half the herbs in the pan. If the mix is too sticky, add water. Add the fresh herbs on top after liberally seasoning with salt and black pepper and drizzling with olive oil.

Nutritional values per serving:
Total Calories: 203kcal, **Fats:** 10.7g, **Carbohydrates:** 23.7g, **Protein:** 5.2g, **Fiber:** 3.5g, **Sodium:** 253mg, **Potassium:** 480.8mg

21. Mushroom Tomato Spaghetti Squash

Prep time: 30 mins.
Cook time: 10 mins.
Total time: 40 mins.
Serves: 6
Difficulty: easy
Ingredients:

- 2 cups of tomatoes diced
- 1 spaghetti squash (large), cooked, about 6 cups.
- 4 cloves of garlic minced
- 1/3 cup of chopped shallots or onions, about 1 small
- 8 ounces of mushrooms sliced
- 1/4 cup of pine nuts, toasted
- 3 tbsp. of olive oil
- a handful of fresh basil, cut chiffonade
- Pinch of flakes of red pepper, if desired
- Kosher salt & black pepper, to taste

Optional: Parmesan cheese
Directions:

- Squash spaghetti is ready. Slice in half when cold enough to handle, take out the seeds and stringy parts, and shred using two forks. Put squash aside.
- Oil should be heated to medium heat in a big sauté pan. After approximately 3–4 minutes of continuous stirring, add the onions and mushrooms. Stir in the garlic for one or two more minutes, just until fragrant. Keep garlic from oxidizing.
- Stir in the tomatoes after adding them.
- When the cooked spaghetti squash is hot, and the veggies are spread equally, add it.
- Add toasted pine nuts and fresh basil before tossing. Add kosher salt, pepper, and, if preferred, a dash of some red pepper flakes to taste. (Add fresh parmesan cheese, if preferred.)

Nutritional values per serving:
Total Calories: 173kcal, **Fats:** 12g, **Carbohydrates:** 17g, **Protein:** 4g, **Fiber:** 4g, **Sodium:** 33mg, **Potassium:** 466mg

22. Thai Chicken Coconut Curry

Prep time: 5 mins.
Cook time: 25 mins.
Total time: 30 mins.
Serves: 4

Difficulty: easy

Ingredients:

- 1 1/2 tbsp. of curry powder, divided
- 1 tbsp. of coconut oil
- 1/2 tbsp. of ground turmeric
- 1 tbsp. of grated ginger
- 2 cloves of garlic, minced
- 1 pound of chicken breast (cut in 1-inch pieces)
- 1 sweet potato (large), cubed (400 grams/3 cups)
- 1 cup of diced onion (120 grams)
- 2 bell peppers (large), julienned (400 grams)
- 1 can of coconut milk (full fat)
- 3 heaping cups of broccoli (2 heads/250 grams)
- 1 tbsp. of red curry paste
- 1/2 tsp. of cayenne pepper
- 1 tbsp. of tomato paste
- salt & pepper, to taste

For serving: cauliflower rice, white rice, lime wedges, cilantro.

Directions:

- Over low heat, preheat a big Dutch oven or nonstick pan. About 30 seconds after adding the oil, let it heat up. Stir in 1 tablespoon of curry powder along with the powdered ginger, garlic, and turmeric for approximately 30 seconds, or until the mixture is aromatic. Don't let the garlic burn.
- Stir in the chicken & salt, and pepper after adding them to the spice mixture. Cook for 5-7 minutes, or until the outside is browned. Take out of the pan and place aside.
- Cook for 5 mins, stirring once or twice while adding onion, sweet potato, salt, and pepper. With the lid on, add the broccoli and peppers, and simmer for an additional 3 to 5 minutes while stirring regularly. Combine the cooked chicken with coconut milk, tomato paste, red curry paste, cayenne, 1/2 teaspoon curry powder, and salt & pepper. To blend, stir.
- Let veggies boil for 5 to 10 minutes, depending on how you want your vegetables cooked. As you cook the curry, it will thicken.

Nutritional values per serving:

Total Calories: 511kcal, **Fats:** 25g, **Carbohydrates:** 41g, **Protein:** 31g, **Fiber:** 9g, **Sodium:** 330mg, **Potassium:** 1071mg

23. Moroccan Lamb Stew

Prep time: 30 mins.
Cook time: 50 mins.
Total time: 1 hr. 20 mins.
Serves: 6
Difficulty: medium

Ingredients:

- 1 tsp. of ground cumin
- 1 tsp. of ground cinnamon
- ½ tsp. of ground ginger
- ¼ tsp. of ground nutmeg
- ¼ tsp. of ground cloves
- ¼ tsp. of ground turmeric
- 1 tsp. of kosher salt
- ⅛ tsp. of curry powder
- 1 pound of ground lamb
- 1 chopped sweet onion
- 1 tbsp. of butter
- 1 can of organic beef broth (14.5 ounces)
- 2 cans of beef consommé (14.5 ounces)
- 1 can of organic chicken broth (14.5 ounces)
- 1 can of diced tomatoes (14.5 ounces), undrained
- 3 carrots (large), chopped
- 1 tbsp. of honey
- 2 peeled sweet potatoes, diced
- ½ cup of dried apricots, chopped
- 1 can of garbanzo beans (15 ounces), drained & rinsed
- Some black pepper (ground) to taste
- 1 cup of dried lentils, rinsed

Directions:

- In a large bowl, mix the salt, turmeric, ginger, cumin, nutmeg, cloves, and curry powder. Add the ground lamb and combine. Allow the mixture to rest overnight in the refrigerator for the most delicious results.
- In a big saucepan over medium heat, melt the butter. For five to ten minutes, or until the onion is tender and just starting to brown, cook it in the butter. Combine the onions with the spicy lamb mixture. For approximately 5 minutes, cook and toss the meat until it is browned.
- Add the consomme, chicken broth, and beef broth to the pot. Add the tomatoes, honey, lentils, garbanzo beans, dried apricots, and sweet potatoes after stirring. Bring to a boil, then turn down the heat.
- The stew should be simmered for 30 mins or until the lentils and veggies are cooked and soft. Add black pepper according to taste.

Nutritional values per serving:

Total Calories: 465kcal, **Fats:** 13.9g, **Carbohydrates:** 57.3g, **Protein:** 28.2g, **Fiber:** 16.3g, **Sodium:** 1337.4mg, **Potassium:** 1200.9mg

24. Grilled Flank Steak with Caprese Salad

Prep time: 20 mins.
Cook time: 10 mins.
Total time: 35 mins. (Additional 5 mins.)

Serves: 4
Difficulty: easy
Ingredients:

- 1 ball of fresh mozzarella (4 ounces), cut in 1-inch cubes
- 2 tomatoes (medium), diced
- ¼ cup of fresh basil, coarsely chopped
- 4 tbsp. of olive oil, divided
- 2 cloves of garlic, minced & divided
- 1 pound of flank steak
- 1 bag of butter lettuce mix (6.5 ounces)
- salt & black pepper (ground), to taste
- 2 tbsp. of balsamic vinegar

Directions:

- Combine tomatoes, basil, mozzarella, 1 clove of finely chopped garlic, and 1 tablespoon of extra virgin olive oil, and mix to combine. Refrigerate dish with a cover.
- Set an outside grill over medium-high heat and give the grates a quick oiling.
- Add salt, pepper, 1 tablespoon of olive oil, 1 minced garlic clove, and steak to a large resealable bag. Distribute the mixture of oil over the steak before sealing the bag.
- Cook the steak on the grill for 5 minutes each side for medium-rare when it has heated up. The inside temperature should register 140 degrees Fahrenheit on an instant-read thermometer (60 degrees C). Allow standing for five minutes before slicing thinly against the grain.
- Place the lettuce among the four plates. Pour 1 1/2 tablespoons of olive oil and balsamic vinegar over each piece of lettuce. Evenly distribute the steak and tomato combination among the salads.

Nutritional values per serving:
Total Calories: 321kcal, **Fats:** 24g, **Carbohydrates:** 5.8g, **Protein:** 20.2g, **Fiber:** 1.3g, **Sodium:** 114.9mg, **Potassium:** 442.7mg

25. Thai Chicken Pineapple Curry

Prep time: 15 mins.
Cook time: 35 mins.
Total time: 50 mins.
Serves: 6
Difficulty: easy
Ingredients:

- 1-quart water
- 2 cups of uncooked jasmine rice
- ¼ cup of red curry paste
- 2 boneless & skinless halves of chicken breast, cut in thin strips
- 2 cans of coconut milk (13.5 ounces)
- 3 tbsp. of fish sauce
- 1 ½ cups of bamboo shoots (sliced), drained
- ¼ cup of white sugar
- ½ bell pepper (red & green), julienned
- ½ onion (small), chopped
- 1 cup of pineapple chunks, drained

Directions:

- In a saucepan, bring water and rice to a boil. Cover, lower heat to low, and simmer for 25 minutes.
- Combine curry paste and one can of coconut milk in a bowl. Add the remaining coconut milk, fish sauce, chicken, sugar, & bamboo shoots to the pan after transferring. Cook for 15 minutes, or until chicken fluids are clear. Bring to a boil.
- The red, green, and onion bell peppers are combined in the wok. Cook the peppers for a further 10 minutes, or until the chicken juices are clear. Pineapple is added after the heat has turned off. Over the prepared rice, serve.

Nutritional values per serving:
Total Calories: 623kcal, **Fats:** 34.5g, **Carbohydrates:** 77.5g, **Protein:** 20.3g, **Fiber:** 3.5g, **Sodium:** 781.1mg, **Potassium:** 546.1mg

26. Curried Beef & Vegetables

Prep time: 35 mins.
Cook time: 1 hr. 30 mins.
Total time: 2 hr. 5 mins.
Serves: 8
Difficulty: medium
Ingredients:

- 3 tbsp. of olive oil
- ½ pound of beef for stew, like beef chuck roast, in 1-inch chunks
- 2 pieces of ginger root, fresh (3 inches), peeled & diced
- 2 onions, peeled & diced
- 3 cloves of garlic, minced
- 2 chopped celery ribs
- 2 tsp. of coriander powder
- 2 tbsp. of curry powder
- 1 tsp. of five-spice Asian powder
- 2 peeled carrots, sliced
- 1 tsp. of ground turmeric
- Some peeled parsnips, sliced
- 1 sliced zucchini
- 2 peeled potatoes, cubed
- 2 peeled apples, cored & chopped
- 1 cup of cashews
- 1 cup of raisins
- ½ cup of water

Directions:

- Set oven up to 350 degrees Fahrenheit (175 degrees C). Aluminum foil should be used to line a roasting pan.
- Add enough water to the pan to cover the steak. Boil for a few minutes, then turn down the heat & simmer for 30 minutes.
- Olive oil should be heated in the meanwhile over medium to high heat in a large saucepan. Add the ginger, onions, garlic, and celery and stir. Cook for 5 minutes or until veggies is tender. To uniformly coat the onion mixture, combine the curry powder, five-spice powder, coriander powder, and turmeric. Add the apples, zucchini, potatoes, carrots, and parsnips after cooking for an additional 5 minutes. As you mix the ingredients together, add the raisins, cashews, and meat along with any cooking liquid.
- Fill the roasting pan with the meat and vegetable mixture. Sprinkle the mixture with 1/2 cup of water. Wrap aluminum foil around the pan.
- Bake in a preheated oven for approximately an hour or until well cooked.

Nutritional values per serving:

Total Calories: 343kcal, **Fats:** 17.5g, **Carbohydrates:** 40.7g, **Protein:** 10.3g, **Fiber:** 5.1g, **Sodium:** 158.9mg, **Potassium:** 801.4mg

27. Dinner Veggie Curry

Prep time: 15 mins.
Cook time: 5 mins. (Plus 30 mins. for baking)
Total time: 50 mins.
Serves: 6
Difficulty: medium
Ingredients:

- 8.5 oz. of carrots, about almost 3, medium size
- 12 oz. of cauliflower florets
- 16.5 oz. of zucchini, about two large
- ¼ cup of olive oil
- 12 oz. of yellow squash, almost about 2 large
- ¼ tsp. of black pepper, ground
- 1 tsp. of coarse sea salt, plus some more to taste

For sauce:

- 0.5 oz. of chopped garlic clove, about 2-3 large cloves
- 2-3 tbsp. of olive oil
- 3 oz. of chopped shallot, about 2 large
- 1 tsp. of coriander, turmeric & cumin powder each
- 0.6 oz. of chopped ginger
- 14 oz. of coconut milk cream (full fat)
- 1 to 1.5 tbsp. of tamarind concentrate or some lime juice to taste
- 1.5 tbsp. of SunButter, or almond butter or cashew butter

Directions:

- Set the oven up to 400 degrees (204C). Cut the veggies into bite-sized pieces using a knife.
- Vegetables should be spread out evenly across a large parchment-lined sheet pan while roasting. Add salt, pepper, and olive oil as seasonings. Combine by tossing. Middle rack, 20 minutes of baking
- Make the sauce in the last 8-10 minutes of baking, just before removing the veggies from the oven. In a 12-inch Dutch oven or large pan that has been preheated, add 2-3 tbsp. of olive oil. With a sprinkle of salt, sauté the shallot, garlic, and ginger on medium heat for approximately 2 minutes, or until fragrant.
- Lower the temperature. Add the cumin, coriander, and turmeric powder and stir. Sauté for 30 seconds. Add tamarind concentrate, almond butter, and coconut cream. About 2-3 minutes are needed for the almond butter to thoroughly dissolve with frequent stirring. Adjust to taste. The sauce ought to have a savory, earthy, somewhat sweet, and acidic flavor.
- Add the curry sauce to the roasted veggies. Gently blend by tossing. Serve warm or hot.

Nutritional values per serving:

Total Calories: 354kcal, **Fats:** 31g, **Carbohydrates:** 20g, **Protein:** 6g, **Fiber:** 5g, **Sodium:** 452mg, **Potassium:** 933mg

28. Brussels Sprout & Sweet Potato Tacos

Prep time: 15 mins.
Cook time: 15 mins.
Total time: 30 mins.
Serves: 8
Difficulty: medium
Ingredients:

- 1 finely diced green bell pepper
- ½ finely diced sweet onion
- 3 tbsp. of olive oil
- 1 lb. of Brussels sprouts ends trimmed, thinly sliced
- 1 lb. of peeled sweet potatoes, cut in ½-inch pieces
- 2 cloves of garlic crushed
- 2 tsp. of apple cider vinegar
- 2 tbsp. of maple syrup
- 1 tsp. of hot sauce or sriracha sauce
- ¼ tsp. of ground sage
- 1 tsp. of salt

Optional:

- Cilantro
- Cheese Mozzarella (dairy-free)

- Coarsely chopped Pecans, toasted
- 8 Cassava tortillas (flour) or other tortillas (gluten-free)

Directions:

- Add 2 tablespoons of olive oil, the onion, and the bell pepper to a large pan set over medium heat. Onions should be sautéed for two to three minutes, or until they start to become transparent.
- Sweet potatoes and more olive oil should be added. For 6 to 8 minutes, sauté.
- Add the Brussels sprouts and simmer, covered, for 3 to 4 minutes, or until they are nearly soft.
- In a medium bowl, mix together the garlic, vinegar, syrup, sriracha sauce, salt, & ground sage while the veggies are cooking.
- When adding the sauce, make sure to scrape any browned pieces off the pan's bottom. Cook potatoes and sprouts for 2 to 3 minutes, or until done.
- Serve with nuts, dairy-free cheese, & cilantro in a cassava tortilla or another kind of Paleo tortilla. Enjoy!

Nutritional values per serving:

Total Calories: 283kcal, **Fats:** 13g, **Carbohydrates:** 39g, **Protein:** 3g, **Fiber:** 4g, **Sodium:** 303mg, **Potassium:** 460mg

29. Mushroom Cauliflower Skillet

Prep time: 10 mins.
Cook time: 10 mins.
Total time: 20 mins.
Serves: 4
Difficulty: easy
Ingredients:

- 1 stick of celery sliced
- 2 tbsp. of olive oil
- ½ cup of onion chopped
- 3 cups of mushrooms, sliced
- 1 big clove of garlic, minced
- 14 oz. of cauliflower rice
- Soy sauce, to taste
- 1/3 cup of organic vegetable broth
- 2 cups of spinach
- 1 tbsp. of fresh parsley chopped
- Salt & black pepper to taste

Directions:

- In a food processor, pulse cauliflower florets for 25 to 30 seconds, or until they resemble rice. Place aside.
- Over medium heat, add olive oil to a big skillet. Cook the celery and onions for approximately 5 minutes, or until they are soft.
- For 30 seconds, add the garlic and sauté it.
- Add the mushroom and cook it thoroughly in the pan.
- Add the soy sauce, vegetable broth, and cauliflower rice. Permit the veggie broth to seep into the cauliflower rice. It should be cooked till tender but not mushy.
- Cook the spinach for 2 minutes after adding it. To taste, add salt & pepper to the food. Prior to serving, garnish with freshly cut parsley. Enjoy!

Nutritional values per serving:

Total Calories: 125kcal, **Fats:** 7.3g, **Carbohydrates:** 9.8g, **Protein:** 4.6g, **Fiber:** 4.2g, **Sodium:** 30omg, **Potassium:** 420mg

30. Salmon-Stuffed Dinner Avocados

Prep time: 15 mins.
Cook time: 0 mins.
Total time: 15 mins.
Serves: 4
Difficulty: easy
Ingredients:

- ½ cup of diced celery
- ½ cup of plain Greek yogurt (non-fat)
- 2 tbsp. of chopped fresh parsley
- 2 tsp. of mayonnaise
- 1 tbsp. of lime juice
- 1 tsp. of Dijon mustard
- ⅛ tsp. of ground pepper
- ⅛ tsp. of salt
- 2 cans of salmon (5 ounces), flaked, drained & skin & bones removed
- Chives (chopped), for garnish
- 2 avocados

Directions:

- In a medium bowl, combine the yogurt, celery, lime juice, parsley, mustard, mayonnaise, salt, and pepper. Stir in fish well.
- Pit avocados and cut them in half lengthwise. From each avocado half, remove approximately 1 tablespoon of flesh and place it in a small bowl. With a fork, mash the avocado flesh that has been removed and combine it with the salmon mixture.
- Place a heap of the mixture of salmon, equal to 1/4 cup of each avocado half, on top of each avocado half. If desired, add chives as a garnish.

Nutritional values per serving:

Total Calories: 293kcal, **Fats:** 19.6g, **Carbohydrates:** 10.5g, **Protein:** 22.5g, **Fiber:** 7g, **Sodium:** 399.8mg, **Potassium:** 807.2mg

31. Tofu Poke

Prep time: 30 mins.

Cook time: 0 mins.
Total time: 30 mins.
Serves: 4
Difficulty: easy
Ingredients:

- ¼ cup of tamari (reduced-sodium)
- ¾ cup of scallion greens (thinly sliced)
- 1 ½ tbsp. of mirin
- 1 tbsp. of sesame seeds, toasted
- 1 ½ tbsp. of toasted sesame oil (dark)
- 2 tsp. of grated fresh ginger
- 1 package of extra-firm tofu (12 ounces), drained & cut in 1/2-inch pieces
- ½ tsp. of red pepper, crushed (Optional)
- 4 cups of zucchini noodles
- 2 cups of shredded carrots
- 2 tbsp. of rice vinegar
- 2 cups of pea shoots
- ¼ cup of chopped fresh basil
- ¼ cup of chopped peanuts, toasted

Directions:

- In a medium bowl, combine the scallion greens, mirin, tamari, oil, ginger, sesame seeds, and red pepper, if using. 2 tbsp. of the sauce should be saved in a small dish. In the medium bowl, combine the sauce and tofu. Gently toss to combine.
- In a large bowl, mix the vinegar and zucchini noodles. Add 3/4 cup of tofu, 1/2 cup of carrots, 1/2 cup of pea shoots, & 1 tbsp. Each of peanuts and basil to each of the four dishes. Serve with a drizzle of the sauce you set aside.

Nutritional values per serving:
Total Calories: 262kcal, **Fats:** 15.5g, **Carbohydrates:** 19.2g, **Protein:** 15.9g, **Fiber:** 5.4g, **Sodium:** 800.3mg, **Potassium:** 601.2mg

32. Roasted Rosemary Salmon with Potatoes and Asparagus

Prep time: 5 mins.
Cook time: 25 mins. (Roasting)
Total time: 30 mins.
Serves: 4
Difficulty: easy
Ingredients:

- 1 tbsp. of fresh rosemary, chopped
- 3 tbsp. of olive oil
- 2 tsp. of minced garlic
- 1 tsp. of salt, divided
- 1 ¼ pound of Yukon Gold potatoes, in 1-inch pieces
- ¾ tsp. of ground pepper, divided
- 4 skinless (5 ounces) salmon fillets, wild
- 1 pound of asparagus, trimmed
- 1 lemon (medium)
- ½ tsp. of whole-grain mustard
- 2 tbsp. of balsamic glaze

Directions:

- Set oven up to 425 degrees Fahrenheit.
- Into small bowl, combine oil, rosemary, and garlic. Put the potatoes into large bowl & season with salt & pepper and 1 tbsp. of the oil mixture. Place the potatoes on a large baking sheet with a rim in an equal layer. About 20 minutes of roasting time will result in tenderness. Potatoes should be pushed to 1 end of the pan.
- In a large bowl, combine the asparagus with 1 tbsp. of the mixture of oil, 1/4 tsp. Salt, and 1/8 tsp. Pepper. Toss to combine. On the other end of a baking sheet, arrange the asparagus. It takes around 3 minutes to roast asparagus to brilliant green color. To make room in the middle, push the veggies to the pan's edges.
- The additional 1/4 tsp. Salt and 1/8 tsp. Pepper should be added after brushing the salmon with the rest of 1 tablespoon of the oil mixture. The salmon should be in the middle of the pan. Slice the lemon in half, then arrange the segments over the fish and veggies. Roast for five minutes more. The rest of the lemon half should be cut into wedges.
- In a small dish, combine the mustard and balsamic glaze. Apply the salmon with 1 tbsp, of the mixture. Continue roasting for a further 5 minutes, or until the veggies are soft and the salmon is barely cooked through. Pour the remaining sauce over the veggies. With the lemon wedges, serve.

Nutritional values per serving:
Total Calories: 400kcal, **Fats:** 15.9g, **Carbohydrates:** 34.1g, **Protein:** 32.5g, **Fiber:** 4.4g, **Sodium:** 711mg, **Potassium:** 682.7mg

33. Roasted Root Veggies on Spiced Lentils

Prep time: 5 mins.
Cook time: 40 mins.
Total time: 45 mins.
Serves: 2
Difficulty: easy
Ingredients:
Lentils:

- 1 ½ cups of water
- ½ cup of French green lentils or black beluga lentils
- ½ tsp. of ground coriander
- 1 tsp. of garlic powder
- ½ tsp. of ground cumin
- ¼ tsp. of kosher salt

- ¼ tsp. of ground allspice
- ⅛ tsp. of sumac (optional)
- 1 tsp. of olive oil
- 2 tbsp. of lemon juice

Vegetables:

- 1 clove of garlic, smashed
- 1 tbsp. of olive oil
- 1 1/2 cups of roasted root vegetables
- 1 tsp. of ground coriander
- 2 cups of chopped beet greens or kale
- ⅛ tsp. of ground pepper
- 2 tbsp. of tahini or plain yogurt (low-fat)
- Some kosher salt
- Parsley (fresh), for garnish

Directions:

- Lentils should be cooked by combining water, garlic powder, lentils, 1/2 teaspoon each of coriander, cumin, allspice, and salt (if used) in a medium saucepan. Bring to a boil. Cook for 25 - 30 minutes with the lid on at a simmering temperature.
- After approximately five more minutes, remove the top and continue to boil the liquid until it slightly reduces. Drain. Add 1 teaspoon oil and lemon juice and stir.
- A big skillet with medium heat is used to heat the oil. Add the garlic and simmer for 1 to 2 minutes, or until fragrant. Add the roasted root vegetables & simmer for 2 to 4 minutes, stirring often, till heated through. Add the beet greens (or kale) and stir; simmer for 2 to 3 minutes, or until just wilted. Add the salt, pepper, and coriander.
- With tahini on top, serve the veggies over the lentils (or yogurt). If desired, add parsley as a garnish.

Nutritional values per serving:

Total Calories: 453kcal, **Fats:** 22.4g, **Carbohydrates:** 49.7g, **Protein:** 18.1g, **Fiber:** 13.9g, **Sodium:** 346.1mg, **Potassium:** 465mg

34. Roasted Sheet-Pan Salmon and Vegetables

Prep time: 15 mins.
Cook time: 40 mins. (Baking)
Total time: 55 mins.
Serves: 4
Difficulty: easy
Ingredients:

- 2 tbsp. of olive oil
- 1 pound of fingerling potatoes, lengthwise halved
- 5 cloves of garlic, coarsely chopped
- ½ tsp. of black pepper, freshly ground
- ½ tsp. of sea salt
- 4 frozen or fresh (5 - 6-ounce) skinless salmon fillets
- 2 cups of cherry tomatoes
- 2 red, orange, and/or yellow sweet peppers (medium), cut into rings
- 1 ½ cups of fresh parsley, chopped (1 bunch)
- ¼ cup of fresh oregano, finely snipped or 1 tbsp. of oregano (dried), crushed
- ¼ cup of pitted kalamata olives, halved
- 1 lemon

Directions:

- Set oven up to 425 degrees Fahrenheit. Add potatoes to a large bowl. Toss to coat with 1 Tbsp. of oil, 1/8 tsp. of salt and black pepper, garlic, and 1 Tbsp. of oil. Wrap in foil and transfer to a baking tray (15x10-inch). Roast for 30 minutes.
- If the salmon was frozen, defrost it now. Sweet peppers, parsley, tomatoes, oregano, olives, and 1/8 teaspoon each of salt & black pepper should all be combined in the same bowl. Add the last 1 Tbsp. of oil and drizzle, then toss to coat.
- Dry off salmon after rinsing. Add the last 1/4 tsp. of salt & black pepper. Salmon should be placed on top of the sweet pepper combination and potatoes. 10 more minutes of roasting, uncovered, or until fish flakes.
- Lemon zest must be removed. Lemon juice should be squeezed over the fish and veggies. Add a little zest.

Nutritional values per serving:

Total Calories: 422kcal, **Fats:** 18.6g, **Carbohydrates:** 31.5g, **Protein:** 32.9g, **Fiber:** 5.7g, **Sodium:** 593.1mg, **Potassium:** 1740.6mg

35. Tofu & Mushroom Stir-Fry

Prep time: 10 mins.
Cook time: 10 mins.
Total time: 20 mins.
Serves: 5
Difficulty: easy
Ingredients:

- 1 pound of mushrooms (mixed), sliced
- 4 tbsp. of canola oil or peanut oil, divided
- 1 red bell pepper (medium), diced
- 1 tbsp. of grated fresh ginger
- 1 bunch of trimmed scallions, cut in 2-inch pieces
- 1 clove of garlic (large), grated
- 3 tbsp. of vegetarian oyster sauce or simple oyster sauce

- 1 container of baked or smoked tofu (8 ounces), diced

Directions:

- In a large cast-iron pan or wok with a flat bottom, heat 2 tablespoons of oil over high heat. Add the bell pepper and mushrooms; simmer for 4 minutes, stirring occasionally, until tender. Add the scallions, ginger, garlic, and sauté for an additional 30 seconds. Place the veggies in a bowl.
- Tofu and the 2 tablespoons of residual oil are added to the pan. Cook for 3 to 4 minutes, turning once, until golden. Oyster sauce and the veggies are combined. Cook for approximately a minute while stirring until heated.

Nutritional values per serving:
Total Calories: 171kcal, **Fats:** 13.1g, **Carbohydrates:** 8.6g, **Protein:** 7.7g, **Fiber:** 2.3g, **Sodium:** 309.2mg, **Potassium:** 468.7mg

36. Mediterranean Quinoa & Arugula

Prep time: 25 mins.
Cook time: 3 hrs.
Total time: 3 hrs. 25 mins.
Serves: 6
Difficulty: medium
Ingredients:

- 1 ½ cups of uncooked quinoa, rinsed
- 2 ¼ cups of unsalted vegetable stock
- 1 cup of red onions, sliced (from 1 onion)
- 1 can of chickpeas (garbanzo beans), no-salt-added (15.5 ounces), drained & rinsed
- 2 cloves of garlic, minced (about 2 tsp.)
- 2 ½ tbsp. of olive oil
- 2 tsp. of lemon juice, fresh (from 1 lemon)
- ¾ tsp. of kosher salt
- ½ cup of chopped, drained red bell peppers, roasted (from a jar)
- 2 ounces of crumbled feta cheese (about 1/2 cup)
- 4 cups of baby arugula (almost about 4 ounces)
- 2 tbsp. of fresh oregano, coarsely chopped
- 12 pitted kalamata olives, halved lengthwise

Directions:

- In a 5 - 6-quart slow cooker, combine the stock, onions, quinoa, garlic, 1 1/2 tsp. of olive oil, chickpeas, and 1/2 teaspoon of salt. For 3 to 4 hours, with the lid on, simmer the quinoa on LOW until it is soft and the liquid has been absorbed.
- Cut the slow cooker off. With a fork, fluff the quinoa mixture. Lemon juice, the remaining 2 tablespoons of olive oil, and 1/4 teaspoon of salt are all combined in a bowl. Red bell peppers and the olive oil combination should be added to slow cooker and gently mixed together. Fold the arugula in slowly. For approximately 10 minutes, or till the arugula is just beginning to wilt, cover and leave out. The oregano, feta cheese, and olives should be distributed equally over each dish.

Nutritional values per serving:
Total Calories: 352kcal, **Fats:** 13g, **Carbohydrates:** 46g, **Protein:** 12g, **Fiber:** 7g, **Sodium:** 575mg, **Potassium:** 450mg

37. Stuffed Potatoes with Beans & Salsa

Prep time: 5 mins.
Cook time: 20 mins. (Microwave)
Total time: 25 mins.
Serves: 4
Difficulty: medium
Ingredients:

- ½ cup of fresh salsa
- 4 russet potatoes (medium)
- 1 ripe of avocado, sliced
- 4 tsp. of pickled jalapeños, chopped
- 1 can of pinto beans (15 ounces), warmed, rinsed & lightly mashed

Directions:

- Use a fork to pierce potatoes all over. For around 20 minutes, on Medium, flip the food once or twice until soft. (Alternatively, bake potatoes for 45 to 1 hour at 425 degrees F until they are soft.) After transferring, let it cool somewhat on a clean cutting board.
- Make a longitudinal incision, but do not cut all the way through to open the potato while holding them with a dish towel. To reveal the flesh, pinch the ends.
- Add some salsa, avocado, beans, and jalapenos on top of each potato. Serve hot.

Nutritional values per serving:
Total Calories: 324kcal, **Fats:** 8g, **Carbohydrates:** 56.7g, **Protein:** 9.2g, **Fiber:** 11g, **Sodium:** 421.7mg, **Potassium:** 1415.5mg

38. Oven-Baked Ginger-Tahini Salmon & Vegetables

Prep time: 15 mins.
Cook time: 35 mins. (Roasting)
Total time: 50 mins.

Serves: 4
Difficulty: medium
Ingredients:

- 1 pound of cremini mushrooms or white button (6 cups), cut in 1-inch pieces
- 1 sweet potato (large), cubed (12 oz.)
- 2 tbsp. of olive oil, divided
- 1 pound of green beans, trimmed
- ½ tsp. of salt, divided
- 2 tbsp. of soy sauce (reduced-sodium)
- 1 tbsp. of honey, plus 1 tsp.
- 1 tbsp. of tahini, plus 2 tsp.
- 1 ½ tsp. of fresh ginger, finely grated
- 2 tsp. of rice vinegar
- 1 ¼ pound of salmon, preferably wild, cut in 4 portions
- 2 tbsp. of fresh chives, chopped (Optional)

Directions:

- Put a large baking sheet with a rim in the oven. One rack should be placed in the center of the oven, and the other should be placed approximately 6 inches from the broiler. Heat up to 425 degrees Fahrenheit.
- In a large bowl, mix the mushrooms, sweet potato, 1 tablespoon of oil, and 1/4 teaspoon of salt. Toss to combine.
- The baking sheet has to come out of the oven. On the pan, evenly distribute the vegetable mixture; roast for approximately 20 minutes, stirring once, or till the sweet potatoes are beginning to brown.
- Green beans should be mixed with the remainder of 1 Tbsp. oil & 1/4 tsp. Salt in the meanwhile. Into a small bowl, mix the soy sauce, honey, tahini, and ginger.
- Pan should be taken out of the oven. Place green beans onto the other side of the sweet potatoes and mushrooms. If necessary, nestle the salmon on top of the veggies and place it in the center. On top of salmon, spread half of tahini sauce. For a further 8 to 10 minutes, roast the fish until it flakes. Broil for approximately 3 minutes, or till the salmon is glazed, after turning the broiler to high.
- The leftover tahini sauce should be mixed with vinegar before being drizzled over the fish and veggies. If preferred, top with chives before serving.

Nutritional values per serving:
Total Calories: 555kcal, **Fats:** 29.9g, **Carbohydrates:** 37.3g, **Protein:** 37.7g, **Fiber:** 7.6g, **Sodium:** 718.4mg, **Potassium:** 1387.7mg

39. Sheet-Pan Dinner Chicken Fajita Bowls

Prep time: 20 mins.
Cook time: 20 mins. (Roasting)
Total time: 40 mins.
Serves: 4
Difficulty: easy
Ingredients:

- 2 tsp. of ground cumin
- 2 tsp. of chili powder
- ¾ tsp. of salt, divided
- ½ tsp. of smoked paprika
- ½ tsp. of garlic powder
- ¼ tsp. of ground pepper
- 1·¼ pound of chicken tenders
- 2 tbsp. of olive oil, divided
- 1 yellow onion (medium), sliced
- 1 green bell pepper (medium), sliced
- 1 red bell pepper (medium), sliced
- 4 cups of stemmed kale, chopped
- ¼ cup of plain Greek yogurt (low-fat)
- 1 can of black beans, no-salt-added (15 ounce), rinsed
- 2 tsp. of water
- 1 tbsp. of lime juice

Directions:

- Pre-heat the oven to 425 degrees F and place a big rimmed baking sheet inside.
- In a large bowl, combine the chili powder, cumin, 1/2 teaspoon salt, paprika, garlic powder, and ground pepper. One teaspoon of the mixture of spices should be added to a larger bowl and left aside. The remaining mixture of spices in the big bowl should be incorporated with 1 Tbsp. oil. Toss to coat the onion, chicken, and red & green bell peppers.
- When done baking, remove the pan and spray it with cooking spray. On the pan, distribute the mixture of chicken in a uniform layer. Roast for 10-15 minutes.
- In the meanwhile, place the kale & black beans in a large bowl and add the remaining 1/4 teaspoon of salt and 1 tablespoon of olive oil. Toss to coat.
- Pan should be taken out of the oven. Chicken and veggies are stirred. Evenly distribute the greens and beans over the top. Cook the chicken for a further 5 to 7 minutes, or until it is well done.
- In the meanwhile, combine the saved spice mixture with the yogurt, lime juice, and water.
- The chicken & vegetable mixture should be divided into 4 bowls. Serve after drizzling with the yogurt dressing.

Nutritional values per serving:
Total Calories: 343kcal, **Fats:** 9.9g, **Carbohydrates:** 23.7g, **Protein:** 42.7g, **Fiber:** 8.2g, **Sodium:** 605.1mg, **Potassium:** 579.8mg

40. Zucchini Noodles with Shrimp & Avocado Pesto

Prep time: 25 mins.
Cook time: 10 mins.
Total time: 35 mins.
Serves: 4
Difficulty: easy
Ingredients:

- ¾ tsp. of salt, divided
- 5-6 zucchini, medium (2 & 1/4-2 & 1/2 pounds in total), trimmed
- 1 avocado (ripe)
- ¼ cup of shelled pistachios, unsalted
- 1 cup of fresh basil leaves, packed
- 2 tbsp. of lemon juice
- ¼ cup of olive oil, plus 2 tbsp., divided
- ¼ tsp. of ground pepper
- 3 cloves of garlic, minced
- 1-2 tsp. of Old Bay seasoning
- 1 pound (21-25 count) of raw shrimp, peeled & deveined, tails can be left on if desired

Directions:

- Slice the zucchini lengthwise in thin, long strands or strips using a vegetable peeler or a spiral slicer. When you get to the seeds in the center, stop. Put the "noodles" of zucchini in a strainer and sprinkle with 1/2 tsp. salt. After 15 - 30 minutes, let drain, then firmly squeeze to get rid of any extra water.
- Avocado, pistachios, basil, lemon juice, pepper, and the last 1/4 teaspoon of salt should be combined into a food processor in the meanwhile. To finely chop, pulse many times. Blend in 1/4 cup of oil after adding it.
- In a big skillet over medium to high heat, warm 1 tablespoon of oil. For 30 seconds, while stirring, add the garlic. Add the shrimp and Old Bay seasoning; simmer, stirring occasionally, for 3 to 4 minutes, or until the shrimp is nearly cooked through. Place in a large bowl.
- To the pan, add the last tablespoon of oil. Add drained zucchini noodles & stir gently for three minutes, or until heated. Transfer it to the bowl, stir in the pesto, and serve.

Nutritional values per serving:
Total Calories: 446kcal, **Fats:** 33.2g, **Carbohydrates:** 15.8g, **Protein:** 25.9g, **Fiber:** 6.6g, **Sodium:** 712.9mg, **Potassium:** 1271.2mg

41. Beef Tenderloin

Prep Time: 20 mins.
Cook Time: 25 mins.
Total Time: 45 mins.
Serves: 12
Difficulty: Easy
Ingredients:

- 1 tsp. of sea salt
- 3 pounds of beef tenderloin roast
- black pepper, to taste
- 4 cloves of garlic, minced
- 4 tbsp. of butter, salted
- 1 tsp. of Dijon mustard
- 1 tbsp. of rosemary, chopped

Directions:

- Use kitchen thread to tie the tenderloin roast. Every two to three inches along the roast, separate lengths of twine are spaced apart to achieve this.
- Add salt and pepper to the roast to season it. Overnight, put it in the refrigerator unattended.
- For 15 minutes, preheat the Oven to Steam/Roast at 450° F.
- Put the melted butter, garlic, rosemary, and Dijon in a small bowl. The components should be carefully combined.
- Apply the butter mixture to the roast.
- After roasting the steak for 15 minutes, click "additional time" and add 8-10 minutes. Check the roast's internal temperature with a meat thermometer at the end of the ten minutes. Until the roast reaches the desired temperature, cook it for an additional 5 to 10 mins. At a time.
- Before slicing the meat, let it for 10 minutes to rest.

Nutritional Values per serving:
Total Calories: 346kcal, **Fat:** 29g, **Carbohydrates:** 1g, **Protein:** 21g, **Fiber:** 1g, **Sodium:** 288mg, **Potassium:** 349mg

42. Spaghetti Squash Sausage Boats

Prep Time: 20 mins.
Cook Time: 45 mins.
Total Time: 1hr 5 mins.
Serves: 4
Difficulty: Easy
Ingredients:

- 1 tbsp. of avocado oil
- 1 baked spaghetti squash
- 1/2 cup of onion chopped
- 1/2 cup of black olives, sliced
- 1/2 cup of chopped green bell pepper

- 1 package of Golden Brown sliced Chicken Sausage
- 1 cup of mozzarella cheese
- 1 1/2 cups of marinara sauce

Directions:

- Achieve a 450°F oven temperature. Prepare to fill a roasted spaghetti squash that has been cut in half.
- Add bell peppers, onions, and avocado oil to a skillet. When they are transparent, sauté them for approximately 10 minutes at medium-low heat.
- Sausage slices, olives, and marinara sauce should all be added to the skillet. After bringing to a gentle simmer, turn off the heat.
- Place the spaghetti squash, sliced side up, in a baking dish. To remove the threads from each squash half, use a fork.
- Half the sauce and half the cheese should be placed into each half of the squash.
- For approximately 10 minutes, or till the cheese is bubbling and beginning to brown, bake the filled squash.

Nutritional Values per serving:
Total Calories: 361kcal, **Fat:** 22g, **Carbohydrates:** 28g, **Protein:** 18g, **Fiber:** 6g, **Sodium:** 1542mg, **Potassium:** 648mg

43. Pad Thai

Prep Time: 20 mins.
Cook Time: 5 mins.
Total Time: 25 mins.
Serves: 4
Difficulty: Easy
Ingredients:

- 1 beaten egg
- 1 tbsp. of olive oil or sesame oil
- 1/2 pound of shrimp
- 1 clove of garlic minced
- 1/2 pound of chicken breasts, cut in small cubes
- 2 large zucchini, spiralized
- 1 cup of sliced thinly purple cabbage
- 1 large carrot, spiralized
- 3 sliced green onions in 1-inch pieces
- lime wedges & cilantro to garnish, optional

Pad Thai Sauce:

- 3 tbsp. of unsweetened rice wine vinegar
- 3 tbsp. of SunButter, No Sugar Added
- 3 tbsp. of fish sauce or coconut aminos
- 1 1/2 tbsp. of lime juice
- 3 tbsp. of honey
- 1/4 tsp. of salt or some more, to taste
- 1 tbsp. of sriracha or some more, to taste

Directions:

- To make the sauce, put all the ingredients in a medium mixing bowl and whisk to incorporate. Place aside.
- A large skillet is heated at high heat. Add the chicken after the sesame oil. Add shrimp after browning chicken for around 7 minutes. Continue to cook for a further 4-5 minutes, or until the chicken and shrimp are fully cooked. Take out of skillet and place in dish.
- Add egg to the same skillet. Scramble in a stir-fry, then take from the pan and leave away.
- Put garlic in the same skillet. Sauté for 5-7 minutes, or until aromatic and softened.
- Zucchini noodles, red bell pepper, carrot noodles, and purple cabbage should all be added to the skillet. Stir-fry for approximately 4-5 minutes at high heat, or until cooked thoroughly. Vegetable noodles that have been overcooked will produce a watery meal.
- Add shrimp, chicken, and an egg after taking the skillet off the heat. After drizzling the sauce, mix the veggies to coat them.
- Add lime wedges, cilantro, and sunflower seeds as garnish.

Nutritional Values per serving:
Total Calories: 400kcal, **Fat:** 19g, **Carbohydrates:** 28g, **Protein:** 32g, **Fiber:** 3g, **Sodium:** 1036mg, **Potassium:** 726mg

44. Mushroom Veggie Burger

Prep Time: 15 mins.
Cook Time: 30 mins.
Total Time: 45 mins.
Serves: 6
Difficulty: Easy
Ingredients:

- 3 packages of fresh mushrooms, sliced (8 ounces)
- 2 tbsp. of olive oil
- ½ finely chopped onion
- 1 tsp. of salt
- 4 cloves of garlic, minced
- ½ tsp. of black pepper
- ⅔ cup of rolled oats
- ½ tsp. of dried oregano
- ¾ cup of dry bread crumbs
- ½ cup of Parmigiano-Reggiano cheese, freshly shredded
- 2 beaten eggs
- 2 tbsp. of olive oil

Directions:

- In a large pan, heat 2 tablespoons of olive oil over medium heat. Add the mushrooms, onion, and garlic. Season with salt, pepper, and oregano. For approximately 10 minutes, cook and stir the mushroom mixture until the liquid has nearly completely evaporated. Slice the cooked mushrooms into tiny pieces with a knife on a chopping board.
- Place the mushrooms in a large bowl. Add the bread crumbs and rolled oats after tasting for salt & black pepper and adding more as desired. Add eggs and Parmigiano-Reggiano cheese to the mixture and stir. Allow mixture to sit for approximately 15 minutes to allow the crumbs to absorb any extra liquid. (At this stage, if preferred, you may chill the mixture and cook it later.) Pick up approximately 1/4 cup of the mixture, moisten your hands with either water or vegetable oil, and shape into patties.
- Burgers should be pan-fried in the remaining 2 tablespoons of olive oil for 5 to 6 minutes, or till browned and cooked through.

Nutritional Values per serving:
Total Calories 255, **Fat:** 14.2g, **Carbohydrates**: 22.5g, **Protein:** 11.4g, **Fiber:** 4g, **Sodium:** 630.3mg, **Potassium:** 1100mg

45. Steamed Veggie Fish Fillet

Prep Time: 25 mins.
Cook Time: 15 mins.
Total Time: 40 mins.
Serves: 4
Difficulty: Easy
Ingredients:

- 1 fennel bulb (small)
- 1 shallot
- 1 carrot (small)
- 3 tbsp. of vegetable broth
- Salt & peppers
- 2 stalks of smooth parsley
- 3 oz. of catfish (organic)
- ½ lime (small)

Directions:

- Chop the shallot finely after peeling.
- Trim and rinse the carrot and fennel. To peel the carrot create little matchsticks out of both.
- In a non-stick pan, warm the broth. Cook for approximately 3 minutes after adding the shallot, fennel, and carrot. Use salt and pepper to taste to season.
- Fish fillets should be rinsed, dried off, and placed in the pan along with the broth. For 8 to 10 minutes, cook covered over low heat.
- Meanwhile, rinse the parsley, shake it dry, remove the leaves, and use a big knife to cut it finely.
- Squeeze the remaining lime and pour the juice all over the fish. To taste, add salt & pepper to the food. Serve after adding parsley.

Nutritional Values per serving:
Total calories: 100kcal, **Fat:** 2g, **Carbohydrates:** 5g, **Protein:** 13g, **Fiber:** 5g, **Sodium:** 450mg, **Potassium:** 355mg

46. Sardines with Parsley & Garlic

Prep Time: 50 mins.
Cook Time: 30 mins.
Total Time: 1hr. 20 mins. (Baked)
Serves: 4
Difficulty: Easy
Ingredients:

- 2 cloves of garlic
- 1 kg of fresh sardine
- 2 bunches of flat-leaf parsley
- Lemon juice
- 4 tbsp. of olive oil
- Salt & peppers

Directions:

- Sardines should be rinsed, dried, and gently salted inside before being layered closely together in an oven-safe dish. Sliced garlic has been peeled. Clean the parsley, slice it into little pieces, and add 1/2 the garlic. Add lemon juice, salt, and pepper to the mixture after adding the olive oil.
- The sardines should be marinated, then baked for about 30-35 minutes at 180°C (or 350°F). Garnish with the leftover parsley just before serving.

Nutritional Values per serving:
Total calories: 490kcal, **Fat:** 37g, **Carbohydrates:** 6g, **Protein:** 29g, **Fiber:** 1g, **Sodium:** 52mg, **Potassium:** 0mg

47. Moroccan Spicy Chicken Skewers with Tomato-Arugula Salad

Prep Time: 1hr.
Cook Time: 15 mins.
Total Time: 1hr. 15mins.
Serves: 2
Difficulty: Easy
Ingredients:

- 1 red onion
- 7 oz. of chicken breasts
- 1 clove of garlic
- 2 sprigs of thyme
- 3 oranges

- 1 tsp. of ground paprika
- 1 pinch of cinnamon
- 1 pinch of cayenne pepper
- Salt & peppers
- 4 oz. of cherry tomatoes
- ½ bunch of arugula
- 2 tbsp. of olive oil

Directions:

- Chicken breast should be rinsed, dried with paper towels, and then cut into roughly 1/2-inch broad strips.
- Four long wooden skewers with chicken strips on them are placed in a baking dish (rectangular).
- Finely cut onion and garlic after peeling. 2 oranges should have their skins cut off, with the white pith completely removed.
- Using a sharp knife, cut segments of fruit between the membranes that separate them, catching the juice into a bowl. Place orange segments on a platter for later.
- Measure 5 tbsp. of the third orange juice after halves and pressing it.
- Thyme leaves should be rinsed, dried, and picked. Thyme should be mixed with paprika, cayenne, cinnamon, orange juice, garlic, onion, and salt & pepper to taste.
- The chicken skewers should be covered and marinated in the marinade for 20 minutes in the refrigerator.
- Spin the arugula dry after rinsing. Rinse after halving cherry tomatoes.
- Chicken skewers should be taken out of the marinade and placed on a platter. The marinade should be heated in a skillet with 1 tablespoon of oil, then added. Reduced by half after cooking
- The reduced marinade should be poured into a small dish. Clean the pan. The chicken skewers should be cooked for approximately 6 minutes, flipping them over regularly in the remaining oil.
- Place tomatoes, orange segments, and arugula on a platter. On top, arrange the chicken skewers, sprinkle with the cooled marinade, and serve.

Nutritional Values per serving:

Total calories: 276kcal, **Fat:** 11g, **Carbohydrates:** 16 g, **Protein:** 26g, **Fiber:** 10g, **Sodium:** 650mg, **Potassium:** 785 mg

48. Zucchini Chicken with Pecans

Prep Time: 30mins.
Cook Time: 25 mins.
Total Time: 55mins.
Serves: 4
Difficulty: Easy
Ingredients:

- 18 oz. of chicken breasts
- 3 zucchini
- Salt & peppers
- 1 clove of garlic
- 4 tbsp. of olive oil
- Some mint
- 3 oz. of pecan
- Some lemons

Directions:

- Slice the cleaned, trimmed, and thinly sliced zucchini. Chicken should be washed in cold water, dried off, and seasoned with salt & pepper.
- In a pan, heat two teaspoons of oil. For approximately 10 minutes, sear the chicken on medium heat on both sides until golden brown. Simmer the heat down.
- Heat the remaining oil in a different pan. Over medium heat, lightly sauté zucchini slices for 4 minutes. Garlic cloves are peeled and squeezed into the pan using a press.
- Mint should be washed, dried, and the leaves are taken. Squeeze the lemon's half.
- Chicken should be taken out of the pan, patted dry with paper towels, and sliced into thin slices. Pecans should be roughly chopped and combined with chicken, zucchini, mint, and lemon juice. Serve in dishes after adding salt and pepper to taste.

Nutritional Values per serving:

Total calories: 400kcal, **Fat:** 26g, **Carbohydrates:** 6 g, **Protein:** 36g, **Fiber:** 13g, **Sodium:** 623mg, **Potassium:** 804mg

49. Sicilian-Style Veal Fillet with Grapefruit and Orange Salad

Prep Time: 30mins.
Cook Time: 15 mins.
Total Time: 45mins.
Serves: 2
Difficulty: Easy
Ingredients:

- 1 grapefruit (pink)
- 2 oranges
- Salt & peppers
- 1 red onion
- 1 oz. of pistachio
- 1 fennel bulb, small (about 5 ounces)
- ½ lemon
- 6 fillets of veal (2 ounces each)
- 4 tbsp. of olive oil
- 2 sprigs of rosemary

Directions:

- Peel the grapefruit and oranges by going with the fruit's natural curve and removing the white, bitter pith.
- Slice the oranges and grapefruit thinly, arrange on a platter, and sprinkle with salt and pepper.
- Cut the red onion into thin rings after peeling.
- Cut the fennel bulb into extremely tiny cubes or strips after trimming, rinsing, and drying. Fennel fronds should be rinsed, shaken dry, and coarsely chopped.
- Pistachios should be finely chopped and gently toasted in a skillet over medium heat, regularly shaking the pan.
- On a dish, arrange the orange grapefruit slices together with the onion, fennel, and pistachios. Juice a lemon.
- 2 teaspoons of lemon juice, 3 tablespoons of oil, and salt & pepper to taste should all be whisked together. Add to the slices of orange and grapefruit, and then wait 10 to 20 minutes.
- Dry the veal by patting it, then arrange it between the layers of plastic wrap. Making use of a meat mallet, pound to an equal thickness.
- Shake the rosemary dry after rinsing it. In a nonstick pan, heat the remaining oil. For approximately a minute total, add the veal, rosemary, and heat until the meat is well-browned on both sides. Serve the salad with a dash of salt and pepper.

Nutritional Values per serving:

Total calories: 585kcal, **Fat:** 29g, **Carbohydrates:** 27 g, **Protein:** 48g, **Fiber:** 20g, **Sodium:** 1ooomg, **Potassium:** 1,268 mg

50. Pepper Veggie Steak

Prep Time: 20mins.
Cook Time: 30 mins.
Total Time: 50mins.
Serves: 4
Difficulty: Easy
Ingredients:

- 4 tbsp. of olive oil
- 4 steak (180g or 6 ounces)
- Sea salt & peppers
- 200g of oyster mushrooms
- 6 Hungarian (green, red, and yellow) wax peppers

Directions:

- The oven should be preheated to 100°C (about 200°F).
- Steaks should be rinsed, dried off, then seared on each side in 2 teaspoons of heated oil. Place on a baking pan after seasoning with salt and pepper. Depending on how well-done you want your steak, cook it in a preheated oven for 20 to 25 minutes. Cooking involves one rotation.
- Peppers should be rinsed, trimmed, and cut in rings for the veggies. Cut the oyster mushrooms into strips after rinsing. Mushrooms should be prepared for 1-2 minutes in the leftover oil. Add the peppers and cook the mixture for two to three minutes. Distribute on plates after seasoning with salt and pepper. Serve with steaks on top.

Nutritional Values per serving:

Total calories: 160.5kcal, **Fat:** 8g, Carbohydrates: 19.7g, **Protein:** 7.7g, **Fiber:** 5.6g, **Sodium:** 527.1mg, **Potassium:** 686.9mg

Chapter 5: Pegan Diet - Snacks

1. Pancetta and Peas

Prep time: 10 mins.
Cook time: 10 mins.
Total time: 20 mins.
Serves: 4
Difficulty: easy
Ingredients:

- 2 ounces of pancetta, chopped
- 2 tbsp. of olive oil
- 3 tbsp. of chopped onion
- ¼ cup of dry white wine
- 1 pound of frozen peas, thawed
- salt & black pepper (ground), to taste
- 1 ½ tbsp. of fresh thyme leaves, chopped

Directions:

- The pancetta and onion should be cooked and stirred in the heated oil for approximately 5 minutes or until the pancetta are transparent. Bring to a boil the pancetta mixture after adding the peas, thyme, white wine, salt, and pepper.
- Reduce heat, cover, and simmer for 3 to 5 minutes, or until peas are cooked, and liquid has somewhat decreased.

Nutritional values per serving:
Total Calories: 189kcal, **Fats:** 9.1g, **Carbohydrates:** 17g, **Protein:** 7.7g, **Fiber:** 5g, **Sodium:** 232.2mg, **Potassium:** 222.1mg

2. Stuffed Pico de Gallo Avocado

Prep time: 15 mins.
Cook time: 0 mins.
Total time: 15 mins.
Serves: 6
Difficulty: easy
Ingredients:

- 3 tbsp. of diced onions
- 2 Roma tomatoes
- 2 tbsp. of cilantro minced
- 1 tbsp. of lime juice
- 1 tbsp. of minced jalapeno, optional
- 3 avocados
- 1/2 tsp. of salt

Directions:

- Dice onion and tomato. Drain juice from the tomatoes (optional). Jalapeno and cilantro are minced.
- Combine chopped tomatoes, diced onions, cilantro, and jalapenos in a bowl. Salt and lime juice should be added together.
- Remove the avocado seeds after cutting them in half. Make an oval hole (where seeds are) bigger by using a spoon to carefully enlarge the hole (wider, not deeper).
- Put pico de gallo into the avocados.
- Serve this as a side dish or snack with your preferred main entrée! Enjoy!

Nutritional values per serving:
Total Calories: 168kcal, **Fats:** 15g, **Carbohydrates:** 10g, **Protein:** 2g, **Fiber:** 7g, **Sodium:** 202mg, **Potassium:** 554mg

3. Roasted Garlic Balsamic Brussels Sprouts & Bacon

Prep time: 5 mins.
Cook time: 30 mins.
Total time: 35 mins.
Serves: 5
Difficulty: easy
Ingredients:

- 4-6 slices of bacon, nitrate free & sugar-free
- 1 lb. of halved Brussels sprouts (or quartered for bigger ones)
- Salt & pepper
- 2 tbsp. of balsamic vinegar
- 4 cloves of garlic, minced

Directions:

- Set your oven's temperature to 425. On a big baking sheet, spread the Brussels sprouts in one single layer. Sprinkle chopped bacon liberally over the Brussels sprouts.
- Bake for 15 minutes in a preheated oven, mix, then restore to a single layer and roast for an additional 5 to 10 minutes, or until the bacon is crisp. Sprinkle the garlic on top after drizzling the vinegar all over.
- Roast for a further 5-7 minutes, or until golden and crispy.

Nutritional values per serving:

Total Calories: 82kcal, **Fats:** 6g, **Carbohydrates:** 2g, **Protein:** 2g, **Fiber:** 1g, **Sodium:** 118mg, **Potassium:** 51mg

4. Roasted Broccolini

Prep time: 5 mins.
Cook time: 15 mins.
Total time: 20 mins.
Serves: 4
Difficulty: easy
Ingredients:

- 2 tbsp. of olive oil
- 2 bunches of broccolini, washed
- 2 tsp. of garlic chopped
- salt & black pepper, to taste
- ½ lemon

Directions:

- Set the oven to 425°.
- Broccoli should be spread out on a sheet pan covered with parchment paper.
- Sprinkle with olive oil, then massage with your hands after adding the garlic, salt, and pepper. Make careful to season and oil each piece of broccolini.
- Roast for 12 to 15 minutes, checking at least once.
- Serve right away with some freshly squeezed lemon juice.

Nutritional values per serving:
Total Calories: 102kcal, **Fats:** 7g, **Carbohydrates:** 7g, **Protein:** 3g, **Fiber:** 1g, **Sodium:** 25mg, **Potassium:** 18mg

5. Pizza Dough Bites

Prep time: 5 mins.
Cook time: 15 mins.
Total time: 20 mins.
Serves: 5
Difficulty: easy
Ingredients:

- 1/4 cup of coconut flour
- 1/4 cup of cassava flour
- 1/4 cup of tapioca starch
- 1 tsp. of onion powder
- 1 tsp. of garlic powder
- 2 tsp. of dried basil
- 1/2 tsp. of dried parsley
- 1 tsp. of dried oregano
- 2 tsp. of nutritional yeast
- 1/2 tsp. of sea salt
- 1/8 tsp. of baking soda
- 2 tbsp. of olive oil

For gelatin egg (substitute 1 regular egg if possible):

- 1 tbsp. of gelatin
- 1/4 cup of water

For serving:

- Marinara sauce, any of choice

Directions:

- Bake at 375 degrees Fahrenheit and cover a baking sheet using parchment paper.
- Sift the flours in a medium dish until well mixed.
- Stir in the nutritional yeast, baking soda, spices, and seasonings after that.
- Add the water into a small saucepan and add the 1 tbsp. Gelatin, stirring constantly, to make the gelatin egg (substitute 1 real egg if acceptable). If necessary, softly combine; avoid clumps. Give the mixture 2-3 minutes to sit and bloom. Set the saucepan on low heat and place it on the stove. Gelatin should be slowly melted (it won't take long) and then removed from heat.
- The gelatin egg should be rapidly whisked until frothy after being taken from the fire. Immediately add gelatin egg into the mixture and stir to incorporate.
- Once the dough is well incorporated, add the olive oil & thoroughly mix.
- Make 4-5 little snack bits out of the dough (more than one batch are shown in the photo). If dough is very dry, add 1 teaspoon extra of olive oil.
- The dough balls should be placed on a baking pan and baked for 12 to 15 minutes.
- After taking the dish out of the oven, let it cool while cooking marinara sauce.
- Enjoy serving with sauce for dipping!

Nutritional values per serving:
Total Calories: 163kcal, **Fats:** 8.6g, **Carbohydrates:** 17.5g, **Protein:** 4.8g, **Fiber:** 5.3g, **Sodium:** 70mg, **Potassium:** 35mg

6. Blueberry Muffins

Prep time: 10 mins.
Cook time: 25 mins.
Total time: 35 mins.
Serves: 12
Difficulty: medium
Ingredients:

- ⅓ cup of sweetener of choice
- 2 ½ cups of almond flour
- 1 tbsp. of baking powder
- ½ tsp. of salt
- ½ tsp. of baking soda
- ½ cup of melted butter cooled
- ⅓ cup of coconut or almond milk
- 3 eggs
- 1 tsp. of vanilla

- ⅓ cup of dried blueberries
- ½ tsp. of almond extract
- ½ cup of fresh blueberries

Directions:

- Turn the oven on to 350 degrees. Apply cooking spray to a muffin pan.
- Almond flour, baking powder, sweetener, baking soda, and salt are all combined in a bowl.
- Add milk, eggs, melted butter, and extracts. Stir well.
- Add both fresh and dried blueberries. Stir well.
- In order to fill the muffin cups 3/4 full, use the ice cream scoop.
- Cook thoroughly for 20 to 25 minutes in the oven. For a delicious treat, add some peanut butter or almond on top!

Nutritional values per serving:
Total Calories: 237kcal, **Fats:** 20g, **Carbohydrates:** 10g, **Protein:** 6g, **Fiber:** 3g, **Sodium:** 243mg, **Potassium:** 154mg

7. Cinnamon Apple Granola Bars

Prep time: 20 mins.
Cook time: 0 mins.
Total time: 50 mins. (30 mins. to chill)
Serves: 20
Difficulty: medium
Ingredients:

- 1 cup of raw almonds
- 1 cup of walnuts halves or pecan (raw)
- 1 cup of raw cashews
- 1 tbsp. of cinnamon
- 1 cup of unsweetened coconut flakes
- 1/4 tsp. of nutmeg
- 1/2 tsp. of fine grain sea salt (or 1/4 tsp. for less salty)
- 1/8 tsp. of allspice optional
- 1 cup of apples (dried), chopped
- 1/4 cup of nut butter almond or cashew (smooth)
- 1/4 cup of organic coconut oil, melted
- 1 tsp. of pure vanilla extract
- 1/4 cup of raw honey or pure maple syrup (+ 2 tbsp.)

Directions:

- Don't over-mix; just pulse the nuts into a food processor a few times until they resemble crumbles. A few bigger bits are okay.
- Add the nuts into a large mixing bowl, then evenly whisk in the coconut flakes, salt, cinnamon, and dried apples.
- Melt the coconut oil, then add the almond butter, maple syrup, honey, and vanilla to a different mixing dish.
- Use a silicone spatula to properly incorporate the ingredients after adding the wet mixture to the big dish of dry ingredients. Make sure the dry ingredients are completely covered by mixing well.
- With additional parchment paper extending up the edges for easy removal, line the bottom & sides of an 8 x 8" or 9 x 9" square pan. Transfer the mixture to the pan and compact it there with your hands or a different piece of parchment paper.
- If you have time, place the top into the freezer for 30 minutes at least to firm up before covering it with parchment paper or plastic wrap.
- Cut the dish into 20 bars with a long, razor-sharp knife. They may be frozen for a longer period of time or individually wrapped in parchment and stored in the refrigerator for up to 2 weeks.
- Because of the coconut oil in the bars, they must be kept cold to prevent melting at room temperature. Enjoy!

Nutritional values per serving:
Total Calories: 203kcal, **Fats:** 16g, **Carbohydrates:** 12g, **Protein:** 4g, **Fiber:** 3g, **Sodium:** 82mg, **Potassium:** 187mg

8. Oatmeal Bars

Prep time: 10 mins.
Cook time: 0 mins.
Total time: 1 hr. 10 mins. (1 hr. to chill)
Serves: 8
Difficulty: easy
Ingredients:

- 1/2 cup of almonds (75 g)
- 1 cup of pitted, packed soft dates (225 g)
- 3/4 cup of oats (75 g)
- 1/4 cup of natural peanut butter (70 g), or any other seed or nut butter)
- 1/4 cup of hemp seeds (40 g)
- Some salt, optional
- 1 tbsp. of maple syrup (15 mL)

Directions:

- The almonds & dates should be combined in a powerful blender or food processor to create a crumbly mixture.
- Oats, peanut butter, hemp seeds, and maple syrup should all be added at this point. Process until a thick dough forms that you can compress into a tiny ball.
- After using parchment paper to line a loaf pan of standard size, firmly push the dough in the

pan. Spend some time smoothing the top and squeezing it into the corners.

- To solidify, place it in the freezer for approximately an hour.
- After removing the bars from the pan with the help of the parchment paper, cut them into 6 bars or 8 squares, and store them in an airtight container in the refrigerator.

Nutritional values per serving:
Total Calories: 259kcal, **Fats:** 12g, **Carbohydrates:** 32g, **Protein:** 8g, **Fiber:** 5g, **Sodium:** 110mg, **Potassium:** 150mg

9. Chocolate Truffles

Prep time: 15 mins.
Cook time: 0 mins.
Total time: 15 mins.
Serves: 16
Difficulty: easy
Ingredients:

- 20 g of cacao butter (0.7 oz.)
- 120 g of cashew nuts, raw (1 cup), soaked overnight in cold water or put in boiling water for 10-15 minutes
- 2 heaped tsp. of cocoa powder
- 1 tsp. of vanilla extract
- 3 tbsp. of maple syrup, to taste (or substitute any other sweetener)
- 2 tsp. of cocoa powder to dust
- Salt to taste

Directions:

- Drain the soaked cashews, then combine them with the other ingredients in a food processor.
- Blend until absolutely smooth.
- Taste, then adjust flavor as necessary.
- Place the mixture in the refrigerator for two hours to solidify. It should be firm enough to form into balls easily. If you'd like, you may move the dough to a bowl.
- On a plate, sift the cocoa powder.
- Make tsp.-sized balls of a mixture using two teaspoons, and then roll the balls into the cocoa powder using your hands.
- Repeat with the remaining mixture.
- For up to five days, store truffles in the refrigerator in an airtight container.

Nutritional values per serving:
Total Calories: 63kcal, **Fats:** 4g, **Carbohydrates:** 4g, **Protein:** 1g, **Fiber:** 2g, **Sodium:** 1mg, **Potassium:** 57mg

10. Sweet Potato Brownies

Prep time: 15 mins.
Cook time: 40 mins.
Total time: 55 mins.
Serves: 16
Difficulty: easy
Ingredients:

- 200 g of pitted dates (1 ⅛ cup), soaked in cold water overnight or put in boiling water for 10 minutes
- 500 g of sweet potatoes (17.5 oz.), peeled & diced
- 50 g of cocoa powder (½ cup)
- 180 ml of almond milk, unsweetened (¾ cup) (or substitute any other milk, plant-based)
- 2 tbsp. of almond butter, smooth (or substitute peanut butter)
- Some salt, to taste
- 2 tsp. of baking powder (gluten-free)
- 200 g of ground almonds (1 ⅔ cup)

Directions:

- Set the oven up to 180 degrees Fahrenheit (350 degrees Fahrenheit).
- Put sweet potatoes into a pot and add water to cover them.
- When the mixture is soft enough to be lightly pierced with a fork, bring to a boil and simmer for 15 minutes over low heat.
- Drain the dates that have been soaked in water as well as the sweet potatoes.
- In a blender or food processor, combine drained dates, the cooked sweet potatoes, chocolate powder, almond milk, almond butter, and salt.
- Blend well, scraping down the sides a number of times if required.
- Additionally, put the baking powder and powdered almonds in a quick blender.
- Pour the mixture onto a square or rectangle baking pan coated with oiled baking paper.
- Bake for 25 minutes in the oven. Be cautious not to overcook them; they should have a little top crack and be somewhat hard within but still rather mushy.
- Before cutting into squares, let it cool.
- Keeps for a few days when covered in the refrigerator.

Nutritional values per serving:
Total Calories: 154kcal, **Fats:** 7g, **Carbohydrates:** 20g, **Protein:** 4g, **Fiber:** 4g, **Sodium:** 33mg, **Potassium:** 300mg

11. Orange Spice Cheesecake

Prep time: 15 mins.
Cook time: 0 mins.
Total time: 2 hr. 15 mins. (2 hr. to chill)
Serves: 10
Difficulty: easy
Ingredients:
Crust:

- 1/2 cup of pepitas (roasted) or any other nut/seed
- 1 cup of roasted almonds
- 2 Tbsp. of coconut oil
- Some pink salt
- 1 Tbsp. of monk fruit granules
- 1-2 Tbsp. of water

Cheesecake:

- 1 cup of cashews (raw), soaked
- 1 cup of skinless, blanched almonds, soaked
- 1/2 cup of pure maple syrup or Lakanto maple syrup
- Zest juice of one orange (large), 1/4 cup of juice plus 1 Tbsp. of zest
- 1/2 cup of melted coconut oil
- 1/4 cup of coconut cream
- dash of ginger, nutmeg, or cloves - optional
- 3/4 tsp. of cinnamon - to taste
- Some pink salt

Garnish:

- Coconut whipped cream, orange zest, orange slices, orange slices, and cinnamon

Directions:

Making the crust:

- Almonds and pepitas should be processed in the food processor a few times to break them down. Salt, monk fruit, coconut oil, and other blending ingredients are added till a sticky dough is formed. Water is then added to help the dough come together.
- Press into a parchment-lined 7" springform pan. In contrast, you make the filling, freeze.

Creating the filling:

- (Use nuts that you have soaked for at least two hours in hot water.) Almonds and cashews should be drained, rinsed, and shaken dry before being processed in the food processor for five minutes at least to create a thick paste.
- Blend well while adding the other ingredients.
- Taste and make taste adjustments (more zest, sweetener, spice) over the crust.
- Frozen for approximately two hours or until stiff, wrap in foil. When ready to serve, remove from the springform and place in the refrigerator.
- Add whipped coconut cream, an orange slice, and a sprinkle of cinnamon for decoration.

Nutritional values per serving:

Total Calories: 411kcal, **Fats:** 37g, **Carbohydrates:** 15g, **Protein:** 10g, **Fiber:** 7g, **Sodium:** 30mg, **Potassium:** 150mg

12. Roasted Soy-Lime Tofu

Prep time: 1 hr.
Cook time: 20 mins. (Roasting)
Total time: 1 hr. 20 mins.
Serves: 4
Difficulty: easy
Ingredients:

- ⅔ cup of soy sauce (reduced-sodium)
- 2 packages of water-packed, extra-firm tofu (14 ounces), drained
- 6 tbsp. of toasted sesame oil
- ⅔ cup of lime juice

Directions:

- Cut tofu into half to 3/4-inch cubes after patting it dry. In a big sealable plastic bag or medium bowl, combine lime juice, soy sauce, and oil. Toss the tofu in after adding it lightly. Marinate for up to 4 hours in the refrigerator while giving it a little toss every so often.
- Set oven up to 450 degrees Fahrenheit.
- With the use of a slotted spoon, take the tofu out of the marinade (discard marinade). Make sure the pieces aren't touching when you spread them out on 2 big baking sheets. Roast for approximately 20 minutes, carefully turning once halfway through, till golden brown.

Nutritional values per serving:

Total Calories: 163kcal, **Fats:** 2g, **Carbohydrates:** 2.2g, **Protein:** 19g, **Fiber:** 1.9g, **Sodium:** 110.9mg, **Potassium:** 2.8mg

13. Roasted Mexican Cauliflower

Prep time: 10
Cook time: 30 mins.
Total time: 40 mins.
Serves: 4
Difficulty: easy
Ingredients:

- 2 tbsp. of avocado oil
- 1 head of cauliflower (large), cut into florets
- 1 tsp. of chili powder
- 1/2 tsp. of onion powder
- 1/2 tsp. of garlic powder
- 1/4 tsp. of cumin
- 1/4 tsp. of black pepper
- 3/4 tsp. of salt
- 1/4 cup of cilantro
- 3 lime wedges (fresh)
- 1/4 cup of red or green onion diced
- 1/2 sliced avocado

Directions:

- Set oven up to 425 degrees Fahrenheit.
- Sprinkle salt, pepper, cumin, garlic powder, chili powder, onion powder, and avocado oil over the cauliflower florets. Assure even distribution of the spices.

- Spread evenly and roast for approximately 20 minutes on a baking sheet coated with parchment paper.
- To ensure equal cooking, take the cauliflower out of the oven and turn it. 10 to 12 minutes of further roasting is required to achieve tenderness and crispy edges.
- Remove from the oven, then top with avocado, lime wedges, fresh cilantro, and onions.

Nutritional values per serving:
Total Calories: 167kcal, **Fats:** 11g, **Carbohydrates:** 16g, **Protein:** 5g, **Fiber:** 7g, **Sodium:** 511mg, **Potassium:** 804mg

14. Cranberry Bliss Bars

Prep Time: 30mins.
Cook Time: 30 mins.
Total Time: 7 hrs. (6hrs. Additional)
Serves: 16
Difficulty: Medium
Ingredients:

- ½ package of cream cheese (8 ounces), softened
- 3 cups of confectioners' sugar
- 1 tsp. of vanilla extract
- 1 tbsp. of lemon juice

Cake:

- ¾ cup of butter softened
- 1 cup of dark brown sugar (packed)
- 3 eggs
- 1 tsp. of vanilla extract
- 2 tbsp. of minced candied ginger
- ½ tsp. of salt
- ½ tsp. of baking powder
- 1 ½ cups of all-purpose flour
- 1 cup of white chocolate chips
- ¾ cup of chopped dried cranberries, sweetened

Topping:

- 2 tbsp. of minced candied ginger
- ¼ cup of chopped dried cranberries, sweetened
- 1 tbsp. of heavy whipping cream
- ½ cup of confectioners' sugar

Directions:

- Using an electric mixer, combine 1 teaspoon vanilla extract, 3 cups of confectioners' sugar, lemon juice, cream cheese, and in a large bowl. In contrast, making the cake, cover dish with plastic wrap & chill.
- Set oven up to 350 degrees Fahrenheit (175 degrees C). Grease a 9x13-inch baking dish with butter.
- In a large bowl, combine the brown sugar, butter, and eggs. Using an electric mixer, whip the ingredients until smooth. Add the eggs one at a time. Salt, 1 tsp. extract, 2 tablespoons ginger, and the brown sugar-butter combination should all be well combined.
- Brown sugar and butter mixture should be smooth after adding flour and baking powder; add 3/4 cup of dried cranberries & white chocolate chips after that. Spread the batter evenly after pouring it into the prepped baking pan.
- For approximately 30 minutes, or until a toothpick placed in the middle of the cake comes out clean, bake into the preheated oven. In between four and eight hours, totally cool the cake. One hour before icing the cake, remove the frosting from the refrigerator.
- Spread icing evenly over the cake and top with 2 tablespoons ginger and 1/4 cup dried cranberries.
- Pour cream and 1/2 cup of confectioners' sugar into a bowl and whisk until smooth. Drizzle over a cake that has been decorated. Wrap the cake in plastic wrap and chill for approximately two hours.
- Cake should be divided into equal 8 rectangles after being cut in half lengthwise. 16 triangle-shaped bars are produced by cutting each rectangle in 1/2 diagonally.

Nutritional Values per serving:
Total calories: 414 kcal, **Fat:** 16 g, **Carbohydrates:** 64 g, **Protein:** 3g, **Fiber:** 1g, **Sodium:** 200mg, **Potassium:** 97 mg

15. Chinese Stir-Fry Broccoli with Garlic Sauce

Prep Time: 10 mins.
Cook Time: 10 mins.
Total Time: 20 mins.
Serves: 6
Difficulty: Easy
Ingredients:

- 2 tbsp. of avocado oil
- 3 to 4 lbs. of Chinese broccoli (6 8 cups, tightly packed)
- 2 tsp. of grated garlic cloves
- 1-2 tsp. of sesame oil, toasted (garnish)
- 1/2 tsp. of coarse sea salt (divided)
- 1 tbsp. of coconut aminos (garnish)

Directions:

- Cut off the base of Chinese broccoli stems (1-inch) & discard. To remove their stems from the leafy portions, make another incision. Cut the stems at a diagonal angle to a length of about 2 to 2-12 inches. Divide the leafy sections in half.

Stems and leafy portions should be washed and rinsed separately. Put them aside in separate bowls to drain.

- Add 2 tbsp. Frying oil to a big skillet (or wok) that has been preheated. Place the stems in a pot and cook them over medium-high until they become brilliant green (about 2 minutes). Sprinkle on 1/4 teaspoon of coarse salt. With a wooden spoon, smash and distribute the grated garlic over the veggies after adding it.
- Add leafy parts. The stems & garlic should be tossed and scooped over the leaves quickly. Place a lid on top. Heat is reduced to medium. The leaves should be cooked for 3 minutes or until they are a dark green color. Sprinkle on 1/4 teaspoon of coarse salt. Toss the ball quickly. Dispose of heat and transfer to a big platter.
- Add coconut aminos and toasted sesame oil for seasoning. Serve warm or cold.

Nutritional Values per serving:
Total calories; 86 kcal, **Fat:** 7 g, **Carbohydrates:** 4 g, **Protein:** 1g, **Fiber:** 2g, **Sodium:** 148mg, **Potassium:** 236 mg

16. Avocado Baked Fries

Prep Time: 10 mins.
Cook Time: 15 mins.
Total Time: 25 mins. (Baked)
Serves: 4
Difficulty: Easy
Ingredients:

- 1/2 cup of almond meal
- 1 avocado (large), not too ripe
- 1/4 cup of almond milk
- 1 tsp. of Cajun seasoning

Directions:

- Set oven temperature to 450 degrees Fahrenheit.
- Twist the avocado's halves apart after cutting them lengthwise. Peel skin off after removing the pit. Wedges should be cut.
- Fill a small bowl with almond milk. Combine almond meal & Cajun spice in a separate bowl.
- Slices of avocado are coated on both sides after being dipped in almond milk and then pressed into an almond meal. This process is simpler and less messy if the almond meal is applied to the avocado using a spoon.
- Fries made from avocado should be baked for 15 to 18 minutes, or until they are just beginning to become brown.
- Remove from the oven, then let it cool for a few seconds. Eat right away.

Nutritional Values per serving:
Total calories: 206 kcal, **Fat:** 19 g, **Carbohydrates:** 7 g, **Protein:** 3g, **Fiber:** 5g, **Sodium:** 18mg, **Potassium:** 370 mg

17. Sweet Potato Fries

Prep Time: 5 mins.
Cook Time: 25 mins.
Total Time: 30 mins. (Baked)
Serves: 4
Difficulty: Easy
Ingredients:

- 1 1/2 tbsp. of olive oil
- 1 lb. of sweet potatoes (washed & cut in 1/4-inch matchsticks)
- 2 tsp. of Cornstarch
- 1/2 tsp. of smoked paprika
- 1/2 tsp. of garlic powder
- 1/4 tsp. of sea salt (or some more to taste)
- 1/2 tsp. of freshly cracked black pepper

Directions:

- Set the oven up to 425 °F. Use a silicone mat or parchment paper to line a sheet tray.
- Sweet potatoes should be thoroughly rinsed in the cold, running water till the water is clear. Dry off by evaporating on paper towels. Try your best to completely dry each sweet potato before placing it in a large mixing dish.
- Combine the garlic powder, cornstarch, black pepper, smoked paprika, & salt into a separate small bowl. Olive oil should be drizzled over potatoes & combined by tossing. Potatoes should be equally covered after being sprinkled with the cornstarch mixture and tossed. Transfer the potatoes to the sheet tray, placing them as evenly apart as you can in a single layer. Use a second tray if necessary (this would give you crispier fries).
- For 12 minutes, bake. Flip the potatoes with a spatula.
- If necessary, taste and adjust the seasoning. Serve warm.

Nutritional Values per serving:
Total calories: 150 kcal, **Fat:** 5 g, **Carbohydrates:** 25 g, **Protein:** 2g, **Fiber:** 4g, **Sodium:** 210mg, **Potassium:** 397 mg

18. Roasted Cabbage Steaks

Prep Time: 5 mins.
Cook Time: 1 hr.
Total Time: 1hr 5 mins.
Serves: 4
Difficulty: Medium
Ingredients:

- 2 tbsp. of olive oil
- 1 tbsp. of salt-free seasoning blend (all-purpose)
- 1/2 tsp. of black pepper

- 1 tbsp. of fresh dill (chopped)
- 1 head of green cabbage

Directions:

- Set the oven to 350° F. cabbage head into six slices, each 1" thick.
- On a baking sheet, arrange the cabbage pieces and sprinkle them with olive oil. Over the cabbage, add a spice mixture and dill weed. Use aluminum foil to protect.
- For 45 minutes, bake. Remove the foil and bake the cabbage steaks for a further 15 minutes to brown.

Nutritional Values per serving:

Total calories: 90 kcal, **Fat:** 5 g, **Carbohydrates:** 9 g, **Protein:** 2g, **Fiber:** 3g, **Sodium:** 25mg, **Potassium:** 265 mg

19. Rigatoni with Pesto, Sun-Dried Tomatoes, and Olives

Prep Time: 15 mins.
Cook Time: 20 mins.
Total Time: 35 mins.
Serves: 6
Difficulty: Easy
Ingredients:

- 1 cooking spray (Olive oil)
- 8 oz. of rigatoni (whole-wheat)
- 1/2 cup of onion (diced)
- 1/2 cup of sun-dried tomatoes, rehydrated (sliced, not soaked in oil)
- 2 cloves of garlic (minced)
- 1/2 cup of dry white wine
- 2 tbsp. of toasted pine nuts
- 4 tbsp. of pesto sauce (bottled)
- 1/4 cup of Kalamata olives (coarsely chopped & pitted)
- black pepper (freshly ground), to taste
- 2 tsp. of fresh lemon zest

Directions:

- Large saucepan of slightly salted water should be brought to a boil. When the rigatoni is al dente, add it and simmer for 8 to 10 minutes.
- Meanwhile, spray frying oil in a big skillet. Over medium heat, sauté the onion & garlic for approximately 6 minutes. Sun-dried tomatoes should be added and sautéed for 2 minutes. Cook after adding the wine until it nearly completely evaporates.
- In order to save roughly 1/3 cup of pasta water, drain the pasta. Separate the pasta. After cooking for one minute, add pasta water into the onion mixture. Pine nuts, olives, lemon zest, and pesto should all be added. Use pepper to season. Toss the rigatoni in after adding it.

Nutritional Values per serving:

Total calories: 245 kcal, **Fat:** 8 g, **Carbohydrates:** 36 g, **Protein:** 7g, **Fiber:** 5g, **Sodium:** 235mg, **Potassium:** 260 mg

20. Onions & Portobello Mushrooms with Balsamic Glaze

Prep Time: 10 mins.
Cook Time: 20 mins.
Total Time: 30 mins.
Serves: 15
Difficulty: Easy
Ingredients:

- 2 cups of onion (thinly sliced)
- 2 tsp. of olive oil
- 2 cloves of garlic (minced)
- Sea salt, to taste
- 6 (1/4-inch thick) Portobello mushrooms (sliced), or any other mushroom)
- Black Pepper, to taste
- 3/4 cup of balsamic vinegar
- red pepper flakes, crushed (optional), to taste

Directions:

- Put some olive oil in a sauté pan that is already hot. Add the mushrooms, onion, and garlic. Cook until onions are transparent and tender. Add red pepper, if preferred, along with salt and pepper, to taste.
- Balsamic vinegar is heated in a small pot, brought to a boil, and then simmered. Cook for 20 minutes or until syrupy or the vinegar barely coats the backside of a spoon. Place aside.
- On grilled bread, spread the mushroom mixture and drizzle with the balsamic vinegar.

Nutritional Values per serving:

Total calories: 30 kcal, **Fat:** 1 g, **Carbohydrates:** 5 g, **Protein:** 1g, **Fiber:** 0g, **Sodium:** 5mg, **Potassium:** 170 mg

21. Poached Pears & Pomegranate Sauce

Prep Time: 10 mins.
Cook Time: 5 mins.
Total Time: 15 mins.
Serves: 2
Difficulty: Easy
Ingredients:

- 2 tsp. of sugar
- 1/3 cup of pomegranate juice (100%)
- 1 peeled pear (cut in half & cored)
- 1 tbsp. of water
- 1/4 tsp. of Cornstarch
- 1/4 tsp. of lemon zest
- 2 tbsp. of almonds, sliced (toasted & crumbled)
- 1/4 tsp. of vanilla extract

Directions:

- Pomegranate juice & sugar should be combined in a small pot. Place the cut-side-down pear halves into the bowl. Using high heat, bring to a boil. Reduce the heat, cover the pan, and simmer for five minutes, or until the meat is cooked, stirring periodically. Get rid of the heat. Transfer the halves of pear to dessert plates with the sliced side facing up, leaving the juice in the pan.
- In a small bowl, place the cornstarch. While stirring to help the cornstarch dissolve, add the water. Add liquid to the pot. Over medium-high heat, bring to a boil while whisking continuously. For one minute, boil. Get rid of the heat. Add the vanilla and lemon zest after that. Toss the pears on top. Sprinkle almonds on top.

Nutritional Values per serving:
Total calories: 120 kcal, **Fat:** 3 g, **Carbohydrates:** 22 g, **Protein:** 2g, **Fiber:** 3g, **Sodium:** 0mg, **Potassium:** 210 mg

22. Cranberry, Peanut Butter & Walnut Apple Slices

Prep Time: 10 mins.
Cook Time: 0mins.
Total Time: 10 mins.
Serves: 6
Difficulty: Easy
Ingredients:

- 4 tbsp. of creamy peanut butter
- 2 medium apples (cored & cut in six slices each)
- 3 tbsp. of dried cranberries
- 2 tbsp. of coconut flakes, unsweetened
- 3 tbsp. of chopped walnuts

Directions:

- On a level surface, arrange the 12 apple slices. One spoonful of peanut butter should be spread on each piece.
- Combine the walnuts, cranberries, and coconut flakes in a small bowl.
- Sprinkle roughly 1 spoonful of the mixture of cranberry evenly over each apple.

Nutritional Values per serving:
Total calories: 140 kcal, **Fat:** 9 g, **Carbohydrates:** 13 g, **Protein:** 3g, **Fiber:** 3g, **Sodium:** 50mg, **Potassium:** 150 mg

23. Red Pepper & Hummus Celery Logs

Prep Time: 10 mins.
Cook Time: 0mins.
Total Time: 10 mins.
Serves: 4
Difficulty: Easy
Ingredients:

- 4 tbsp. of hummus
- 4 ribs of celery
- 1/2 red bell pepper (1/4-inch pieces, square)

Directions:

- Cut each celery rib into three equal pieces after filling with 1 tbsp. of hummus. Each celery piece should have 2 red bell peppers on it.

Nutritional Values per serving:
Total calories: 40 kcal, **Fat:** 2 g, **Carbohydrates:** 4 g, **Protein:** 2g, **Fiber:** 1g, **Sodium:** 90mg, **Potassium:** 145 mg

24. Roasted Red Bell Pepper & Eggplant Relish

Prep Time: 10 mins.
Cook Time: 30mins.
Total Time: 40 mins. (Baked)
Serves: 6
Difficulty: easy
Ingredients:

- 1 tbsp. of olive oil (divided use)
- 1 unpeeled eggplant (cut in 12 slices, 1/2 inch each)
- 1/8 tsp. of salt
- 1 tbsp. of chopped parsley (fresh) or 1/4 tsp. of oregano (dried), basil, or thyme (crumbled)
- 1/2 cup of red peppers, roasted (drained & chopped)
- 1 clove of garlic, small (minced)
- 1/2 tsp. of red wine vinegar
- 1 Pinch of black pepper

Directions:

- Set the oven up to 425 °F. Spray cooking spray in a big baking dish sparingly.
- Apply two tablespoons of oil sparingly to each side of the eggplant pieces. On top of the slices, season with salt. Place in a baking dish in a single layer.
- Roast the eggplant for 18 to 20 mins, or till the bottom is just starting to brown. Flip over. Cook for 8 mins, or till the bottom is browned. Place the eggplant on serving dishes.
- In the meanwhile, combine the other ingredients, including the last 1 teaspoon of oil, in a small dish. Spoon it over the eggplant.

Nutritional Values per serving:
Total calories: 50 kcal, **Fat:** 3 g, **Carbohydrates:** 7 g, **Protein:** 1g, **Fiber:** 3g, **Sodium:** 200mg, **Potassium:** 280 mg

25. Roasted Corn on the Cob

Prep Time: 30 mins.
Cook Time: 5mins.
Total Time: 35 mins.
Serves: 10
Difficulty: Easy
Ingredients:

- 1 tsp. of cayenne pepper
- 5 ears of corn (7¾ to 9-inch-long), large (husks on)
- 1/4 tsp. of cumin (ground)
- 3 limes, fresh (halved)
- 1/2 tsp. of sea salt

Directions:

- For 30 minutes, soak corn (husks on) in a big bowl or saucepan of water.
- Take off the corn's husks and silk. (Alternatively, you could roast the corn while the husks are still on and take them off afterward. This enables the corn to cook without charring and instead caramelize.)
- Cook corn on the grill or over a medium to high gas flame (gas burner). To ensure that the corn is evenly roasted, rotate each ear about every 30 seconds. (While cooking, some kernels may pop.) Roasted ears should be taken from the heat or grill and put aside.
- Salt, cumin, and cayenne are combined in a bowl.
- If you haven't previously, carefully remove husks & silk from the corn. Squeeze the lime juice while rubbing the spices into the corn after dipping halves of lime into the spice mixture to pick up the flavours. Serve.

Nutritional Values per serving:
Total calories: 60 kcal, **Fat:** 1 g, **Carbohydrates:** 13g, **Protein:** 2g, **Fiber:** 2g, **Sodium:** 110mg, **Potassium:** 140 mg

26. Bbq Popcorn

Prep Time: 5 mins.
Cook Time: 10mins.
Total Time: 15 mins.
Serves: 2
Difficulty: Easy
Ingredients:

- 1/2 tsp. of smoked paprika
- 1 tbsp. of barbecue sauce (no-sugar-added), or Sweetened Bbq Sauce (Fruit)
- 1/8 tsp. of salt
- 1/4 cup of popcorn kernels
- 2 tsp. of avocado or sunflower oil

Directions:

- Combine the salt, smoked paprika, and barbecue sauce in a small bowl; reserve.
- Heat the oil completely in a big saucepan over medium heat. When you observe the popping start, add the kernels of popcorn, cover using a lid, & shake the pan occasionally. Uninterrupted popping should continue for roughly 3 minutes. Remove the cover with caution.
- Over medium heat, immediately ladle the mixture of barbecue sauce mixture over the popcorn. After about 2 minutes of vigorous stirring later, the popcorn should be lightly coated and crisp again. Serve.

Nutritional Values per serving:
Total calories: 130 kcal, **Fat:** 6 g, **Carbohydrates:** 18g, **Protein:** 3g, **Fiber:** 3g, **Sodium:** 200mg, **Potassium:** 100 mg

27. Artichokes with Garlic Oil

Prep Time: 15 mins
Cook Time: 35mins.
Total Time: 50 mins.
Serves: 4
Difficulty: Medium
Ingredients:

- Juice of 2 lemons, divided
- 12 baby artichokes, fresh
- 3 tbsp. of Olive Oil
- 1/4 tsp. of unrefined sea salt
- 4 cloves of garlic, minced
- 1/8 tsp. of black pepper, freshly ground
- 1 tsp. of flat-leaf parsley (fresh), finely chopped
- 1 pinch of red chile flakes, crushed

Directions:

- Artichokes should be cleaned by soaking in water; drain, then repeat until the water is clear. Remove the bottom 1/2 of the artichokes' outer leaves by peeling them off. Remove the artichoke's top quarter. Peel any remaining stiff, dark green leaves as well. Clean artichokes should be placed in a bowl with 1 lemon juice added to them to prevent discoloration.
- Add cleaned artichokes to a big saucepan of boiling water. High heat, bring it back to a boil. Artichokes should be simmered for 25–30 mins, or unless they are soft, over medium-low heat. Artichokes should be thoroughly drained, dried using paper towels, and placed aside.
- Olive oil should be heated in a big pan over medium heat. Add the garlic and cook for about a minute or until the garlic starts to release its scent. When the artichokes are

added, flip them over to coat them in oil and season with pepper, salt, and red chili flakes. Serve heated and top with parsley.

Nutritional Values per serving:

Total calories: 150 kcal, **Fat:** 10 g, **Carbohydrates:** 14g, **Protein:** 4g, **Fiber:** 6g, **Sodium:** 210mg, **Potassium:** 420 mg

28. Spicy Air Fried Green Beans

Prep Time: 10 mins
Cook Time: 10 mins.
Total Time: 20 mins.
Serves: 4
Difficulty: Easy
Ingredients:

- 1 tbsp. of olive oil
- 12 oz. of green beans, fresh (trimmed)
- 1 tsp. of chili garlic paste, Thai-style
- 1/4 tsp. of salt
- 1 tbsp. of panko bread crumbs, whole-wheat

Directions:

- Toss the green beans into a medium bowl with the panko bread crumbs, salt, chile garlic paste, and olive oil.
- Put the green beans into the basket of the air fryer. Heat the oven to 400 degrees Fahrenheit and air fried it for 4 minutes. Shake the basket of the air fryer. Add another 5 to 7 mins to the air fryer. Serve hot.

Nutritional Values per serving:

Total calories: 60 kcal, **Fat:** 3 g, **Carbohydrates:** 7g, **Protein:** 2g, **Fiber:** 2g, **Sodium:** 160mg, **Potassium:** 115 mg

29. Dried Apple Delicious Rings

Prep Time: 30 mins
Cook Time: 5 hr.
Total Time: 5 hr. 30mins. (Baked)
Serves: 2
Difficulty: Easy
Ingredients:

- 50 ml lemon juice
- 1 tsp. of salt
- 1 ½ kg apple

Directions:

- 750 ml (or around 3 cups) of water, salt, and lemon juice should all be combined. Wash each apple separately. Dry the peel before removing the core and chopping it into 5 mm-thick rings. Put the rings right away in the lemon juice mixture (so they don't discolor). Ten minutes of soaking the apples in the mixture.
- Remove the rings from solution, then pat them dry using paper towels. Clean off.
- Place the rings side by side on a double sheet of cheesecloth. Between the cooling rack and a frying grate, sandwich the cheesecloth.
- Place the apple rings on the cooking grate and wire rack in a cool oven. Oven temperature should be set at 50°C (around 125°F). When the temperature is attained, keep the oven door slightly ajar (propped with the wooden spoon). The temperature should be raised to 60 °C, or around 150 °F. Keep the oven door slightly ajar while you let the rings dry for approximately five hours. When the apples dry but still malleable and squishy, remove. Before serving, remove from oven and let cool fully.

Nutritional Values per serving:

Total calories: 2 kcal, **Fat:** 0 g, **Carbohydrates:** 0g, **Protein:** 0g, **Fiber:** 1g, **Sodium:** 2mg, **Potassium:** 4 mg

30. Pumpkin Roasted Wedges with Lentils & Tomatoes

Prep Time: 35 mins
Cook Time: 30
Total Time: 1hr. 5mins.
Serves: 2
Difficulty: Easy
Ingredients:

- 1 clove of garlic
- 2 oz. of green lentil, small
- 2 tomatoes
- ½ pumpkin (21 ounces)
- 2 scallions
- 2 tsp. of pumpkin seed oil
- 4 sprigs of smooth parsley
- Some coarse sea salt
- 1 pc of ginger, fresh (approx. 2 inches)
- Salt & peppers

Directions:

- Drain and rinse lentils in a colander.
- In a saucepan, add lentils, 3/4 cup water, and peeled garlic. Bring it to a boil and then cover

and simmer lentils for approximately 30 minutes, or until they are soft.

- Trim the stems from the tomatoes and rinse them in the meanwhile. Remove the seeds from the tomatoes, then quarter them and slice the meat into thin wedges.
- The scallions should be rinsed, dried off, and sliced into thin rings at an angle.
- Slice the pumpkin in half, then remove the seeds. Peel the pumpkin after cutting the meat into 8 wedges.
- Over medium heat, warm the oil in the large nonstick skillet. Cook the pumpkin for approximately 4 minutes, until just barely browned on both sides. Add the scallions approximately 2 minutes later. Add a little sea salt.
- Parsley should be rinsed & dried.
- The ginger root should be peeled before being pressed into the lentils.
- Lentils and tomatoes should be cooked all the way through. After removing the garlic, add salt and pepper to the lentils. On warmed plates, distribute pumpkin wedges, scallions, and the lentil mixture. Garnish with parsley & serve.

Nutritional Values per serving:
Total calories: 228 kcal, **Fat:** 4 g, **Carbohydrates:** 33g, **Protein:** 12 g, **Fiber:** 5g, **Sodium:** 700mg, **Potassium:** 1364 mg

31. Grape Salad with Dates and Figs

Prep Time: 20 mins
Cook Time: 0 mins.
Total Time: 20mins.
Serves: 2
Difficulty: Easy
Ingredients:

- 2 figs
- 4 oz. of purple grape
- 1 pear
- 2 grapefruit
- 4 dried date
- 1 lime
- 1 large pinch of cinnamon (ground)
- 1 large pinch of cardamom (ground)
- 1 tbsp. of pistachio

Directions:

- Wash and cut the grapes in half. Take the seeds out. The figs' skin should be removed, and the meat should be chopped into small pieces.
- Remove the pear's core, then chop it into pieces after rinsing. Dates with pits should be chopped. Cut the grapefruit in half.
- To a bowl, add the chopped fruit. Lime should be squeezed, its juice mixed with the spices, and then the fruit should be added. Pistachios should be chopped, then sprinkled on top as garnish.

Nutritional Values per serving:
Total calories: 133.7kcal, **Fat:** 6g, **Carbohydrates:** 18g, **Protein:** 2.7g, **Fiber:** 1g, **Sodium:** 52mg, **Potassium:** 186.1 mg

32. Ravioli & Butternut Squash

Prep Time: 30 mins
Cook Time: 1hr. 15 mins.
Total Time: 1hr. 45mins.
Serves: 4
Difficulty: Medium
Ingredients:

- 1/2 tsp. of fine sea salt
- 2 1/2 cups of Gluten-Free Flour (or Gluten-Free all-purpose flour)
- 1/2 tsp. of Psyllium husk powder
- 1/4 cup of water
- 4 eggs
- 1 butternut squash, small (about 2 cups)
- 1/2 cup of nutritional yeast
- 1 cup of spinach
- 1 tsp. of garlic powder
- 1/2 tsp. of thyme
- 1 tsp. of basil
- 1/2 tsp. of sage
- Salt & black pepper to taste
- Pinch of cinnamon (optional)

Directions:

- Set the oven to 400°F. Remove the seeds from the butternut squash after cutting it in half lengthwise. Season with salt & pepper and place into a baking dish flesh side up. For 45 to 50 minutes, bake.
- The flour should be measured up and placed in a food processor. Then pulse in the eggs, Psyllium husk, and salt till a thick dough develops. Add the water to a stream and keep pulsing till the dough forms together. Don't over-blend it since the dough may quickly become tough.
- Transfer this dough to the surface dusted with gluten-free flour. Use your hands to knead the

pasta dough until it is smooth and supple. Allow it to settle for 20 minutes, at least with a plastic wrap cover.

- Scoop the cooked squash in the food processor once it has finished cooking. Process the spices and nutritional yeast after adding them till almost smooth. Add the spinach and pulse. Place aside.
- Your dough should be extremely thin after being rolled out on a level surface with a rolling pin. Lower than 1/8 "If it's feasible, in thickness. Cut your ravioli out from the huge sheet of rolled-out dough using a 2 "knife or a biscuit cutter (circular) (square). Add a 1/2 tsp. of filling to one circle, moisten the sides with your finger, and then cover with one other circle of dough. Pinch the sides together with a fork. Repeat with the rest of the filling and dough.
- Heat up some water in a pot with a little salt. Cook the ravioli for 8 to 9 minutes after carefully adding it to the boiling water (till the dough seems to be cooked enough and they're floating at the top part of your pan). They should be cooked in five or six little batches at one time, each pot.
- To serve, top ravioli with some preferred sauce (pesto, red sauce, or basic dairy-free butter all work well), fresh herbs, and red pepper flakes.

Nutritional Values per serving:
Total calories: 370 kcal, **Fat:** 7g, **Carbohydrates:** 66g, **Protein:** 16 g, **Fiber:** 10g, **Sodium:** 363 mg, **Potassium:** 467mg

33. Chewy Ginger Molasses Healthy Cookies

Prep Time: 5 mins
Cook Time: 10 mins.
Total Time: 15 mins.
Serves: 12
Difficulty: Easy
Ingredients:

- 1/2 cup of almond butter
- 1 flax egg
- 1 tbsp. of flaxseed meal plus 3 tbsp. of water
- 1/3 cup of coconut sugar
- 1 tsp. of Organic Vanilla Extract
- 2 tbsp. of molasses
- 1 tsp. of Organic Ginger
- 1/4 tsp. of sea salt
- 1/4 tsp. of Organic Allspice
- 1/4 tsp. of baking soda
- turbinado sugar (Raw) for sprinkling, (optional)
- 3 tbsp. of coconut flour

Directions:

- Set the oven to 350°F Put parchment paper on a baking sheet and put it aside.
- The flax egg, coconut sugar, almond butter, molasses, and vanilla should all be combined in a mixing dish. Until smooth, beat using an electric mixer.
- When a sticky dough starts to form, add the salt, spices, baking soda, and coconut flour & mix again.
- Place the dough on the baking sheet using a cookie scoop, leaving at least 2" between each cookie. Continue until you have utilised all of the dough.
- Spread sugar over the cookies after gently flattening them with your fingertips. For eleven minutes, bake on the middle rack.
- After taking the cookies out of the oven, let them rest for ten minutes on the baking sheet before moving them to a cooling rack to complete cooling.
- After cooling, have fun!

Nutritional Values per serving:
Total calories: 104 kcal, **Fat:** 6g, **Carbohydrates:** 11g, **Protein:** 3 g, **Fiber:** 3g, **Sodium:** 51 mg, **Potassium:** 102mg

34. Gluten-Free Pizzelles

Prep Time: 10 mins
Cook Time: 10 mins.
Total Time: 20 mins.
Serves: 24
Difficulty: Easy
Ingredients:

- 1/2 cup of quinoa flour
- 1 cup of sorghum flour
- 1/2 cup of tapioca starch
- 3 eggs (large)
- 2 tsp. of baking powder
- 1/2 cup of maple syrup
- 1 tsp. of vanilla extract
- 1/3 cup of coconut oil
- 1/4 tsp. of anise extract
- 1/2 tsp. of almond extract

Directions:

- Spray nonstick cooking spray into a preheated pizzelle cookie iron.
- In a medium mixing bowl, sift the dry ingredients together and reserve.
- In a big mixing bowl, beat the eggs until they are creamy and smooth. Whisk in the oil and seasoning gradually. As you proceed to whisk, slowly drizzle in the syrup until everything is combined.
- As a smooth batter develops, gradually add the dry ingredients.

- Place a spoonful or so of dough on the heated pizzelle iron, cover it, and cook as directed. My cookies took around a minute each. Continue by using the remaining batter.
- On a wire rack, let biscuits cool fully. Maintain in a cool, dry area.

Nutritional Values per serving:

Total calories: 95 kcal, **Fat:** 3g, **Carbohydrates:** 13g, **Protein:** 1 g, **Fiber:** 3g, **Sodium:** 11 mg, **Potassium:** 116mg

35. Corn & Cheese Vegetarian Empanadas

Prep Time: 30 mins
Cook Time: 20 mins.
Total Time: 50 mins.
Serves: 10
Difficulty: Medium

Ingredients:

- almond or Soy milk to brush on the top
- 1 cup of queso fresco, diced or crumbled, small
- 1 cup of white corn
- ¼ cup of diced green onions
- Powdered sugar, to dust on top, optional

Directions:

- Combine the corn, cheese, and green onions in a small bowl.
- Set the up oven to 400° F.
- The discs should be spread out on a work surface that has been gently dusted with flour.
- Fill the dough circle's centre with a heaping spoonful of the filling.
- To make a half moon shape, wet the circle's edges with water & fold in half.
- To seal the edges, use a fork.
- Empanadas should be placed on the baking sheet with approximately 1 1/2 inches between each one.
- To create all 10 empanadas, repeat the process using the leftover empanada dough and filling.
- Empanadas' tops are brushed with vegan milk. Put the crust in the oven and bake for 15 to 20 minutes, or until it puffs up and becomes golden.

Nutritional Values per serving:

Total calories: 140 kcal, **Fat:** 4g, **Carbohydrates:** 23g, **Protein:** 5 g, **Fiber:** 2g, **Sodium:** 341 mg, **Potassium:** 181mg

36. Cauliflower Sticky Sesame Wings

Prep Time: 25 mins
Cook Time: 15 mins.
Total Time: 40 mins.
Serves: 6
Difficulty: Easy

Ingredients:

- 1/2 cup of gluten-free flour (all-purpose)
- 1 head of cauliflower (small)
- 1/2 cup of unsweetened almond milk
- 1/2 tsp. of ground black pepper
- 1/4 tsp. of sea salt
- 1/2 tsp. of garlic powder
- 1 cup of crispy/panko breadcrumbs (gluten-free), seasoned with pepper & salt
- 1/4 tsp. of red pepper flakes (crushed)

Sauce:

- 3 tbsp. of soy sauce (low-sodium), or liquid aminos
- 5 tbsp. of maple syrup
- 1/2 tsp. of sesame seeds
- 1/4 tsp. of ground ginger
- 1/4 tsp. of ground black pepper
- 1 tsp. of cornstarch plus 1 tsp. of water, mixed together separately from other ingredients in a bowl for the cornstarch slurry
- Scallions, chopped & sesame seeds, to garnish
- ¼ cup of water

Directions:

- Oven should be heated to 450°F/230°C. A greased foil or silicone baking sheet should be used to line a baking sheet.
- Cut the leaves off of the cauliflower and discard the stalks before removing the florets with a knife. To make the cauliflower pieces seem like wings cut them into smaller pieces.
- To create the batter, combine the almond milk, gluten-free flour, salt, freshly ground black pepper, & garlic powder in a separate bowl. Feel free to add extra milk to the batter to smooth it out if it is too thick. Breadcrumbs should be placed in a separate bowl. Place it next to the batter dish.
- Use a spatula or spoon to evenly coat the cauliflower into the batter mixture (you may add them all at once). Place them on the baking sheet with adequate room between each wing after transferring them to breadcrumbs (you may do this in 2 or 3 batches). Continue till all the wings have been covered.
- For 22 minutes, bake. Please make sure the oven is hot and fully preheated. The ingredients for the sauce should be combined and baked while you are doing this.
- Take out of the oven. Use a spatula to stir the wings about in the sauce once it has been cooked and cooled down. Then, using a spoon or tongs, remove the wings and set them back onto the baking sheet. To allow the sauce to seep into the wings, bake for an additional five minutes.
- Serve right after removing it from the oven. Enjoy!

Nutritional Values per serving:

Total calories: 170 kcal, **Fat:** 1g, **Carbohydrates:** 36g, **Protein:** 6g, **Fiber:** 4g, **Sodium:** 637 mg, **Potassium:** 324mg

37. Zucchini Chicken Poppers

Prep Time: 10 mins
Cook Time: 25 mins.
Total Time: 35 mins.
Serves: 5
Difficulty: Easy
Ingredients:

- 2 cup of zucchini, grated
- 1 lb. of chicken breast, ground (raw)
- 2–3 sliced green onions
- 1 clove of garlic, minced
- 3–4 tbsp. of cilantro, minced
- 1 tsp. of salt
- 3/4 tsp. of cumin (optional)
- 1/2 tsp. of pepper

Optional: avocado oil or coconut oil, for cooking (or ghee)
Directions:

- Combine the chicken, zucchini, green onions, cilantro, salt, garlic, pepper, & cumin in a large bowl (if using). The mixture would be quite moist. Use a tiny scoop or heaping tablespoon to scoop the meatballs, then gently smooth them with your fingertips. Usually, you can get 20 to 24 poppers. Depending on how big you make them, you can receive more or fewer.
- In a medium skillet over medium to low heat, warm a little oil. Cook for 5 to 6 mins on the first side, 4-5 at a time. When the centers are cooked through and golden brown, flip the pancakes over and cook for a further 4-5 minutes.
- Serve with salsa, guacamole, or your preferred dip.

Nutritional Values per serving:
Total calories: 203 kcal, **Fat:** 10g, **Carbohydrates:** 1g, **Protein:** 25g, **Fiber:** 0g, **Sodium:** 635 mg, **Potassium:** 780mg

38. Garlic Cauliflower Crust Breadsticks

Prep Time: 10 mins
Cook Time: 40 mins. (30 mins. baking)
Total Time: 50 mins.
Serves: 10
Difficulty: Easy
Ingredients:
Cauliflower crust:

- 1 free-range egg (organic), lightly beaten
- 1 head of cauliflower (small), cut in small florets (3 cups cauliflower rice)
- ½ cup / 50 g / 1.7 oz. of mozzarella cheese, shredded
- 1 tbsp. of olive oil
- 2 cloves of garlic, minced or grated
- ½ tsp. of sea salt, fine grain
- ¼ tsp. of ground black pepper
- ½ tsp. of Italian herb seasoning (dried)

Toppings:

- A pinch of Italian herb season (dried)
- 2 tbsp. of mozzarella cheese, shredded
- Marinara sauce, to serve (optional)

Directions:

- A loaf pan should be lined with parchment paper so the excess drapes over the edges. Lightly oil the parchment paper. Preheat the oven up to 350°F (175°C). Place aside.
- In a small skillet over low heat, heat the olive oil. Add the garlic, and cook for no more than one minute or until it is fragrant. Remove from heat and put aside.
- The cauliflower florets are riced in a food processor (it must be evenly chopped yet not completely pulverized).
- Put the cauliflower rice in a microwave-safe container and cook it for 8 minutes on high.
- Fill a tea towel with the cauliflower rice, then twist it to extract as much liquid as you can. This has major significance. If the cauliflower rice isn't dry, the breadsticks will turn out to be mushy.
- Cauliflower rice should be transferred to a mixing bowl along with the egg, Italian herb seasoning, mozzarella, garlic oil, salt, and pepper.
- Spread the mixture of cauliflower in the loaf pan that has been prepared.
- Bake for 25 to 30 minutes, or till the loaf is set & beginning to turn brown.
- Line the baking sheet with parchment paper while you wait.
- When the "loaf" is finished cooking, gently tip it over onto the prepared baking sheet using the parchment paper for removing it out of the loaf pan.
- Cook for a further 10 minutes, or until golden.
- Remove it from the oven, then turn on the broiler. Top the loaf with cheese & Italian herb spice.
- For a few minutes under the broiler, till the cheese melts & slightly browned.
- Before slicing into (10) sticks, let to chill for a few minutes.
- Serve warm, hot, or chilled

Nutritional Values per serving:
Total calories: 34 kcal, **Fat:** 3g, **Carbohydrates:** 2g, **Protein:** 2g, **Fiber:** 4g, **Sodium:** 345 mg, **Potassium:** 485mg

39. Corn Fritters

Prep Time: 5 mins
Cook Time: 20 mins.
Total Time: 25 mins.
Serves: 10
Difficulty: Easy
Ingredients:

- 1 jalapeño finely diced and seeds removed (optional)
- 3 cups of corn kernels (thawed, if frozen)
- 2 eggs
- 2 tbsp. of diced cilantro leaves (or use any other herb)
- 1 cup of white flour, whole wheat
- 2-4 tbsp. of Olive oil, to fry
- ½ tsp. of salt or some more to taste

Optional: Lime juice & cilantro for serving
Directions:

- Use a mojito muddler or a potato crusher to smash the kernels of corn in a big bowl until most of the kernels are broken & some liquid is out. You may also briefly pulse corn in the food processor to break it up, but be cautious not to over-process it and create creamed corn.
- Salt through jalapeno, add the remaining ingredients and combine well. In a skillet, heat a few teaspoons of olive oil. To add corn batter to the pan, use a melon baller or a heaping tablespoon. Over medium heat, cook for approximately 3 minutes or till golden brown. Flip the corn fritters carefully, then heat for a further three minutes, or until golden brown and well done.
- Serve with a squeeze of 1 lime and some fresh cilantro.

Nutritional Values per serving:
Total calories: 125 kcal, **Fat:** 3g, **Carbohydrates:** 8g, **Protein:** 3g, **Fiber:** 1g, **Sodium:** 129 mg, **Potassium:** 25mg

40. Plantain Chips

Prep Time: 10 mins
Cook Time: 10 mins.
Total Time: 20 mins.
Serves: 2-3
Difficulty: Easy
Ingredients:

- 1/2 cup of coconut oil (melted)
- 2 peeled green plantains
- Sea salt, to taste — or any other seasoning you want like paprika or chipotle powder

Directions:

- Each plantain may be peeled by first trimming the end & scoring the skin lengthwise numerous times.
- Slice each plantain that has been peeled diagonally.
- In a pan over medium heat, warm a thin layer of coconut oil.
- Slices should be carefully added to the heated oil; try not to crowd the pan. If the temperature is appropriate, the slices should lightly sizzle and move about.
- Slices should be fried for no more than two minutes on each side until they become golden and start to darken at the edges.
- With a perforated spoon or spatula, remove the chips and set them on the paper towels to drain.
- Right away after removal, salt to ensure that the salt adheres to the chips.
- Enjoy right away to get the most crispiness.

Nutritional Values per serving:
Total calories: 220 kcal, **Fat:** 12g, **Carbohydrates:** 25g, **Protein:** 1g, **Fiber:** 2g, **Sodium:** 170 mg, **Potassium:** 310mg

41. Pumpkin Spiced Granola

Prep Time: 15 mins
Cook Time: 1 hr.
Total Time: 1hr. 15 mins. (Baked)
Serves: 10
Difficulty: Medium
Ingredients:

- 1/2 cup of pecans
- 1 cup of walnuts
- 1/2 cup of almonds
- 1/2 cup of flaked almonds
- 1 cup of pumpkin seeds
- 1 cup of coconut flakes
- 3/4 cup of pumpkin puree
- 1/3 cup of raisins
- 1/3 cup of melted coconut oil
- 1/2 tsp. of ground cloves
- 1/3 cup of maple syrup or honey
- 1 tsp. of ground ginger
- 2 tsp. of cinnamon
- 1/4 tsp. of nutmeg
- 1/2 tsp. of salt

Directions:

- Turn the oven's temperature up to 300 degrees Fahrenheit (150 degrees Celsius).
- Place the whole, unflaked almonds, pecans, and walnuts into a food processor & pulse just

long enough to break them up into tiny bits but not long enough to turn them into powder.

- Add the pumpkin seeds, almond flakes, coconut flakes, and raisins to the nuts in the big dish.
- Mix the melted coconut oil, pumpkin puree, honey, all of the spices, and salt in a small bowl. Once everything is well combined, pour the liquid on the nut mixture & swirl to evenly distribute it.
- On a baking sheet, distribute the mixture uniformly, and bake for 50 mins to 1 hour, stirring the pan every 15 mins. To produce an equal browning (do not let it burn!).
- Take everything out of the oven when it is browned and let it cool. As it cools, the granola would become crispy. Transfer to a container that is airtight.

Nutritional Values per serving:
Total calories: 325 kcal, **Fat:** 20g, **Carbohydrates:** 22g, **Protein:** 7g, **Fiber:** 5g, **Sodium:** 123 mg, **Potassium:** 426mg

42. Loaded Cauliflower Nachos

Prep Time: 30 mins
Cook Time: 20 mins. (10 mins. baked)
Total Time: 50 mins.
Serves: 4
Difficulty: Medium
Ingredients:

- 2 tbsp. of taco seasoning plus 1 tsp.
- 1 head of cauliflower
- 2 tbsp. of olive oil plus 1 tsp.
- 1 bell pepper, small (any colour)
- 200 g of ground beef (or pork)
- ½ cup of black olives (sliced)

Tomato Salsa:

- ½ red onion (small)
- 2 tomatoes
- 10 leaves of basil (or 3 cilantro stems)
- ¼ tsp. of black pepper
- ¼ tsp. of Himalayan salt
- 1 stalk of green onion

Avocado Sauce:

- 1 clove of garlic
- ½ avocado
- 1 tbsp. of olive oil
- 1 tsp. of lemon juice
- 2 tbsp. of homemade mayonnaise
- 1 stalk of green onion
- ¼ tsp. of black pepper
- ¼ tsp. of Himalayan salt

Directions:

- Set the oven's temperature to 210C/410F.
- Cut the cauliflower head off at the stalk, then separate the florets. Place two or three slices of each floret in a bowl. Slices of cauliflower are coated with 2 tablespoons olive oil & 2 tablespoons of taco spice; combine well. Bake for 15-20 minutes with the item on a baking sheet covered with parchment paper. Remove the cooked food from the oven.
- Slice the basil & green onion stem, dice the red onion, tomatoes, and red onion. Mix with the salt & pepper in a bowl. Mix well and reserve.
- Dice yellow pepper. Add the chopped pepper to the hot 1 tsp. olive oil in a frying pan. Add ground beef after 2 minutes of cooking on medium heat. Add the 1 teaspoon of taco spice, stir well, and cook the beef thoroughly. Place aside.
- Slice the green onion stem, mince the garlic clove, and peel the avocado. In a food processor, combine all the ingredients for avocado sauce and process until well-combined.
- Place the cauliflower, tomato salsa, taco meat, and black olives on a large serving platter. Fill a spray bottle with avocado sauce and squirt it all over the nachos. Dispense and savour!

Nutritional Values per serving:
Total calories: 397 kcal, **Fat:** 33g, **Carbohydrates:** 27g, **Protein:** 13g, **Fiber:** 8g, **Sodium:** 284 mg, **Potassium:** 400mg

43. Sweet Potato Pretzels

Prep Time: 15 mins
Cook Time: 1 hr. 25 mins. (60 mins. passive time)
Total Time: 1hr 40 mins.
Serves: 4
Difficulty: Medium
Ingredients:

- 1 cup of cassava flour
- 1 cup of sweet potato (mashed)
- 1/4 cup of warm water
- 1 tbsp. of maple syrup
- 2 1/4 tsp. of active dry yeast
- 2 tbsp. of coconut oil
- 1 egg whisked (large), for egg wash
- 1/2 tsp. of salt

Directions:

- For 10 minutes, until the yeast is frothy and active, combine warm water, maple syrup, and yeast in small cup or dish.

- Add all ingredients to a food processor, except the egg (or mix by hand). Once the dough has been formed, cover it with a clean cloth and let it rise for 60 minutes in a warm, quiet spot in the kitchen.
- Set the oven to 350°F. Use parchment paper to line a baking sheet.
- Once the dough has expanded, knead it before dividing it into four equal pieces. Make pretzel forms by rolling out the dough into tubes approximately 3/4" in diameter.
- Put the pretzels on a baking sheet covered with the parchment paper and egg wash them. Sprinkle with salt flakes, then bake for 25 minutes at 350°F.

Nutritional Values per serving:

Total calories: 219 kcal, **Fat:** 5g, **Carbohydrates:** 43g, **Protein:** 2g, **Fiber:** 3g, **Sodium:** 429 mg, **Potassium:** 445mg

44. Banana Bread Cookies

Prep Time: 5 mins
Cook Time: 30 mins. (Baked)
Total Time: 35 mins.
Serves: 15
Difficulty: Easy
Ingredients:

- 1/4 tsp. of baking soda
- 1 1/2 cups of almond flour
- 1/8 tsp. of sea salt
- 1 tbsp. of pure maple syrup
- 1/4 tsp. of cinnamon
- 1 1/4 cup of mashed bananas (overly ripe), 4 medium
- 1 egg (sub with 1 flax egg)

Optional Add-ins:

- 2 tbsp. of nut butter
- 1/2 cup of chocolate chips
- Some chopped nuts
- extra 1/4 tsp. of cinnamon
- 1/2 tsp. of vanilla extract
- A pinch of ground cloves

Directions:

- Put a baking sheet in the oven and preheat it to 350 degrees. In a bowl, combine the baking soda, almond flour, salt, and cinnamon.
- With a fork, mash the bananas and combine them with the dry ingredients. Add the egg, if using, and the maple syrup. Mix everything well to combine it all.
- The dough should be plopped onto a baking sheet using a 1.5 tbsp. Cookie scoop. Use the backside of a spoon or a fork to gently press down on the cookies. Bake for 26 to 30 minutes, or until the middles are no longer runny
- Place the freshly baked cookies on a cooling rack to cool after removal from the oven. Before eating, let the cookies warm up to room temperature.
- For up to five days, keep in the refrigerator in an airtight container.

Nutritional Values per serving:

Total calories: 103 kcal, **Fat:** 5g, **Carbohydrates:** 10g, **Protein:** 3g, **Fiber:** 2g, **Sodium:** 46 mg, **Potassium:** 119mg

45. Blueberry Lemon Donuts

Prep Time: 15 mins
Cook Time: 25 mins. (Baked)
Total Time: 40 mins.
Serves: 9
Difficulty: Easy
Ingredients:

- 1/3 cup of full-fat coconut milk, canned
- 3 eggs (large)
- 1/3 cup of pure maple syrup
- 1/4 cup of fresh lemon juice
- Grated Zest of one med lemon
- 2 tbsp. of coconut oil melted & cooled
- 2/3 cup of coconut flour
- 1 tsp. of pure vanilla extract
- 1/4 cup of tapioca flour
- 1/4 tsp. of salt
- 1/2 tsp. of baking soda
- 2/3 cup of fresh blueberries

For glaze:

- 2-3 tsp. of fresh lemon juice
- 1/2 cup of maple sugar (powdered) or powdered sugar (organic)

Directions:

- Use a silicone pan for donut for easier removal. Preheat the oven up to 350 degrees F. Grease or coat your donut pan gently with cooking spray or coconut oil.

- Combine the eggs, maple syrup, coconut milk, lemon zest & juice, coconut oil, and vanilla in a big bowl with an electric hand mixer. Combine the tapioca flour, salt, baking soda, and coconut flour in a separate bowl.
- A thick batter will develop after thoroughly combining the dry and wet ingredients. Before pouring the mixture into the donut moulds, fold in the blueberries. Make nine doughnuts that are the full size.
- Bake for 23 to 25 minutes in the preheated oven, then remove and let cool into the pan for 10-15 minutes. Remove the donuts with care, then place them to cooling racks to finish cooling.

For glaze:

- The glaze ingredients should be well combined and drizzle-like while the donuts are cooling. Pour the glaze on the mostly-cooled donuts using a small whisk or spoon, and then let them cool for an additional 15 minutes to let the glaze set. For up to 4 days, keep leftovers closed in the refrigerator. Enjoy!

Nutritional Values per serving:

Total calories: 159 kcal, **Fat:** 8g, **Carbohydrates:** 20g, **Protein:** 3g, **Fiber:** 3g, **Sodium:** 177 mg, **Potassium:** 85mg

46. Air Fried Chicken Wings & Spicy Asian Sauce

Prep Time: 10 mins
Cook Time: 20 mins.
Total Time: 30 mins.
Serves: 24
Difficulty: Easy

Ingredients:

- Some sea salt, to taste
- 2 pounds of chicken wings or 22-24 wings
- Some black pepper, to taste
- 2 tsp. of baking powder

Spicy Chicken Wing Asian Sauce:

- 1/4 cup of coconut aminos or 2 tbsp. of soy sauce or tamari
- 1/4 cup of water
- 2 tbsp. of honey
- 2 tbsp. of sriracha sauce
- 2 tbsp. of SunButter Organic or No Sugar Added
- 1 tsp. of ginger powder
- 2 tbsp. of unsweetened rice wine vinegar

Directions:

- Either allow the wings to air dry at normal temperature or use paper towels to absorb any remaining moisture. Sprinkle them with some baking powder after lightly seasoning them with salt and pepper.
- An air fryer should be preheated for 5 minutes at 390° F. When it is ready, add chicken wings and reheat the air fryer for 15 minutes at 390° F.
- In a pan, add the ingredients for the wing sauce and whisk to incorporate. The sauce should be heated over medium heat, smoothed out with a whisk, and given a few minutes of light boiling. Don't over simmer the sauce since it will proceed to thicken as it cools.
- Take the air-fried wings out and coat them with the spicy Asian wing sauce. If preferred, serve them with sliced green onions and sesame seeds as garnish.

Nutritional Values per serving:

Total calories: 62 kcal, **Fat:** 4g, **Carbohydrates:** 3g, **Protein:** 4g, **Fiber:** 1g, **Sodium:** 72mg, **Potassium:** 66mg

47. Buckwheat Crackers

Prep Time: 10 mins
Cook Time: 25 mins. (Bake)
Total Time: 35 mins.
Serves: 25
Difficulty: Easy

Ingredients:

- 1 tsp. of Thyme (Dried)
- 1 cup of Buckwheat Flour
- 1 tsp. of Dried Oregano
- 1 tsp. of Red Chilli Flakes
- 1 tsp. of Sesame Seeds
- 1/2 tsp. of Salt
- 4 tbsp. of Water for the dough
- 2 tbsp. of Olive Oil

Directions:

- In a large bowl, sift the buckwheat flour and set it aside. Thyme, sesame seeds, oregano, red pepper flakes, & salt to taste are now added.
- Add olive oil after combining all the ingredients. In order for the oil to cover the flour, thoroughly combine all the ingredients.
- Using a spoon, incorporate water and knead a compact, flexible dough. Roll the dough out into a circle, then sprinkle some buckwheat flour on the wooden board. With a cookie cutter, cut the dough into the required shapes after forking it.
- Gather the remaining dough, shape it into a ball, and then re-roll it. Use a cookie cutter once again and/or cut the paper into long strips.
- For 10 minutes, preheat oven to 180 degrees Celsius.
- Put all of these crackers on a baking sheet that is flat and covered with parchment paper.

- When the oven is ready, put the tray inside, lower the temperature up to 150 degrees C, and bake the dish for 25 minutes.
- When the tray has finished baking, take it out of the oven, let it cool on a cooling rack, and then store the cookies in an airtight container. This cracker's shelf life is at least two weeks.

Nutritional Values per serving:

Total calories: 280 kcal, **Fat:** 3g, **Carbohydrates:** 52g, **Protein:** 12g, **Fiber:** 0g, **Sodium:** 108mg, **Potassium:** 216mg

48. Air-Fried Crispy Chickpeas

Prep Time: 20 mins
Cook Time: 15 mins.
Total Time: 35 mins.
Serves: 4
Difficulty: Easy
Ingredients:

- 1 ½ tbsp. of toasted sesame oil
- 1 can of unsalted chickpeas (15 ounce), rinsed & drained
- ¼ tsp. of smoked paprika
- ⅛ tsp. of salt
- ¼ tsp. of crushed red pepper
- 2 lime wedges
- Cooking spray

Directions:

- On multiple layers of paper towels, spread the chickpeas. Roll the chickpeas beneath paper towels for them to dry on all sides, then add additional paper towels on top and pat until extremely dry.
- In a medium bowl, mix the oil and chickpeas. Salt, crushed red pepper, and paprika should be added. Pour into a cooking spray-coated air fryer basket. Cook for 12 to 14 minutes at 400 degrees F, shaking the basket regularly until very nicely browned. Serve the chickpeas with lime wedges on top.

Nutritional Values per serving:

Total calories: 132 kcal, **Fat:** 5g, **Carbohydrates:** 14g, **Protein:** 4g, **Fiber:** 3g, **Sodium:** 85mg, **Potassium:** 151mg

49. Broccoli Tater Tots

Prep Time: 20 mins
Cook Time: 10 mins.
Total Time: 30 mins.
Serves: 4
Difficulty: Easy
Ingredients:
Broccoli Tater Tots:

- 1 tbsp. of olive oil
- ½ cup of shallot, minced (about 1 large)
- 3 cups of broccoli, grated (from the crown)
- 4 cloves of garlic, minced
- ½ tsp. of fine sea salt
- ½ tsp. of lemon zest, packed (optional)
- ½ tsp. of black pepper
- 2 eggs (large)
- ⅔ cup of breadcrumbs (gluten-free)
- ⅔ cup of cheddar cheese, grated (smoked cheddar)
- Oil spray (neutral oil or olive oil)

Creamy Buffalo Dip:

- ½ tsp. of garlic powder
- ½ cup of plain Greek yogurt
- ¼ tsp. of packed lemon zest
- Sea salt, to taste
- 1 to 2 tsp. of hot sauce

Directions:

- In a pan over medium heat, warm the olive oil. Add the shallot & garlic, and simmer, stirring often, for approximately two minutes, until aromatic. Add the broccoli and simmer for approximately 3 minutes, stirring periodically, until bright green.
- A mixture of broccoli should be transferred to a big basin. Add the salt, black pepper, & lemon zest, and mix well. To create a well, push this mixture to the sides of the bowl. The eggs should be cracked in the center and then whisked together. Combine the broccoli mixture with the beaten eggs. Add breadcrumbs and cheddar cheese and mix well.
- Gather the ingredients and form 20 little balls (about 2 tbsp. each). To avoid sticking, lightly wet your hands before forming the balls into little cylinder tots. Place the tots in the basket of an air fryer in a single layer.
- Spray some oil on the tots lightly. For 10 minutes, bake in an air fryer at 400°F (200°C) without preheating (or till golden brown).
- In the meanwhile, combine Greek yogurt, garlic powder, spicy sauce, lemon zest, and salt in a small bowl. Serve the heated tots with the dip.

Nutritional Values per serving:

Total calories: 266 kcal, **Fat:** 14g, **Carbohydrates:** 21g, **Protein:** 15g, **Fiber:** 3g, **Sodium:** 637mg, **Potassium:** 334mg

50. Carrot Fries

Prep Time: 5 mins
Cook Time: 15 mins. (Baked)
Total Time: 20 mins.
Serves: 24
Difficulty: Easy
Ingredients:

- 2 tsp. of olive oil
- 1 bag of carrot sticks (12 oz.)
- Salt, to taste

Directions:

- Heat the air fryer up to 400 degrees. Wash, peel, and cut carrots into sticks if you aren't using previously prepared carrot sticks to make fries.
- Place them in the air fryer until they are ready.

Nutritional Values per serving:
Total calories: 99 kcal, **Fat:** 3g, **Carbohydrates:** 18g, **Protein:** 2g, **Fiber:** 6g, **Sodium:** 205mg, **Potassium:** 410mg

Conclusion

The "Pegan" diet is a cross between the paleo diet, which emphasizes entire foods that may have been obtained by hunting or gathering, such as fruits, vegetables, meats, and nuts, & the vegan diet, which calls for the consumption of exclusively plant-based meals. According to the Pegan principle, you should eat a diet high in nutrients that are composed of around 75% plant-based foods and 25% animal-based foods. It emphasizes consuming fresh, whole foods that are produced responsibly and have a little environmental impact. The diet excludes processed foods as well. Gluten and dairy products are forbidden.

The Pegan Diet was not intended to be something you go "on" and "off" of, as many of you are used to thinking of diets as something you do briefly and without much pleasure. The Pegan Diet particularly is a way of life rather than a diet. Keep in mind that the objective is to have clear, uncomplicated guidelines that will help to maintain our health for many years, not to be flawless. This Diet is a way of thinking about health. Doing your best while letting go of tension and anxiety related to eating is important. Pegan tries to use the benefits that each of the dietary philosophies offers while minimizing the drawbacks of both the Paleo & Vegan extremes. It ought to be a win-win situation.

Most importantly, the Pegan diet is actually not a diet at all, at least not in the sense that you describe it in contemporary society, which emphasizes weight reduction, fat loss, and restriction. Instead, this diet adheres to the Latin term dieta's original definition, which is: a certain way of life. Pegan represents how people used to eat before labels, Paleo & Vegan treats, Instagram, and diet books ever existed. You can expect that this book's guidelines will help you feel at ease and confident about your general health and well-being. Remember that genuine health is about feeling well, being present, and sharing your finest talents with the world. It isn't only about dropping some pounds or being free of chronic illness.

Made in the USA
Middletown, DE
08 October 2022